A Practical Guide to Co: Interpretation

A Practical Guide to Costumed Interpretation is just that – a book that takes you through the various stages of becoming an historical costumed interpreter.

Jackie Lee has worked in this area of heritage interpretation for more than twenty years and sets out what it takes to develop the persona for a character from the past. The methods she shares focus on first-person delivery of an historic character. Lee introduces the reader to two new methods she has developed that support character creation and delivery. The "three realms" highlight the importance of research and making the character believable and the "crystal ball", which enables the costumed interpreter to look into the future when the occasion demands it. The book is full of practical help on all aspects of the costumed interpreter's craft including costume making and how to prepare personally for stepping out full of confidence, ready to engage visitors of all ages.

A Practical Guide to Costumed Interpretation is aimed at those interested in becoming costumed interpreters as well as those who wish to develop or revise their techniques. It will also be useful for students of museum practice and heritage interpretation considering costumed interpretation as a means of on-site delivery.

Jackie Lee is a heritage interpretation consultant specialising in costumed interpretation. She began her professional career as a history teacher, establishing her own business in 2000. Jackie works with museums, galleries and heritage sites. In 2019, she received the Communication Award from Scottish Women in Business. www.artemisscotland.com.

Routledge Guides to Practice in Museums, Galleries and Heritage

This series provides essential practical guides for those working in museums, galleries, and a variety of other heritage professions around the globe.

Including authored and edited volumes, the series will help to enhance practitioners' and students' professional knowledge and will also encourage sharing of best practices between different countries, as well as between different types and sizes of organisations.

Titles published in the series include:

Applying for Jobs and Internships in Museums
A Practical Guide
Martha Schloetzer

Welcoming Young Children into the Museum
A Practical Guide
Sarah Erdman and Nhi Nguyen with Margaret Middleton

Museums and Interactive Virtual Learning
Allyson Mitchell, Tami Moehring and Janet Zanetis

The Sustainable Museum
How Museums Contribute to the Great Transformation
Christopher J. Garthe

Museums and Well-being
Rose Cull and Daniel Cull

A Practical Guide to Costumed Interpretation
Jackie Lee

For more information about this series, please visit: www.routledge.com/Routledge-Guides-to-Practice-in-Museums-Galleries-and-Heritage/book-series/RGPMGH

A Practical Guide to Costumed Interpretation

Jackie Lee

Routledge
Taylor & Francis Group
LONDON AND NEW YORK

Cover image: Washing day at the National Museum of Rural Life's Fabulous Fifties event © Keith Shaw Buckley/Eilidh McCormick, costumed interpreter for Artemis Scotland

First published 2023
by Routledge
4 Park Square, Milton Park, Abingdon, Oxon OX14 4RN

and by Routledge
605 Third Avenue, New York, NY 10158

Routledge is an imprint of the Taylor & Francis Group, an informa business

British Library Cataloguing-in-Publication Data
A catalogue record for this book is available from the British Library

ISBN: 978-1-032-19653-4 (hbk)
ISBN: 978-1-032-19651-0 (pbk)
ISBN: 978-1-003-26022-6 (ebk)

DOI: 10.4324/9781003260226

Typeset in Times New Roman
by Apex CoVantage

To my grandson, Joseph, who shows all the signs of a future in costumed interpretation.

Contents

Figures

Tables

Acknowledgements

While it is supremely satisfying to see my name on the cover of this book, it certainly would never have happened without the encouragement and support of many wonderful people. In providing the inspiration throughout my career, taking the first steps to write the book, chatting with me over ideas, providing help and reassurance in the process of the manuscript's creation and finally in the production of the book, all of you have given your time and effort with great kindness. I am grateful to you all.

In constructing this book, I wanted it to reflect the opinions of the people I have worked with over the last twenty or so years. To those who have most kindly contributed comments on their experiences, reflecting what they enjoy most about being costumed interpreters and how they perceive their work being appreciated by visitors, my thanks goes to Karen Bartke, Helen Cuinn, Laverne Edmonds, Stephanie Falls, Dr Richard Irvine, Mark Kydd, Chris Lee, Fergus John McCann, Eildih McCormick and Vera Rennie.

My thanks also goes to Laura Bennison, community engagement officer, and Alison Rae, family engagement officer, both of the Learning and Engagement Team at National Museums Scotland and Craig Fletcher, head of learning and inclusion, at Historic Environment Scotland for providing comments on work I have delivered within their organisations and giving me permission to use feedback from visitor evaluation they carried out. Also, to Claire Allan, head of engagement at National Museums Scotland, who provided some much-needed help towards the end of my writing – thank you so much for your prompt replies.

The wonderful photographs in the book are thanks to the amazing skills of Ruth Armstrong, Clare McIntyre of Witch Creations and Keith Shaw Buckley. Also, I am very grateful to Karen Ashfield, who has worked with me for many years, creating and making most of the costumes featured in the pages of this book. Together, we have learned about how to cut a few corners and make costumes more comfortable and practical, as you will discover later. Those not made by Karen have been hired from the Wardrobe of Scottish Opera; my thanks to them for letting me lose myself in their fabulous costume store.

In particular, I would like to thank Bill Bevan, Jude Knowles, Abbey Lee, Steve Slack, John Taylor and Abigail Young for their advice and reassurance during the writing process.

As to the publication, the team at Routledge have been superb in helping me through the whole production process from the first meeting to the point I am at now with the book in my hand. My thanks goes to you all and in particular Heidi Lowther, Manas Roy and Matthew Gibbons for their supreme patience throughout. Also to Jayachandran Rajendiran for answering all my questions related to copyediting, thank you.

Last but not least, a big thank-you to my husband, Chris, for being the greatest inspiration and source of encouragement in my career and in writing this book. Also, to my sons Matthew and Jonathan, who have put up with their mother appearing in a variety of strange costumes over the years and provided great enthusiasm and support in my decision to write this book.

Introduction

Performing as a professional, historic costumed character at heritage sites, museums and galleries has been one of the greatest privileges and pleasures of my life. I would like to share with you some of the knowledge and practical experiences I have gained in nearly twenty-five years of working in this form of heritage interpretation.

This book will provide a practical guide for both practitioners and managers as well as offering useful background for heritage academics working in this often misunderstood and sometimes contentious interpretive technique. Costumed interpretation has been on the receiving end of harsh criticism by academics, as will become evident in Chapter 1, and indeed is often confused by heritage professionals with similar but ultimately different ways of explaining the past. To some, it is seen as just a bit of dressing up, to others a waste of time. Needless to say, I do not agree with this, as I will demonstrate in this book, as my belief comes very much from on-the-ground experience or, more accurately, from castle ramparts, the Georgian ballroom, the prison cell, a battlefield nursing station, a heritage learning or museum learning centre, a school classroom.

How Did I Become a Costumed Interpreter?

In all honesty, my career as a costumed interpreter began by accident. I had no idea that such a job existed, but I suppose, looking back, the elements I could later draw upon were always there.

As the only child of older parents brought up in middle-class Glasgow, I spent a great deal of time on my own with my imagination for a friend. I played at being a princess, as many little girls still do, and I also liked to play at being a Victorian. This was facilitated by access to a trunk belonging to my grandmother full of Victorian clothes that were now for me to dress up in. My grandmother lived with us, and after the death of my mother when I was eight, she largely brought me up. She was herself a Victorian, born when Gladstone was prime minister and the clothes in the trunk were originals. Her attitudes were Victorian, and I was treated as a child would have been decades earlier. Dressing up and pretending to be other people was definitely a great escape valve for me as a child.

DOI: 10.4324/9781003260226-1

At school, I developed a great interest in history, which resulted in my history degree from the relatively new and cutting-edge Strathclyde University, followed by teacher training college, where I received a distinction in teaching practise and thus began my working life as a secondary school teacher in the east end of Glasgow. I thoroughly enjoyed teaching here and did my best to enthuse my classes with the same excitement I felt for the stories of the past and the things we could all learn from them. I always enjoyed the opportunity to get the pupils out of the classroom to see where great events of the past had taken place.

Life and family came along, and my career was put to one side, as I wanted to be around for my young children, but eventually, the time came to consider a return to work. An invitation to an exhibition opening turned my life around. For this event, an actor had been employed to take on a character and interact with the guests in a 1930s office setting, appropriate to the exhibition. I enjoyed her portrayal as a secretary during that period and the fact that she was dressed in historical costume. I felt that you could really understand what her working day was like from what she was describing, and the click of the typewriter and the background ring of a phone occasionally really brought the whole exhibition to life. However, what became clear quite quickly was that she could only answer questions relevant to the script she had learnt; anything outside that was a problem. It made me wonder if my historical knowledge could be used in a new way to teach history in a slightly different way. Mulling this over, I eventually took the plunge in 2000 and set up my business, Artemis Scotland, my aim being to provide costumed characters that fitted with periods of history being taught at primary and secondary levels. I took my first bookings from several local primary schools for a Victorian servant, a Victorian schoolteacher and a Second World War home-front housewife. Word spread about what I was doing, and I started getting bookings further afield. I did not really know what to call what I was doing until I came across the Association for Heritage Interpretation (AHI) and an article on costumed interpretation at Hampton Court Palace, and this was when I realised that I was in fact a costumed interpreter, using my skills on a much smaller scale. From these humble beginnings, I now work with organisations such as Historic Environment Scotland, National Museums Scotland, the Scottish Portrait Gallery and the National Trust for Scotland as well as directly with schools across Scotland and northern England. I train others to be costumed interpreters at sites and museums and also employ people to work for Artemis, and I have even run a course on costumed interpretation at Hampton Court Palace for the AHI, of which I am now a trustee.

When I began, I was not aware of much written about costumed interpretation and its benefits. What I did discover was that in 1957, Freeman Tilden (regarded by many as the "father" of heritage interpretation) had written in his book, *Interpreting Our Heritage*, about avoiding the situation in which heritage sites appeared to "be frozen at a moment in time when nobody was at home" (Tilden, 1957). He clearly liked the idea of something going on at certain places. Tilden later went on to suggest what he calls "animation" as a way to avoid the "frozen" experience and referenced several historic sites that are "peopled" by those representing historic characters who once lived there, in the costume of the period. To me, this is costumed interpretation – animating and peopling historic places.

Who Have I Been?

It has been my good fortune to have played many of the "great figures" of the past. I have been Mary of Guise, mother of Mary, Queen of Scots, and also Mary, Queen of Scots herself in the sites key to her story – the palace where she was born, the castle in which she gave birth to the future King James VI and the abbey at which she spent her last night on Scottish soil before her escape to England and subsequent imprisonment and execution. As Queen Elizabeth I, I found myself granting an audience to supposed fellow travellers at an inn after our coach en route for London lost one of its wheels, especially as the invited audience of my client were performers from the London stage, many prominent in musical theatre. Fortunately, I was assisted by my partner, who portrayed her astrologer, John Dee, who had the ability to see into the future! The event provided an opportunity to engage in conversation about the court, its manners and especially food. Being Queen Victoria, often accompanied by my private secretary, Sir Henry Ponsonby, I have met many people in great halls, art galleries and on tours of textile mills, as well as at late nights in museums with rock bands and cocktails!

Not all of my roles have been royal, but they have admittedly tended to be strong women, as theirs are the stories that survive. I have been Florence Stacpoole, a suffragist who wrote on women's health in magazines around the time of the First World War as well as examining how housewives coped with food shortages during that war. I also portrayed a generic female journalist researching an article while on board one of the little-known passenger steam ships that sailed between Edinburgh and London in the 1920s. This forgotten voyage offered a more leisurely mode of travel than the dirty steam engines provided by the railway companies, which "travel too fast". One of my physically least demanding (but arguably most restful) roles was as Mrs Cardeza, the richest woman on the *Titanic*. She was probably the character on whom Rose is based in the 1997 film, as Mrs Cardeza had had the most expensive suite on board and made the highest insurance claim of all the passengers, which included $20,000 for one diamond. While she looked splendidly of her time, she was really a foil for my partner, the put-upon and exhausted chief steward, charged with recruiting and training stewards from school audiences or groups of older people at a senior citizens' lunch club. On one occasion, Mrs Cardeza's supremely "fine sitting" was interrupted by a fourth-wall moment when she was required by her employers to receive the Commonwealth Games baton, which was passing through the town. The audience took it in good part.

At the other end of the social scale, my costumed interpretation roles have included numerous domestic servants – cooks, maids, laundresses and ladies' maids – working in country houses. I think I have done more housework in the course of costumed interpretation than I have ever done in my own home! There have been numerous occasions when I have been required to be a Victorian or Second World War teacher, and during the four-year commemorations for the centenary of the First World War, as a VAD nurse, I prepared thousands of primary school children for service at the front while a colleague demonstrated how and why so many young men willingly agreed to go to war. As a Second World War housewife in a costume made appropriately from other costumes, I have demonstrated "make do and mend" and have eked out rations with some truly ghastly recipes. I have trained spies going into occupied France and protested with the suffragettes. My portrayal of a suffragette at Glasgow's People's Palace Museum received unexpected praise from the nephew of Paul Robson, who happened to be visiting the city and took part in the presentation and interaction on the day.

On some occasions, I have had the opportunity to challenge accepted ways of thinking about people in the past. One of my favourite characters is Jean Armour Burns, the wife of poet Robert Burns. His nearly untouchable status as the voice and image of Scotland includes the belief that his wife, Jean Armour, was an insignificant woman who just stayed in the background and put up with her husband's philandering ways. As a result of my research, I have been able to present her as a much more three-dimensional character who very much knew how to take charge of her husband's legacy and, indeed, as the "canny" woman she was, played a considerable role in his continued fame and iconic status. Equally, in my portrayal of Flora MacDonald, I was able to challenge perceptions about this woman and her role in the flight of Bonnie Prince Charlie made famous in the song "Over the sea to Skye". We will meet her again in Chapter 5, when I explain how costumed interpretation can be used to explore the real stories rather than the romanticised myths and legends which have grown up around certain characters of history.

Not all of the characters I have developed for my business, Artemis Scotland Ltd, have been women, and therefore, not all have been played by me! Through my business, I have managed costumed interpretation programmes and coached others to become monarchs, mill owners, sea captains, dancing masters, soldiers and writers. I have been fortunate to work with some of the best and most talented interpreters, usually drawn from the ranks of the acting profession. My colleagues have presented, for me, among others, Bonnie Prince Charlie visiting Linlithgow Palace, which he did in September 1745; a Russian princess celebrating Easter at the Palace of Holyroodhouse; Robert Louis Stevenson showing the places in New Town Edinburgh that inspired him; Catherine Sinclair, a forgotten writer who was the most popular children's author until Lewis Carol wrote *Alice in Wonderland* as well as a friend of Sir Walter Scott and responsible for much philanthropy within Edinburgh; and Edward Lear, author of the nonsense poems. Costumed interpretation is ideal as a means of challenging preconceptions and reviving long-forgotten heroines and, of course, sometimes heroes.

Costumed Interpretation Works

Costumed interpretation does work. I know it does because I have seen it in the faces of the public when, for that brief moment, they are transported back to another time through my character – a time past but one which has helped to make them and me. They know, of course, it is make-believe (or mostly they do), but for many, the swish of a skirt, the removal of a glove, the flick of a fan or an instruction about sitting appropriately to have one's portrait painted from a costumed interpreter provides an immediate and unforgettable moment of access to elements of our shared stories. It is not perfect; it does not work in all circumstances, and there is room for improvement and development. This is, as I am all too aware, particularly true with regard to diversity. The characters I have been asked to play as myself or through my business, Artemis Scotland, do not reflect multicultural Britain. There is no reason why this could not happen. The challenges of interpreting issues of ethnicity, sexual orientation and gender by costumed interpreters are full of exciting possibilities.

Things are beginning to change, as you will see in Chapter 3. It is not so long ago since my reference to the African background of Queen Charlotte received a rebuke from those employing me. Now, if you type her name into Google, the first thing that comes up refers to her African ancestry. Some of the costumed characters I or those who have worked with me have portrayed may have been queer, but so far such stories have not been revealed or yet been given the green light as a key message. We need to change mindsets and tell new stories, and while I touch on this, this development will be mainly up to all you costumed interpreters of the future. The tools and methodology I offer here are just as valid for the1950s Windrush immigrant or the 1960s Asian shopkeeper as the 18th-century Edinburgh housewife and the new stories that you will tell in the future.

What I enjoy about my work as a costumed interpreter is being able to provide a window into the past which reveals interesting details to visitors of all ages that gives them a glimpse into what life was like for their ancestors. By being in costume and adopting an historic persona, it is far easier to engage with people on what appears a more personal, almost intimate level, sharing stories in a conversational manner. For me, the key to this form of interpretation is to make it look natural and effortless, which makes people curious and entices them to chat and, on occasion, participate with an activity. The feedback I have received over the years has reinforced my feeling that costumed interpretation really does work. Who cannot be delighted when a child comes up at the end of a school workshop and says, "Meeting you has just been the best day of my life; I will remember this day forever". Written evaluation from teachers has expressed similar comments. "From Castle to Palace", a workshop about Mary, Queen of Scots and her connections with the castle, which I created for the Learning Team of Historic Environment Scotland's Edinburgh Castle, has run for more than fifteen years and produced some fabulous responses from teachers, such as "I think the children will remember this all their lives".[1] The very fact this school session ran for so long is testament to its success. In 2010, Historic Environment Scotland's Learning Team created an event, known as a "Glow Meet", within the Scottish schools' intranet service in which Mary, Queen of Scots answered questions from pupils around Scotland in a live "Audience with the Queen", setting the date to 15 May 1568, her last day on Scottish soil before sailing to England. Seventy schools, both primary and secondary, signed up for it, and the feedback again made me feel I had made a very satisfying career choice and that costumed interpretation can have a significant impact through digital delivery too:

> Jackie's performance was outstanding. She answered a huge range of questions as queen, from how she felt getting married so young to how different it was living in France compared to Scotland, convincing all present, both physically and via "Glow Meet", that was indeed the Queen![2]

A comment from parents at a family gallery session at the National Museum of Scotland again demonstrates that costumed interpretation is a most enjoyable way to explain history and provide memorable experiences that conveys our heritage with all ages: "Absolutely fantastic, the children loved it. The Victorian lady was so informative and held the children in awe; very interesting and informative. It made our daughter's day. And we enjoyed it too – who knew that drinking tea was so complicated?"[3]

In sharing these moments with you from my working life, I hope I have enthused you to read on and discover for yourself how to be a costumed interpreter.

How to Use This Book

The book is here to be read as a whole. However, it may well be that you are only interested in certain sections, and that too is fine. Chapter 1 gives you an introduction to the evolution of costumed interpretation, focussing on definition of the various forms of live interpretation, the form it takes around the world and what has been written on the subject. Chapters 2 and 3 concentrate on the most important aspect of the work, building your character. All the examples provided in the detailed character realms are there to be used by you. The principles used to create these three examples can be used with any of the character types you encounter in your career, no matter where you are based. Costume is of course a must, and Chapter 4 sets out how to go about getting the right costume for you as well as some tips on how to use the costume itself. The techniques and tips in Chapter 5 will help all new costumed interpreters and may also be of use to those well established in the field who want to brush up on their methods of delivery. Chapter 6 provides strategies for different visitor groups that you may encounter. Perhaps you are reading the book because you have been asked to run a costumed interpretation programme for the first time. If this is the case, Chapter 7 sets out how to go about this along with how to evaluate the programme.

Everything here has been tried and tested in my twenty-plus years of experience delivering costumed interpretation. I have also included anecdotes from my work which I hope will shine a light on the pleasure that such work brings, as well as comments from others who have worked for or with me over the years just to prove that it is not just me who thinks that costumed interpretation is a fabulous means to convey the past to others. This observation from Karen Bartke, who has worked with me for many years and is very experienced in the world of costumed interpretation, reinforces everything I feel about my work:

> There is a huge amount of joy to be had in working so closely with the audience. Each little performance or interaction is a unique, unrepeatable moment and I can't really express how satisfying it is to see a visitor lose themselves in the moment and start to believe that I might, truly, be an echo of the past appeared here just briefly to speak to them and them alone.

Enjoy reading the book. Do not be daunted by the work involved in being a costumed interpreter. It is such a rewarding way to tell the stories of the past and make a difference. I wait with interest to see a new generation of costumed interpreters emerge portraying a whole host of fascinating characters who have made the world we live in. If I have played a small part in helping you on that journey, I will be mightily pleased about it!

Notes

1 Comment provided by Craig Fletcher, Head of Learning and Inclusion at Historic Environment Scotland
2 Comment provided by Craig Fletcher, Head of Learning and Inclusion at Historic Environment Scotland
3 Comment provided by Alison Rae, Family engagement Officer at NMS, Chambers Street Museum

1 It's Not Just Dressing Up

There is no doubt that there is great fascination about the clothes worn by our ancestors, be it is what lies beneath what is seen in the form of underwear or the visible outfit. At events, children and adults alike enjoy having the chance to try on a very simplified form of costume and have their photo taken against a suitable background or with the costumed interpreter, if that is on offer. This kind of activity has, unfortunately, resulted in a belief that for the costumed interpreter it is also a bit of "dressing up", even if they are Victorian servants who are far from dressed up by the standard of that time.

History and Heritage – What Is the Difference?

Working within the field of costumed interpretation, I regularly find that people do not appreciate the difference between history and heritage. It might seem a little pedantic to worry about such definitions, as this is a book about how to be a costumed interpreter. However, for those of you who decide this is the way you want to interpret the past, the distinction is important, as you will utilise both. You will also find that costumed interpretation comes under the umbrella of heritage interpretation, so it is good to know what it is all about.

In theory, it should be quite easy to explain – history refers to the study of the written record of the past as a whole, whereas heritage relates to what history leaves behind as evidence of the past, for example buildings, ruins, the man-made landscape, artefacts and literature, now often referred to as heritage assets. Heritage is then further sub-divided into two distinct strands. The first is tangible heritage, which is associated with the landscape, buildings, artefacts – basically, things people can see around them. The second is intangible heritage, often referred to as cultural heritage, and this is made up of people's stories, beliefs, customs, skills, traditions, music, manners and etiquette – all the things that you cannot see but that have been influenced by what happened at a particular period of time in the past.

For those who decide to pursue a career in costumed interpretation, you will be interpreting cultural heritage for a large part of the time. Whether you are portraying someone of considerable historical significance, a minor figure from the past or in some cases a generic character who is a combination of many elements (of

DOI: 10.4324/9781003260226-2

which more in Chapter 2), cultural components of the period they inhabited will have influenced their behaviour and actions, as will significant historical facts relating to them. You might be working within the tangible heritage – a castle, a country house, the ruins of a building or a landscape – giving a voice through your character portrayal to the intangible heritage of beliefs, songs and etiquette which determines how you behave. All the information you require will have come from your historical research and deepening understanding of tangible and intangible heritage.

Live Interpretation Definitions

As definitions are essential, this first chapter is the best place to define the various forms of live interpretation that involve people in costume. This is particularly important, as even within the professional world of museums and heritage, there are many who get confused with the various forms live interpretation takes. There are, in essence, four disciplines which come under the overarching banner of live heritage interpretation. These are:

- re-enactment
- living history
- museum theatre
- costumed interpretation

Within all these forms of live interpretation at heritage sites, historic houses, museums and galleries, those delivering the experience seek to portray some sense of what life was like in the past; to convey the flavour of what a particular period was "really like"; to be authentic.

Re-enactment

It is re-enactment with which most people will have had some kind of encounter, probably at a location associated with a battle. Re-enactors seek to create specific events from history associated with combat which create a spectacle and involve a lot of action, usually featuring some form of fighting or weapon demonstration. Re-enactment societies exist all over the world, and some are international. For example, the Society for Creative Anachronism (SCA), founded in 1966 in Berkeley, California, which specialises in combat re-enactment and living history from early Middle Ages to the early Renaissance period, has branches in the USA, Canada, Australia, New Zealand, Israel, Japan, South Korea, Thailand, Europe and South America. Here in the UK, the best known of re-enactment societies is the Sealed Knot, founded in 1968, which is well known for its re-creation of the English Civil War and also has links with groups in Germany and the Czech Republic.

Re-enactment societies' events are usually at weekends, as all of the members are volunteers, and for them, re-enactment is a hobby. Sometimes re-enactors are referred to as "hobbyists". Most of the societies have events booked quite far in advance to enable the preparation required for the actual event, as they involve a considerable amount of organisation. That said, very often, the same battle is re-enacted year after year and naturally has the same result each time. However, given the numbers involved (anything from 100 to more than 1,000 depending on the battle's size), careful planning is required, because the society will be presenting both the winners and the losers. All the societies, without exception, emphasise that they exist to research and study the particular period of history in which they specialise and use their knowledge to show the public that whatever they are re-enacting is a carefully crafted portrayal of time past. Their delivery at events has at its heart the creation of spectacle and drama – hearing what they say is of less importance, as it is what you can see happening that matters. There is little or no audience participation, because taking part could in reality cause injury to participants. Increasingly, the societies describe themselves as re-enactment and living history societies. The living history part of their re-enactments, usually delivered in third-person, does allow for some involvement of the public.

Living History

"Living history" is a broad term to describe the historically accurate presentation of crafts or skills associated with everyday living in an appropriate setting by people in costume. It can be delivered in first-person – "Do come into my home. My name is Sir Winston Churchill and I played a very important role in the Second World War" – but is very often in third-person – "Winston Churchill lived here, and he was important in the Second World War". Very occasionally, delivery will be in the second-person – "You are coming to the home of Winston Churchill, and as you know, he was important in the Second World War".

"Bringing history to life" is a term often associated with living history. While re-enactment societies are now incorporating living history into their events, often portraying the support network that would have accompanied the particular army they are re-enacting, this form of live interpretation is most commonly associated with large living history museums. The following museums fall into this category, Colonial Williamsburg, Virginia, and Conner Prairie Living History Museum, Indiana, in the USA, Skansen in Stockholm, Sweden, Weald and Downland Living Museum in Sussex in the UK and the Black Forest Open Air Museum in Germany. These museums are also often referred to as outdoor living museums.

The emergence of outdoor museums began in Europe at the end of the 19th century. This was because of the move to industrialisation and a fear that the old ways of rural life would be lost forever if something was not done to preserve traditional skills and customs, these being seen as important to the concept of identity. Skansen, founded by Artur Hazelius in Stockholm in 1891, was one of the first and now advertises itself on its website as the "oldest outdoor museum". Travelling all over Sweden, Hazelius "collected" more than 150 buildings representing rural life from different time periods and had them rebuilt at Skansen. Only three of the buildings on site are not original, and these were carefully reconstructed from buildings he had seen and wanted at his museum. His plan was to create pictures of life with real people rather than static displays with models as he had done within the Nordic Museum, which he had also established some years before. Everything at Skansen had to live. Here, then, was the birth of living history.

There are now many such museums across the European Continent, sometimes referred to as folklife museums. The majority involve buildings that have been brought from some other part of the country and re-assembled at a dedicated site where people demonstrate domestic and agricultural skills of the past such as those of the wheelwright and blacksmith, as well as traditional customs that might otherwise be forgotten. Most of the delivery at these sites is in third-person.

Living history museums are not confined to the interpretation of rural life. Many feature industrial heritage. Most notably in the UK, the birthplace of the Industrial Revolution, there is Ironbridge Gorge, a World Heritage Site comprised of ten museum sites representing different aspects of industrialisation with Blists Hill Victorian Town and its nearby coalmine using living history interpreters to cover the whole gamut of life. Beamish in County Durham and the Black Country Living Museum near Birmingham are also well-known examples in England of industrial outdoor museums interpreting industrial heritage through this medium. Many of the industrial outdoor museums begin life on an original site rather than "importing" buildings from elsewhere, though they often become home to good examples of other forms of industrial heritage that would otherwise be lost. As with their rural counterparts, the emphasis is on the preservation of skills and ways of life that might otherwise be lost, interpreted to visitors by people in costume of the period, most usually in third-person.

The original Skansen model to demonstrate old skills, crafts and customs by real people, copied by industrial sites, has also developed into portraying everyday life in a town. Nowhere is this more obvious than in Colonial Williamsburg in Virginia, USA, which not only reveals 18th-century life under British rule but also undertakes a much harder task of depicting the seeds of revolution, walking a fine line between being overtly political and historically accurate. At Colonial Williamsburg, they use living history to tell the story of the city. Museum theatre, set within particular buildings or just outside them, is also part of their programme. During the day, they also provide what they describe as "Intersections", which take place in first-person at a set location on the site. These Intersections provide the visitors with an insight into life at a particular date in the history of the city. For example, on some days of the week, the date is 26 July 1776, independence has been declared – what is happening in the city is revealed. On other days, if you are in Colonial Williamsburg, you can hear about what happens when the city loses its position as state capital of Virginia to Richmond in 1780. Throughout the Intersections, costumed interpreters make themselves available to interact on a one-to-one basis with visitors in first-person, initiating conversation on the topic being portrayed.

The popularity of living history has spread round the world, and museums can be found as far away as Ballarat in Australia, where you will find Sovereign Hill, which captures life in the 1850s with the discovery of gold in the area. At Min Sok Chon in Yongin, South Korea, many traditional buildings from the 15th-century Joseon period have been reassembled to provide examples of official buildings as well as living accommodation at all levels of society. Within this site is also the Korean Folk Museum that portrays farming of this period. Across the site, there are demonstrations of traditional skills and crafts in costume of the period. On the African, continent the only example seems to be the Pharaonic Village at Giza, which recreates the daily life of Ancient Egyptians in reconstructed buildings using costumed interpreters. The website suggests that while the site's name implies all things associated with Ancient Egypt, it does in fact tell the story of Egypt right up to modern times, as there are also several museums on site. However, it is interesting to discover that the interpreters are in costume, demonstrating ancient crafts and inviting visitors to try their hand at them, too, as well as to dress the part.

Museum Theatre

Museum theatre employs theatrical techniques and takes the form of a scripted piece performed for an audience by professional actors. It is often used to address difficult topics in history, such as slavery, as in the case of Colonial Williamsburg, which can be too demanding on a face-to-face basis with an interpreter in character, who, by the nature of the character they are, may seem to reinforce stereotypes. The theatrical presentation allows different opinions to be voiced on the chosen topic among the characters on stage. Depending on the subject, it may be that influence is brought to bear to change the mind of one of the characters, who, within the performance, explains why they have reached these new views. Museum theatre, therefore, gives the audience time to reflect on what is happening and whether they agree or disagree with what is being portrayed. There is very often a discussion after the performance, when the actors come out of character, answer questions and explain why they chose to portray their character in a particular way. Sometimes, the writer, director and museum professional who commissioned the piece are also present for the discussion.

While it is called museum theatre, the performance does not often take place in a traditional theatre. More usually, it is in a museum gallery, part of an historical house or castle or outside in a courtyard or garden – it is rarely in a theatre. However, no matter where the performance takes place, there is a defined area for the audience and a defined acting area, thus ensuring adherence to theatrical practices. The important thing to remember about museum theatre is that the audience are museum or heritage site visitors. They attend the performances in the hope of discovering some new information about a particular topic or the site itself rather than going for the love of theatre in itself. The piece will have been designed to inform and educate the audience about some aspect of the museum's collection/current exhibition, heritage site's history or a particularly difficult topic in an engaging way, often seeking to evoke an emotional connection with the subject matter. It will also follow the conventions of traditional theatrical performances with a beginning, middle and end but in a considerably shorter time (usually about thirty minutes) than a play in a theatre. Sometimes there will also be audience participation.

Costumed Interpretation

Last but not least of the four disciplines covered by the term "live interpretation", there is costumed interpretation, which is the focus of this book.

Costumed interpretation is delivered by an interpreter as a character from history in costume at a heritage site, museum or gallery, using first-person. The focus of the interpretation is to deliver key messages selected by the organisation regarding a specific period in the past (it could be a particular year or even a day in that year) which reveals a variety of things such as an aspect of life, an event or how people behaved at a certain point in time. The costumed interpreter's mode of delivery aims to engage and educate (and perhaps even entertain!) the visitor and encourage participation in the surroundings in which they find themselves and can be achieved through interpretive conversation or a short presentation. Within a museum or gallery setting, it is likely that the costumed interpreter will interact with visitors with regard to an object or set of objects within an exhibition and interpreting their relevance to the historic period and to the people of that time. As with the heritage site, certain messages are intentionally conveyed in their interaction with visitors so that they feel involved in the overall interpretation of the museum or gallery.

Costumed interpreters use the first-person, thus "pretending" to be from the time period that they portray.[1] Interaction with visitors is often more intimate and informal through conversational encounters, which can lead to a more prolonged engagement with an individual or group who are interested in finding out more and are actively participating with the character through handling objects, copying actions or questioning. Visitors may have different opinions from those portrayed by the character, but that is fine. It gives the costumed interpreter the prospect to introduce other ideas for visitors to consider and to discuss these with them. The opportunity to go beyond the myths that are inevitably associated with famous people and endeavour to show more of who they really were is a very satisfying outcome for any costumed interpreter. For example, on several occasions, I have taken on the persona of Queen Victoria. Most people associate this queen with the famous saying "We are not amused". There is no evidence to suggest that she ever said such a thing. It may well be that this myth has arisen because portraits, both painted and photographic, show her in a dignified manner rather than full of smiles. However, this phrase haunts any portrayal of this queen. When I have interpreted her, a large percentage of my time has been spent demonstrating that this is not the case at all and that before becoming a widow, she was happy and probably smiled. Even in later widowhood, there is evidence to suggest that she enjoyed herself when taking part in certain activities and therefore very likely smiled.

While these informal conversational encounters are very common at sites and museums, costumed interpretation can also be delivered in presentations at set times, which is useful at busy spells of the year and popular exhibitions, and through the medium of guided walks. It is not just a photo opportunity, though this too has its place, as will be seen in Chapter 6.

Within the heritage world of the UK and Europe, it is exceptionally rare to find a location in which first-person costumed interpretation happens all day, every day. Costumed interpretation is more usually presented by one or two interpreters, sometimes a small group, at a museum, gallery or heritage site on set dates at fixed times and often at a particular location to interact with and engage visitors. This can take the form of informal conversation or a more performed piece, which can involve audience participation. The engagement is designed to convey interpretive messages of an exhibition, a particular object, building, time period – perhaps even all of these – selected by the organisation's curatorial/interpretation team.

Many costumed interpreters pride themselves on not being trained actors; their emphasis is on interpreting. In many ways, this is really splitting hairs, as being a costumed interpreter does inevitably involve some kind of performance. I certainly do not want to give the impression that costumed interpretation is for those who did not quite make the grade in acting school. The difference is that for costumed interpreters, their training has come from the study of heritage interpretation and the desire to portray aspects of heritage, tangible and intangible, that affect how people's lifestyles have evolved over the centuries, the connections that can be made with then and now, the lessons that can be learnt whether in the built or natural environment and why this is important. For actors, their performance is that of the imitation and simulation of life, or even caricature in comedy. Their character portrayal is governed by the mimetic mode, and their performance delivered is heavily influenced by the director, who has creative control of the piece. This is not to say actors cannot take part in costumed interpretation, and I have worked alongside actors within Artemis Scotland. Many of their skills are well suited to work in this field, and the use of acting techniques will be discussed further in Chapter 5. Dr Richard Irvine, who works as a volunteer costumed interpreter at Verdant Works Museum in Dundee, puts it most succinctly:

> Just remember you are here to serve the visitors, so don't be a diva.

What Is the Difference?

There is a degree of crossover between costumed and living history interpreters – both are in costume for one thing. Costumed interpreters also use demonstrations of simple tasks and skills such as using a washboard when portraying a Victorian servant or a cup and saucer when showing how to drink tea 18th-century style. However, there are noticeable differences. The setting in which the interpretation is delivered is very different. Living history interpreters work in museums, where the buildings are complete and set in a particular era and do look the part. By contrast, the costumed interpreter's location may be among ruins, for example,

Linlithgow Palace in Scotland, Corfe Castle in England, Ephesus in Turkey and Klis Fortress in Croatia. Within these ruinous settings, costumed interpreters must create a sense of wholeness for the visitors, giving a sense of "how it once was" for the character they are. Another challenge can be that the site, though not ruinous, is a mixture of different periods, as in the case of the Tower of London or Edinburgh Castle. If the delivery is taking place in museum galleries, there is little chance of there being any kind of background that suggests the period being portrayed. In such circumstances, the costumed interpreter must use their character's costume and demeanour to convey the historical period and use the object(s) provided to create that sense of another time and place.

Although there may be some demonstration within their delivery, costumed interpretation relies heavily on talking, explaining and storytelling in first-person, which is quite different to living history interpretation, which can have a more instructional element to it in the sense of the skill or craft demonstration being "this is how they spun wool in the 16th century" and "this is what the woman would have worn" delivered in third-person.

It is not unusual to find costumed interpreters portraying characters from a variety of periods, spanning several centuries – though not on the same day! It is, however, very unusual for living history interpreters to do so. Their specialised knowledge of certain technical skills used in demonstrations means it is harder for them to cross into other periods of time.

It may also seem that costumed interpretation and museum theatre are one and the same thing. However, costumed interpretation is not theatre. Theatrical performances rely on a script, and many costumed interpreters throw up their hands in horror at the mention of the word "script"! Their character creation, based on their research and historical knowledge, gives them a depth to their character that is not dictated by someone else's direction. And there lies the key to costumed interpretation – research and character creation that enable face to face interaction with visitors. Costumed interpreters are in their element when left to wander around a heritage site, museum or gallery, engaging with visitors in conversation and encouraging them to pose questions and look specifically at objects or features of the historic place or even ask about what they are wearing. For some visitors, seeing someone in costume is enough to give the flavour of the period and capture their imaginations, leading to engagement with the interpreter in some aspect about the location. There are also visitors who are quite happy to watch from afar, and we will think about this in more detail later in the book.

Again, costumed interpretation and re-enactment look very similar. However, in reality, the exact set of circumstances from the past can never be fully recreated no matter how much research has been done. Costumed interpretation seeks to find a way of explaining how and why things happened, accepting that it is a starting point for discussion with the visitor and that there are many ways of interpreting the past. Having said that, there is no doubt that re-enactment often provides people with their first contact with active heritage interpretation and has also provided costumed interpretation with many people who have crossed over into the profession.

Different Approaches to Costumed Interpretation Beyond the Western Hemisphere

I would not want you to think that costumed interpretation is the preserve of the Western Hemisphere, for it is not. In my search for what is happening in Asia, it became apparent there is a different perception of heritage and history on this continent. Being an "authentic experience" in the sense of visiting old buildings or sites or viewing objects is of much less importance. Constructing replica buildings at significant locations or copying these buildings elsewhere is regarded as being as much a part of a nation's heritage as seeing the "real thing". The act of reconstruction honours the skills of the craftsmen of the past, and is recognised to be as much a part of their heritage as an original building or object. This leaves the question of where to go to see these reconstructed sites, and the answer to that is to a cultural theme park.

The idea of the cultural park is not as 20th century as we would like to think. From the Edo period (1603–1867), Japanese rulers have provided parks in the form of botanical gardens to amuse people; over time, these have developed into amusement parks, and from this has emerged the cultural theme park. In 1986, Edo Wonderland was opened which is one of the largest cultural parks in that country. Now known as Edo Wonderland Nikko Edomura, it recreates the Golden Age of the Edo period (1688–1704) in Japanese history, a time of relative economic stability when the arts and culture prospered across the nation. The site provides buildings representing all aspects of society from official government buildings to rural homes, as well as samurai dwellings and merchants' houses. The staff on site are in costumes, interacting with visitors in first-person, portraying the various classes of the period and engaging visitors in activities like learning to play a traditional game, calligraphy and archery. There are also sword demonstrations by samurai and the chance to learn that skill. The interpreters are given some basic information about their character, but it remains for them to do the research and development and construct their delivery to fit in with the others on site. There are no scripts as such – a point we will look at more closely later in the book. There are also seven theatres on site in which performances of traditional customs and plays take place, as do their very popular ninja shows. It is possible to hire a costume on arrival and wander round the site dressed like the interpreters, which is also possible at some western sites like Colonial Williamsburg.

Having the term "theme park" in the title of the site is quite misleading to Western visitors, as Edo Wonderland Nikko Edomura is much more like what would be seen as a re-created living history site, similar to Colonial Williamsburg in the USA, Beamish in the UK or Den Gamle By in Denmark. There are none of the rides and thrills associated with what we think of as theme parks, of which there are many in Japan, the most popular being Tokyo Disney Resort. At Edo Wonderland Nikko Edomura, the visitors are predominantly Japanese, and their reason for coming is to learn about the past and enjoy the experience too. The term "edutainment", first used by Walt Disney in 1954, has become accepted as the way to describe the possibility that one can be educated and entertained at the same time.

This is most certainly the aim here, and its success is based on the provision of spectacle and the interaction of the visitors with the on-site costumed interpreters. The term "re-enactment" is often used with regards to the activities and interaction delivered here. This is confusing for western practitioners of costumed interpretation because, as explained earlier, re-enactment is associated with specific battlefields, and the people who take part do it as a leisure activity. For Japan, the term "re-enactment" has become their definition of costumed interpretation.

Edo Wonderland Nikko Edomura is not, of course, the only "park" of this kind in Japan. Ise Ninja Kingdom represents the Azuchi Momoyama period, when the samurai were dominant; another Edo experience can be enjoyed at Noboribetsu Date Jidaimura historical village, while Meiji Mura concentrates on the period at the end of the 19th century and beginning of the 20th century which witnesses the decline of the feudal system. All follow a similar pattern in which costumed interpreters enable visitors to learn and understand Japanese tangible and intangible heritage in a manufactured space that recreates what no longer exists, because within Japan, very few old buildings have in fact survived. This country is a location for earthquakes, and what has not been destroyed by natural disaster has been by wars. The Japanese understanding of the idea of the cultural park demonstrates a mixture of living history – the reproduction buildings and craft/skill demonstrations and participation – and costumed interpretation – first-person interaction with visitors that reveal the stories related to Edo culture. Interestingly Lam points out that while there are very few visitors from other cultures, all are treated the same way; the aim is for everyone to experience the Golden Age of Japanese culture here at this park, regardless of where they have come from (Lam, 2020).

China has taken to the cultural theme park with great enthusiasm, it also being seen as a way of preserving cultural heritage and aspects of history in the various regions of the country through the spectacle of reconstructed buildings, the performance of traditional dance and drama, visitors' active participation in trying out skills associated with old crafts, learning about certain historical characters and appreciation of classic Chinese gardens. All of their cultural theme parks are designed to reinforce a sense of identity, as they are aimed primarily at the Chinese people. Visitors from other countries do, of course, enjoy visiting them too. Every district in China has at least one cultural theme park reflecting some aspect of heritage important to the area. Most of these parks have some form of costumed demonstration taking place, as can be seen in the Millennium City Park in the city of Kaifeng, Henan Province, which takes its visitors back in time to the Song Dynasty through the re-creation of a famous painting of the 12th century, and Shunde Qinghui Park, Foshan, which blends Ming and Quing dynasty culture in classical garden settings. Many of the cultural theme parks in China have an amusement park nearby.

My quest to find examples of costumed interpretation on the South American continent has drawn a blank. However, there is evidence of cultural tourism developments within parts of South America where festivals celebrate old customs and local people dress in traditional costume. Throughout Mexico, festivals are held in which people dress up in Aztec costumes and take part in parades and dances.

For example, in February every year, the execution of Cuauhtémoc, the last Aztec emperor, by the Spanish is commemorated in a festival at Ixcateopan. Ecuador, Colombia, Bolivia and Peru all hold versions of Inti Raymi, the Inca solstice celebration, held on 24 August, to the sun god, Inti. The largest is held in Cusco in Peru and based on the 1609 writings of Inca Garcilaso de la Vega, who watched the ceremony. The re-creation of the original writings takes place at various key sites across Cusco and features an Inca Emperor borne aloft through the streets, followed by parades of hundreds of people dressed in Inca costume denoting specific roles in the ceremony, which culminates at the temple fortress of Sacsayhuaman. While the costumes worn for all these celebrations are very colourful and extravagant, this is definitely not costumed interpretation. It suggests elements of exploitation for the benefit of tourists rather than developing an understanding of the past and respecting tradition and reinforces such concepts as the "exotic-ness" of faraway lands.

This wander off around the world may seem a little out of place. However, the point is really that no matter where you go, with the exception of most of the African and South American continents, there is a fascination with how people lived and what they wore in the past. Being able to see a person move about in these "strange" clothes or even have a chance to try them on helps in the understanding of how those before us lived their lives. On top of that, there is the opportunity to talk to someone knowledgeable about the particular time period and come as close as possible to an authentic feeling of the past. While the approach in Japan and elsewhere in the world is a bit different, the fundamental principle remains the same – visitors enjoy the experience of interacting directly with people dressed in costume representing the past who can convince them, for the time they are with them, that they have in fact "stepped back in time".

For or Against?

Within the heritage world live, interpretation and its various disciplines have struggled to gain acceptance as a serious form of heritage interpretation. Many critics see it as trivialising history, providing a nostalgic or romantic look at the past set at a time when every servant's uniform was clean and everything was in its place. Equally, it is hard to distinguish which form of live interpretation is being written about – is it re-enactment, living history, museum theatre or costumed interpretation? When Stacy Roth published *Past Into Present* in 1998, she confronted such criticism, highlighting that this was a real dilemma – the apparent inability of writers to distinguish between the various forms of live interpretation or their assumption that it did not matter because they were all the same anyway. As I have already mentioned, this is a challenge that still exists today within the museum and heritage world when defining the various disciplines of live interpretation. I have lost count of the number of times I have been asked what I am re-enacting today! This then makes it harder to work out what is being evaluated in the various books and articles written from the 1980s onwards, most of which have come from the USA.

Having read many articles and the few books that exist, I have found that there is very little written about the single costumed interpreter at a museum, historic site, school or community setting brought in for a specific programme or event who may well be working with a modern backdrop yet providing a sense of what it may well have been like in the past. This has very much been the scenario that I have worked in over the years, and it is rarely evaluated by serious scholars.

This is not to say that you will not find costumed interpreters at living history museums working in first-person. They lead guided walks, deliver character presentations and just chat and answer questions. However, more often within the UK, you will encounter a costumed interpreter at a museum conducting a gallery promenade for a specific period; running a family programme in the holidays; delivering a school education session; participating in a special event; or promoting a new exhibition. You will also meet them at historic sites, frequently standing amid the ruins, helping the visitors to visualise how the site looked in past times. This type of costumed interpretation rarely receives any attention. Nevertheless, it is worth taking a few moments to examine what has been written, as it helps to understand how the confusion has arisen and why costumed interpretation has evolved from the living history movement.

Many of the living history museums in the United States were founded and funded by wealthy businessmen who wanted to promote certain values typified as part of the American pioneer spirit such as economy and industriousness (Allison, 2016). These museums became particularly popular in the 1970s with the American public. By the 1980s, some examination of the popularity of these sites began to take place. Jay Anderson's *Time Machines: The World of Living History*, published in 1984, is regarded as the first serious study and covered the whole gamut of this genre of interpretation, thus beginning the difficulty of distinguishing one discipline from another. He concentrated on the large living history museums of the USA, such as Plimoth Plantation and Old Sturbridge Village, both in Massachusetts, and Iowa's living history farms as well as re-enactment and experimental archaeology. He was very positive about using demonstrations by people in costume to help visitors see links between past and present lives and to learn about how much things had changed and espoused it as the new way to reach visitors. He was also very enthusiastic about re-enactment groups, particularly those who recreated replica ships to test out what conditions were like on voyages of the past, which was a popular experimental archaeological practice in the 1980s. The book had a mixed reception. Those in the living history world were pleased to see that their field of work was getting some recognition. However, the academic world was less enthusiastic and more critical of it. For example, David Glassberg of the University of Massachusetts Amherst, in his article "Living in the Past" in *American Quarterly* (1986), wrote that Anderson had not analysed living history and its constituent elements rigorously enough and concluded that in the end, all living history did was to fulfil visitors' expectations of what they thought was the past from their diet of television's historic drama and films rather than grappling with real stories. Richard Handler of the University of Virginia, who later studied Colonial Williamsburg with Eric Gable, saw political implications in how living history interpreters portrayed past lives because of the composition of the managerial boards of the museums. He felt that ultimately, it was a way of endorsing the views of the founders rather than portraying an authentic past.

At the close of the 20th century, Stacy Roth's book *Past Into Present, Effective Techniques for First-Person Historical Interpretation* (1998) was published, again based around working in the large American living history museums, on this occasion Colonial Williamsburg, Plimoth Plantation and Conner Prairie. This book was the first to provide guidance on characterisation and methods of delivery, which concentrated on what we in the UK know as costumed interpretation that uses conversational techniques in first-person and does not use scripts. Roth's methodology really emphasised the importance of individual research on top of whatever was provided for the interpreter by the institution. This then helped them to make connections with visitors on a one-to-one basis and became the real foundation of excellent costumed first-person interpretation that gave the visitor the feeling of being part of an authentic experience, very much at the heart of American live interpretation.

In 2007, Scott Magelssen wrote *Living History Museums: Undoing History Through Performance* examining the methods used at Plimoth Plantation, Old Sturbridge Village and Colonial Williamsburg. He was extremely critical of all of these sites, arguing that first-person interpretation did not portray history accurately enough, settling for a version of the past that kept the visitor entertained rather than informed, to the detriment of all. The opportunity to do something significant was being lost, and history was being trivialised. He also supported the idea that these sites were being used to promote a particular view of the past with political connotations for the present. His book rang alarm bells in the world of live interpretation in the USA and resulted in an overhaul of their approach. Allison's book of 2016, *Living History: Effective Costumed Interpretation and Enactment at Museums and Historic Sites*, shows how much things had changed in the USA in less than ten years and equally put the case for the form of costumed interpretation that is easily recognisable in the UK and Europe – conversational encounters that are "timelessly effective". He also makes the case that with some topics, there is no reason visitors cannot be entertained as well as educated, a view with which I whole heartedly agree.

The Importance of Learning

The one theme that links all forms of heritage interpretation throughout the world is the desire to help people make sense of the past, whether in the built or natural environment. Education is not just the preserve of school pupils; it is for everyone. Whether you wrap it up as visitor experiences, site engagement or discovery trails, the goal is that those taking part have learnt something new and hopefully enjoyed doing so, without feeling they have been preached at.

For understanding the impact live interpretation can have on learning, the article "'Seeing It for Real . . .?' – Authenticity, Theatre and Learning in Museums" by Anthony Jackson and Helen Rees Leahy examined the use of what they called museum theatre in the Imperial War Museum, London, and the People's History Museum, Manchester, with eight groups of ten-year-old pupils. To measure the effectiveness of "museum theatre", half of the groups participated in a different learning activity from the one involving the performer. Their respective museum visits were followed up two months later, when the research team visited the children in their classrooms to see what recall they had of their activity. The aim of the project was to see "*whether* and *how* the use of theatre and theatre techniques" (Jackson & Leahy, 2005) made any difference to the children's museum visit, if it made any difference to what they learnt on the day and whether they remembered it two months later. Although different periods of history were being portrayed, each museum used the same approach of one interpreter using storytelling techniques. Given the earlier definitions of museum theatre and costumed interpretation, it would seem that this is the latter, because the pupils interact with the character within the museum itself rather than in a theatre setting. However, rather than split hairs at this point, the important aspect of this study is its results.

When the researchers visited the schools two months later, the active learning of those who had been part of the "museum theatre" group resulted in better recall of what they had learnt on their visit as well as a feeling that they had been involved in something very memorable with a person from history. Most of those who had not had the theatre experience did not remember as much as those who had. The exception to this was when object handling had been part of their activity – then they too had retained what they had learnt, which does suggest that some form of participation is vital. While the sample was small, it is still the only study that I can find that has attempted to demonstrate that interaction with a costumed character aids learning and helps children engage with the museum, its objects and its stories.

"Seeing It for Real . . .?" provided insight into the benefit gained for schools interacting with some kind of performance. Jane Malcolm-Davies did the same for the general visitor experience in her article "Borrowed Robes: The Educational Value of Costumed Interpretation". She examined whether costumed interpretation at selected historic sites in Sweden, the UK, the USA and Canada was having the desired impact on visitors, which was to educate them about some aspect of the site. The sites chosen all had costumed interpreters as part of their paid staff rather than freelancers brought in for a particular project, which is more unusual in the UK than in Europe or North America. Interestingly, at the beginning of her article, she made the point that there were few studies that objectively studied the contribution of such interpretation and that existing investigations were either overly positive or very negative; there was "no thoughtful comment" (Malcolm-Davies, 2004) that considered what was good and what required improvement. Her findings revealed that visitors wanted to learn something new at the various sites, have fun while doing so and "feel a sense of the past" (Malcolm-Davies, 2004). The key to this success was investment on the part of the site in staff training and excellent reproduction costumes. It was these that made the difference to the experience of the visitors and the feeling that they had learnt something and had an enjoyable experience. It was only in my research for this book that

I discovered this article, but from my involvement in the profession, I can most definitely confirm that these are the key components to excellence. It is important for a costumed interpreter, like every scout, to "be prepared", as you will discover later in the book.

Providing the Best Possible Visitor Experience

Clearly, I am an enthusiastic and passionate supporter of costumed interpretation and believe that it has many applications in the heritage world. A costumed character can do many things – take people on a guided walk, apparently taking them back into the past, initiate a conversation on a variety of topics, engage adults and children alike in learning manners of a specific period, run a school session that breathes life into a challenging subject and explain a complicated concept using storytelling. However, I am also aware that it is not always the solution and could, on some occasions, cause upset to visitors. Traumatic history that has left a scar on the landscape and in the minds of people and that is often relatively recent requires the provision of reflective spaces to deal with coming to terms with information provided. No one would expect to find costumed interpretation as part of an exhibition about the Holocaust or the impact of 9/11.

There are some for whom costumed interpretation is nothing more than a bit of colour, the "bling" beloved by the marketing department of museums and heritage sites – let's get some people in, dress them up, take a few photos, and they can have a chat with the visitors for a few minutes. This is most definitely not the way to use costumed interpretation, nor is it actual costumed interpretation. It is often what stops curators from using any form of live interpretation, because the people hired to be in costume for the day know nothing of any substance about whatever it is they are there to promote.

Arguments levelled against costumed interpretation are often associated with anachronisms. "They are using microphones – they didn't have them in whatever century they are supposed to be in; there's the smell of burgers cooking in the café – bet they didn't have those in the olden days". For the costumed interpreter in a modern gallery space in a museum, this is a daily occurrence, as they are surrounded by all that is of today except for the object(s) with which they are working. It is no better at a heritage site, as there will also be modern intrusions present – safety information put in place because of lose stonework; the fact that the site is in ruins in some cases; the sound of traffic around the site; visitors with audio guides. These anachronisms are always going to be there unless one is working at a living history museum dedicated to replicating a particular period, and even then their cafes will be powered by modern means providing beverages of everyday life. What has to be remembered is that visitors know perfectly well that neither the interpreter nor themselves have "time travelled". They are experiencing some aspect of the site or museum and have been provided with a person to help explain this, which enhances the enjoyment of their visit. In writing this book, I have approached those with whom I have worked over the years to offer their own insights into aspects of costumed interpretation. Karen Bartke, whose

background is within the world of acting, has worked for Artemis Scotl
many occasions and sums up the versatility of costumed interpreters an
interaction with visitors:

> It's a job where ego about your character is the last thing you can afford to permit. Every visitor is going to want/need something different from you and it's vital to constantly adjust to their cues. Some visitors want to engage with a historical character and will be tickled pink to strike up a conversation about how much you appreciate the reduction in hours at the mill (New Lanark) or the vagaries of growing your own vegetables to help the war effort (National Museum of Rural Life). However, others will feel very uncomfortable if pressed into too much interaction – they may simply want you to point them in the direction of an exhibit and leave them alone. Being willing and able to adjust how you're dealing with the audience moment to moment is crucial to ensuring everyone has a positive experience. . . . I think one of the most important elements is ensuring that your character is always living in the environment they are in – not just standing about waiting for someone to arrive and then switching it on.

Another clue to this not really being someone from the past is in the words "costumed interpreter" – the clothes worn represent the past and are not actual clothes from the past; they too are an interpretation.

The interpretation taking place in the form of speaking to the visitor while wearing a costume is as valid as the audio guide, information panel, guided tour or any other form of on-site interpretation. All are working together to provide the best possible visitor experience. As helping visitors to learn something new is at the core of all heritage interpretation, it is the duty of all interpreters to remember everyone learns things differently. Those who are critical of costumed interpretation are forgetful that for some visitors, it is the spectacle of seeing someone in an historical costume and the chance to interact that is their learning stimulus or the chance to participate in a dance or some form of period etiquette which makes some historical period relevant to them. When done properly, with all the research and preparation that back up the costumed interpretation, it does not detract from all the other forms of interpretation on site; it enriches and complements what is already there. And there lies the key: the absolute importance of preparation.

Note

1 In the United States, costumed interpretation is most usually referred to as first-person interpretation and sometimes as role-play.

2 Building Your Character

It is rare to find an institution that provides an intense training scheme for costumed interpreters. If any training is provided, it is usually because those who are to deliver the costumed interpretation are volunteers, and there is an obligation to provide some form of guidance on the work they are about to deliver. It is often no more than a couple of days. That has certainly been my experience when asked to provide costumed interpretation training to volunteers; very often, it is only one day. There are occasional exceptions as in the case when I delivered a six-week course to the full-time education staff and volunteers of the Tall Ship *Glenlee*, in 2009, taking those attending through the process of character creation and delivery. The *Glenlee* is now part of the Riverside Museum in Glasgow, and I am delighted to say that one of those volunteers is now a full-time member of the learning team and very active in costumed interpretation on board the ship. Such a course is, however, unusual.

As far as I can discover, Stacy Roth's *Past Into Present: Effective Techniques for First-Person Historical Interpretation* (1998), written from an American perspective for the large living history museums, is the only text that provides any guidance on costumed interpretation. While there is useful information in this book, the approach is focussed on costumed interpretation in large organisations with considerable infrastructure to support their staff rather than the freelance experience that is more usual in the UK and Europe. Also, by virtue of its age, this book is now a little outdated, as many of the programmes referenced at sites such as Colonial Williamsburg have changed significantly. Searches on the internet for "how to be a costumed interpreter" will produce tips and hints which often contradict one another; one source even suggests that character building is not required! It is all rather confusing for the budding costumed interpreter. As with all heritage interpretation, planning is of the utmost importance, and for costumed interpretation, that means considerable research into who you are going to be and building your character. Regardless of the situation in which you are performing, you need to know who you are.

Fergus John McCann is a seasoned costumed interpreter who I have had the pleasure of working with for a number of years and who has also delivered several characters for Artemis Scotland. Here is his advice on doing your research:

> Know your onions. You need to do the homework. Most historical interpretation requires improvisation, which will quickly fall apart if you don't know

DOI: 10.4324/9781003260226-3

> what you're talking about. It's also true of delivered interpretation (e.g. monologuing without audience interaction): if you don't understand what you're saying, it's unlikely the audience will. If you haven't done your research and don't know about your character and their context, you're just playing dress-up.

Sound advice on which to begin.

Where to Start

Before embarking on building the character that has been selected for a particular event, the interpreter needs to be provided with certain information by the organisation. It may be that the character can move around the whole site or museum, or it may be that there is a specific *location* in which they will be based. The *key messages* that are to be delivered via the costumed interpreter are also required at this stage, as they will influence how the character will be created and the specific information to be sought out in the character creation. It is also crucial to know the *stories* which the organisation has identified to be told within the key messages being delivered.

For those of you new to the world of costumed interpretation, it is worth taking the time now to highlight the definition of messages and stories and the difference between the two from your point of view. It can happen that you have to work these out for yourself. Sometimes, key messages might be referred to as interpretive messages, but they refer to the same thing and are usually brief. What they do is provide you with what the organisation regards as the significant thing they want visitors to remember when they reflect on their day at the exhibition or site visit. The story (in some cases it will be stories) that is to be told is the vehicle for getting the message(s) across. It is the examples you give to visitors to understand the significance of the message(s).

Now is also the time to know if the organisation has any particular *experiences* they wish the visitors to have at the chosen location with the interpreter, as this will determine the *method of delivery*. Information about the *target audience* at whom the costumed interpretation is being aimed – it may be all visitors on the day, but sometimes, it can be a specific audience like family visitors – should also be included at this point to assist with development.

For my convenience, I find it very helpful to put this information into a checklist to keep the character building that is about to take place on track. It provides an easy way to remind yourself and keep what is required uppermost in mind. Let us imagine that you are to be Queen Victoria in a museum gallery, newly refurbished. This is for a late-night opening associated with an exhibition on jewellery featuring three pieces owned by the queen that are on loan and a re-display of their objects associated with the Crimean War. For this event, the year is to be 1854, as this is when the jewellery was given to the queen and also the year when war was declared in the Crimea. This information has been provided by the museum. Following, you will find a checklist for this imaginary event, which takes the form of what I create for myself. Everything I need to know is in one place.

Table 2.1 A checklist demonstrating how to organise information received from the client that will inform your character development and delivery

Location in Gallery

The re-furbished gallery of 19th-century history with:

- jewellery on loan that belonged to Queen Victoria
- large section of objects, particularly medals, associated with the Crimean War

Key Messages

1 Queen Victoria was known for her love of jewellery, but it was always about more than the sparkles, as the interpreter will illustrate – the three pieces here were gifts from her husband in 1854.
2 The Queen insisted on being kept informed about the progress of the Crimean War, and it was she who decided there should be a medal for all those who had fought at Alma and Inkerman, at the end of 1854.

The Stories

1 Queen Victoria was not interested in the value of her jewellery; it was the sentiment behind the gift. These pieces were anniversary gifts from Albert.
2 Queen Victoria is kept well informed about the Crimean War. In November 1854, she writes to the Duke of Newcastle after the battle of Inkerman to say a medal must be made to recognise those who have fought in these battles. She knows exactly how she wants it to look and even decides on the wording.
3 This medal is NOT the Victoria Cross (VC) – that is a later medal also associated with the Crimea. The museum is keen for the interpreter to highlight the role of Victoria in creating a medal for all men who have fought before the VC is created.

Visitor Experience

The evening will be split into 2 distinct sections:

1 Visitors engage with the queen through conversation, trying on costume and reproduction jewellery.
2 Halfway through the evening, the queen will move into the area of the gallery related to the Crimean War. Here, she will hold "an audience", making a short presentation about her decision to create a medal recognising the service of her armed forces at Alma and Inkerman. There will then be an opportunity to question Victoria after her presentation.

Target Audience

Young adults, couples, friendship groups

Method of Delivery

1 Interpreter walks around the gallery, engaging in conversation about the jewellery on display and encouraging conversation about the significance of certain pieces to her and the importance she attaches to jewellery with a story. She encourages visitors to share stories about what jewellery they are wearing – does it have any sentimental value to them? Photo opportunity wearing costume provided by the museum and reproduction jewellery.
2 In the section on the Crimea, the queen gives a short talk about her concern for her troops and that a medal must be issued for those who have fought here. She then answers questions and poses for photographs.

The costumed interpretation provides the opportunity to demonstrate that Queen Victoria takes a real interest in the country over which she reigns and is not just a figurehead. We at the museum want it shown that there is more to her than her marriage to Albert, though that is important too, as the jewellery shows.

A checklist like this enables you to really focus on what the client wants from you as the costumed character at the event as well as how you will begin to create the backstory and inhabit the persona.

A Site Visit

If at all possible, visit a site before you work there. This can be done at any point in the preparation of your character. Some people like to go after receiving the information relating to the messages and stories to be delivered, and others prefer to go when they have more of an idea of who they are going to be. It is a personal choice. A site visit enables you to get the feel of where you will be working. You may want to spend some time just being in the space, soaking up the atmosphere and imagining yourself as your character – this is certainly something I find very useful. Meeting the staff is also important and makes for a more comfortable work experience when you are in character. This is also the time to sort out practical considerations:

- Arrange a parking place – if you are coming by car and on-site parking is available, make sure you request this in advance, as it is usually dealt with by a different department from the one you are working for.
- If you are coming by public transport, check the timetables as well as working out where the nearest bus stop or train station is with regards to the place of delivery and whether you will have to factor in a taxi as well. Try and work out how long it will take you to get there, as this takes away the stress of arrival on the day.
- Check up on the procedure for getting into the building if you are arriving before it opens to the public.
- Organise a place to get changed into your costume, with access to toilets.
- Make sure there is somewhere secure you can leave your personal items and valuables.
- If the room where you change is unsuitable for your break, find out where this is to be in advance and make sure you can leave your food there, because the last thing you want to be seen doing is carrying your lunch in a plastic bag in full costume!
- Make sure you have contact numbers for those who will be on-site on the day, because sometimes no matter how hard you try, something goes wrong – the bus does not come, the train is cancelled or you are held up in a traffic jam.

Of course, it is not always possible to visit the place where you will be working for a preliminary visit. If you live some distance from where you are booked to deliver a particular character it is going to be expensive to go unless the cost has already been factored in as part of your fee, a worthwhile consideration in many cases. If an advance visit is impossible, ask the organisation for whom you are working to provide as much information as possible on the points I have made. You might even be able to persuade them to send photographs of the area in which you are to work and other aspects of the site or building.

Beginning the Process of Character Creation

Once the time period is known, whether it be several years, a whole year or even just one day in a particular month of a year, it is a good idea to read generally about the period to get the feel of this moment in history and note any significant dates that pop up. A good way to manage this is to create a simple timeline of specific events for the time you are investigating that seem, at least at first, essential to your character. Equally, you do not want to get tied up in knots about dates and remembering them. As an interpreter, you are telling about some aspect of history, not reeling off dates. However, they are important, because you do in fact need to know what has happened after the date you are portraying. While in character, you cannot know the future. It is in reality essential that you do so that you are not pulled out of your period by the questioning of visitors. Mary, Queen of Scots is a good example of this. My portrayal of this queen has often been set in 1566, the year her son was born. Inevitably, visitors will ask things about how I feel about living in England, which, of course, in 1566 is not a consideration as this does not happen until 1568. Equally, mention of the execution always comes up and that is far into the future – 1587 to be precise. Therefore, for the sake of delivering the message of joy about the birth of a male heir to the Scottish throne, I must know the future so that I do not answer anything about it!

A timeline is really to help you find your way about the period and record some significant events that have happened that might influence the character. It need not be many dates at all by the end of the process. Additions can be made as the persona begins to take shape, because other dates may become more of a focus as creation develops. It is, however, important to get a feel of what is going on. It may well be that the organisation that you are working for is able to provide this information. If this is not the case, the internet is a good source, though do stick to reliable sites. As you progress through your career, it is also likely that you will create your own reference library and list of trustworthy online sources.

Authenticity

A common goal in providing heritage experiences at historic sites and museums has become what is commonly described as "being authentic". This means that however the history and heritage of the place or object are presented to visitors, they must be as accurate as possible. Whatever story is being told or engaging activity taking place must rely on thorough research. As a costumed interpreter, this means that when preparing and building your character, the material you ultimately present to visitors has to be as close as possible to how people lived and behaved at the point of time you are presenting, whether it is as a generic or real character. You want to be in the position when someone asks, "Are you being authentic?" to be able to say, "Yes, I am". All this depends on the work you do to create the character.

Creating Who You Are

Once I began my career as a costumed interpreter, it became clear to me quite quickly that I needed to find an easy way to organise the information about what my character definitely knew and, equally, what they might have known, a distinction that will become obvious later in this chapter. The other thing that became apparent was that it is impossible to know everything. One way to reconcile this with yourself is to remember that even within life now, we forget things we have done; no one remembers everything.

Requiring a way to organise the information, I came up with the concept of "realms". Every character I develop has a personal, local and wider-world realm which anchors the character in a particular time and place as well as linking them to what exists further afield. Put plainly, the personal realm is what the character knows about themselves. The local realm relates to what the character knows about the place where he/she works and lives. The wider-world realm links the character to what is going on elsewhere in the world and whether they know anything about this. Clearly a monarch will know a lot about this last realm, but a servant or factory worker less so.

Regardless of whether your character is a "real" person, like Elizabeth I or Dr Samuel Johnson, or a generic person such as a 16th-century courtier, an 18th-century mill worker or a 19th-century housekeeper, you will need to give the character depth, validity and a range of knowledge that makes them believable. These realms give you the context in which your character lives and breathes. The real character may seem like the easiest to work on, because the more famous they are the more evidence there is of their existence. However, this can be problematic, as there is often far too much information. You also have to deal with the fact that if the person being interpreted is very well known, like Mary, Queen of Scots or Queen Victoria, for example, visitors will already have their own view of what this person is like. Equally, that gives you the chance to challenge accepted views that are not historically accurate. The generic characters of the costumed interpretation world seem, therefore, to be easier to construct. However, they are an amalgam of information, as there is little evidence of ordinary lives, and the character has to be brought together from a variety of sources. It is not easy, but it is a very fulfilling process to see a character, whether real or generic, taking shape.

When I created the realms' concept, I had not read Roth's ground-breaking *Past Into Present*, and when I did, I discovered that she referred to "worlds" or "spheres", some with similar titles to my realms. It is therefore appropriate at this point to assess her model, as while there are similarities, there are also significant differences to my concept. It should be noted that her suggestions for character development are based on interpreters working at American living history museums. The character development she suggests has five "worlds" or "spheres", each requiring substantial research. For interpreters working full-time in a reconstructed immersive visitor experience dedicated to one particular period in history, this approach works well, as the detail of the character's life has to be more specific, because many visitors spend several days exploring the whole site, as in the case of Colonial Williamsburg. The characters at these American sites are not just there for one day or perhaps once a week for a month or even just for a single-day event. Their characters require considerable depth to deal with repeatedly meeting the same people over several days. It is in these circumstances that it becomes important to consider things like personal habits such as whether the character likes a particular local ale; health over a period of years of the character and family; what the weather has been like over the last few years. The likelihood that the interpreters will meet the same people over several days means that this minutiae of life becomes essential for the conversational encounters they will have. Observations from a study visit I made to Colonial Williamsburg in 2010 revealed that visitors who were there for several days often sought out interpreters they had previously met, as they had enjoyed their company. Also, some were re-visiting from previous years and reminding the interpreters what they already knew about them and wondering how their fictional families were! It was clear from my visit that some interpreters spent several years refining their characters' knowledge.

My experience is not of that environment. I have worked mainly in museums and heritage sites, each of which has history and heritage associated with several periods, rather than one particular point in time as portrayed at most living history museums in the USA. It is not that I do not provide an immersive experience, but I do have to manage the fact that the setting I am within is rarely exactly right. For example, when I have delivered Mary, Queen of Scots at Edinburgh Castle in the Great Hall, the interior décor is a Victorian reconstruction of a medieval hall rather than as it would have been in the 16th-century court of the queen. However, with a well-developed character and the right techniques, which we will examine in Chapter 5, it is possible to involve the visitors and to suspend reality briefly. The method suggested by Roth also requires a lot of time, a luxury which few freelance interpreters have, as often their character development, sourcing of costume and props and delivery format for the event have to be completed within a short time. Much of the work in the UK and beyond is for a specific event and therefore transient. Character development has to be efficient, as while you are being a 19th-century servant on Saturday, you may well be Henry VIII on Tuesday!

Over the years, I have developed a basic list that I use as building blocks for each of the realms, as there is information that is common to all characters, regardless of whether they are real or generic. Inevitably, other areas of interest will arise as the characterisation proceeds that lead into the interpretive messages that are to be delivered to visitors, but you need to start somewhere, and the realms will enable you to develop your research techniques, which will become second nature to you and prevent you from getting bogged down in unnecessary detail. This is not to say that your characters will not have depth and detail. This method will ensure you do not lose sight of your interpretive goals for the character that you will eventually be.

The Personal Realm

As your character, this realm concerns everything you know about yourself. This list is not exhaustive, nor does everything have to be included. It does, however, include many things that anyone knows about themselves, so it is a useful guide:

- Your date and place of birth
- Your immediate family – Are your parents still alive? Do you have any siblings? What does your father do for a living? Does your mother have a job?

- Education – it could be as basic as reading or writing but might also include university
- Where you live now
- Whether you are married and to whom; have you any children? What work does your spouse do?
- Religion
- Do you need to work? If so, what is your job?
- Hobbies/interests/social life
- How you dress
- Your politics – it may not be relevant to your character
- Friends you have – perhaps some are quite important in your period of history
- How you perceive your position in society

If you are building the character for a person who lived, which I will refer to from now on as real, then this information will be readily available. However, you may well be constructing a generic character from scratch, in which case the first thing you need to do, if your client has not done so already, is choose a name which was common to the period you are interpreting. Using an online source is an option, and it is surprising to see the number of choices that appear. If, for example, you type in "pick a name for a Roman character", you will get a huge variety of suggestions. Further internet searches for medieval names for male and female characters recommend William and Alice as popular choices. The internet can be used for all centuries. It was also quite common to use biblical names in early Christian times. There are certainly plenty from which to choose.

As a generic character, you also have to consider a date of birth. If you are building a character of lowly status, it is extremely unlikely that for early periods, such a person would have known their birthdate. Official recording of births in England and Wales began in 1837; in Scotland, it was not until 1855. Before that reliance was on baptismal church records and while most families had their babies baptised they would often move several times, so they would not be able to check a date. Also, a birth within a family was fairly commonplace and unlikely to be noted in any special way. Working out a date of birth for your generic character should be based on your own age in relation to the period you are depicting. The lack of information on a birthdate makes for good conversation in character. It is also worth noting that birth information for some real characters is also vague and, again, a useful talking point.

With regards to parents and siblings of a generic character, that is entirely up to you. If you are depicting a low-status character, it can be useful to reference family as an indication of the level of your poverty. You might, for example, be a working mother in a mill in 19th-century northern England, sad that your four-year-old has had to start work. The family you create for your character depends very much on who you are interpreting for the client.

For the other aspects of your personal realm, the amount of information you require is dependent on the nature of the portrayal you will deliver. You do not have to fill in every point, nor do you have to follow this order; equally, you may think of things that I have not. I have found that in my work, the points

I have provided here and that are in the other realms cover most of the information I need, but please do not feel they are cast in stone and that you cannot change them as you progress in your career. If you are working at a heritage site, the detail is likely to be greater, as you will have more scope to move around the site and interact with visitors and therefore require to be more embedded into your character. Within a gallery-specific exhibition in a museum or even situated near an object or set of objects, your movement will be quite limited and the dwell time of the visitor much shorter, so you may choose to reduce the amount of detail I suggest. However, from experience, I know that you will feel more comfortable if you have anchored your character with information that you can draw on for the one or two visitors who want just that little bit more detail than anyone else.

The Local Realm

This realm relates to what your character knows about where they live and work, in terms of both the locality and what is going on round about them in this particular place. It also conveys your perception of your social standing within the place. In some ways, the local realm can also be seen as your community realm. Keep in mind the date your character will inhabit.

Here are my suggestions of what to consider as part of your character development at this stage. As with the personal realm, you do not need to include all of them, and there may be others that you think of as more relevant to your character:

- What is happening around where you live on a day-to-day basis
- Has anything of any significance happened in the area where you live, or is anything happening at this moment in time you are interpreting? Also remember to factor in the immediate future too.
- How you find out about what is going on in your area
- Can you travel farther afield? And if not, why not?
- Are there any local people who affect how your life is lived?
- How others see your position in society
- Local customs and traditions

If your character interpretation is taking place in a museum gallery, it may well be that some of these suggested elements are irrelevant to you. However, I suggest that even if you are in a museum rather than a heritage site, you do consider some of these aspects to ground your character. For example, let us imagine you have been given the date of 1771 and are to be a generic 18th-century lady interpreting the "language of the fan" (using your fan as a form of communication in a formal setting) at an exhibition of fans in a museum that itself dates to the 1970s about thirty miles away from Bath. In this instance, it will be important to set the scene, as you will be working in a modern environment, so first, incorporate a few pieces of information from your personal realm. You may decide to inform your visitors that you are doing your second season in the very fashionable city of Bath, and therefore, you know all there is to know about manners and etiquette. You are from a family of landed gentry, and you have married well, your husband owning far more land than your parents; hence your wealth and feeling that you are well regarded by your peers. From your local realm, you can make the point that the new Assembly Rooms are to be opened very soon (they were in use by 1771), and you are sure that those who are standing before you are keen to learn some of the forms used in the "language of the fan" in order not to be obvious as first-time visitors to Bath when they, too, attend the Assembly Rooms, the most fashionable place in town. This is all hypothetical, but it does demonstrate some very basic use of personal and local realm material.

A common assumption is that most people did not travel that far because of poor transport, bad roads and the cost of it. This is not strictly true, and there was more movement around Britain than is usually supposed. For example, Shakespeare travelled from Stratford-upon-Avon to London in the late 16th century, a distance of nearly one hundred miles. In July 1618, Ben Jonson and a friend set out on a "foot voyage" from London to Edinburgh, arriving in September of that year. It is not recorded how they returned. Robert Owen, who owned and ran New Lanark, struggled to employ local people in his mills because they did not want to work inside. He recruited a lot of his workforce from the Highlands. Although this was a time of Highland Clearance, this is not the main reason for their employment, as there was already a seasonal migrant pattern of large numbers of Highlanders coming south for work in the bleachfields. The attraction of better wages lured them into staying on at New Lanark and other mills in lowland Scotland. Pedlars travelled throughout the UK, selling at country markets and around small villages from early on in history. Therefore, from these examples, it is clear that movement around the country did occur, and it may be appropriate to factor this into your character development.

The Wider-World Realm

The third realm sets out the information that your character may have about what exists beyond the locality in which they live – the national and international:

- The reigning monarch
- The government of your period and any particular politicians of note
- Famous people – past and present to your period
- Inventions
- History
- Science
- The economy
- War
- Global events – past and present to your period and a bit of the immediate future so that you know what not to talk about.

If you are approaching the wider realm as a generic low-status character, it is quite probable that you will know very little at all about what is going on beyond your locality. Even if you are able to travel farther afield, your access to news will be limited. To obtain such information requires access to a source of news. The first-ever regular daily newspaper in English, the *Daily Courant*, was published in London in 1702. Newspapers were very expensive and certainly not written for the lower echelons of society to read. Even if you got hold of one, it is doubtful you would have had much time to read it, and that was if you could read. However, you could glean facts from overheard conversations, such as the arrival and departure times of stagecoaches. You would most likely know who the king or queen was of your time and possibly the name of the prime minister and perhaps someone famous, but your knowledge of these people would be very limited. What you would be more likely to know about is inventions, as these might very probably affect your life, because from either an industrial or agrarian perspective, these inventions would be taking away people's jobs. You would also have an opinion on the economy of your time because it would determine wages and living costs. If there was a war on, then your character may well be involved in some way. A direct link could be that you have served in the armed forces or had a relative away fighting. Indirectly, your connection could be through the impact of war on your particular job and way of life. For most low-status characters, the world realm will be smaller, but it will exist. And you may even be in the position to comment on faraway events, as in the case of the catastrophic eruption of Krakatoa in 1883, which affected the world's weather and resulted in people seeing strange sunsets. As you rise through the ranks, the amount of knowledge you can have naturally increases, particularly if your character is male and is educated.

Putting Everything Together

Given that you are likely to have a short time in which to create your character, most of your research will probably be done on the internet. It is now becoming more possible to find primary sources online. For example, all of Queen Victoria's journals are now available, as are the consultation letters of Dr William Cullen, which are an important source of information on 18th-century medical practice. Both are free to use.

How you interpret your character's status, which really is the key to who you are, will be reflected by the manners you adopt. From my experience, the most useful source of information for character building is books on etiquette and manners. Without embarking on a lengthy history lesson, suffice it to say that from what is referred to as the Middle Ages (medieval to late 15th century), people were aware of their position in society, and a primitive form of class structure emerged across Europe. With it arrived aspirational people who wanted to know how to behave in a particular way that would enable them, at best, to rise through the ranks of society and, at worst, not to put their foot in it and spoil the chances of their family. The Renaissance saw the rise of the middle class and a plethora of what are called courtesy books to assist the ascent of the social scale. The etymology of courtesy is from the word "court" and the appearance of ideals of being courtly and chivalrous which related to good manners and a show of respect to everyone. It is from this that we get the word "curtsy", which was not solely the prerogative of women at this time and referred to lowering the body in some fashion as a mark of respect by both males and females.

The first known courtesy book in English is in fact a poem written in Latin, *Urbanus Magnus*, believed to be by Daniel of Beccles, a knight at the court of Henry II. It is also known as *The Book of the Civilised Man*. There is no need to worry about how to read this book, as in 2017, the publication of the excellent *The Making of Manners and Morals in 12th Century England* by Fiona Whelan provides the reader with full access through her examination of the original text, which covers the whole gamut of life at the time. There are also numerous references to *Ubanus Magnus* on the internet. The British Library provides free access to a digitised copy of *The Lytille Childrenes Lytil Boke*, written around 1480, which is another well-known early book of manners, this time focussing on how to behave at mealtimes, though various copies feature other aspects of life such as hunting. It is quite hard to read the actual text, but the library has provided a transcript as well as some general information. It is thought to have been used by socially ambitious adults in addition to as guidance for children. It is extremely useful, and some of what is seen as acceptable then is remarkably similar to modern times, such as recommendations that children, or anyone else at table for that matter, should wash their hands before eating, not burp and certainly not pick their nose!

If your character portrayal requires an insight into manners in Europe, then I suggest you look at Bonvesin da la Riva's *The Fifty Courtesies of the Table*, written in the late 13th century, which provides an insight into Italian table manners. It remains the belief amongst many that the language and manners of the English court were French, but this ended in 1490 when Henry VII declared that English was to be the language used for official documents and all communication. Italy was the focus of inspiration until the 17th century because of the Renaissance and everyone of power and wealth wanted to be seen to emulate the qualities of the Renaissance man (and woman too). In Scotland, Gaelic was the predominant language at court, with a bit of Scots and French, up to the reign of James V; his father, James IV, was the last Scottish king to speak Gaelic. James V used Scots and French at court, and both his wives were French. However, even in the Scottish court, Italian courtesy and manners were obligatory, because from James IV onwards to the end of the 16th century, all the monarchs of Scotland were influenced by the Renaissance. Translations of Bonvesin's book are available, and there are many references to aspects of this book online, which would be sufficient for anyone wanting to reference Italian manners.

Baldesar Castiglione's *The Book of The Courtier*, better known as *The Courtier*, published in Italy in 1528, is the last significant publication of courtesy books in terms of its scope of influence. The first English translation of it was not until 1561, and for some time, it governed the manners of the Elizabethan court and beyond. Allusions to it can be found in Shakespeare, and Ben Jonson directly referenced *The Courtier* in his play *Every Man Out of His Humour*. Castiglione's work is important, as he provides guidance on how women should conduct themselves at court. Most advice before his work focussed on the behaviour of men; anything about women was concerned about their reactions to men's actions.

The emphasis of these books changed in the 17th century from the idea of courtesy, associated which chivalrous behaviour, to a focus on etiquette, the origins of this concept coming from the French court. The word itself originates from an old French word, "etiquette", meaning a small label. It is said that cards were handed out at the French court indicating what constituted desirable conduct and manners in the presence of the king. From these developed whole books setting out codes of acceptable behaviour in different areas of society. To avoid confusion therefore etiquette refers to the specific rules of behaviour and manners are the performance of those rules. They are not interchangeable.

Eighteenth-century Georgian Britain's growing middle class was obsessed with etiquette and the accompanying manners to be learnt in order to rise in society. Many books were published providing the necessary guidance, and these are invaluable in character creation. Over the years, I have used several and particularly like Adam Petrie's *Rules of Good Deportment*, as this is easily accessible online, though as with most of the books I refer to, there is a reprint available. Petrie concentrates on how to stay in favour with your "superior" as well as make your mark in society. There are a surprising number of these etiquette books by other authors still in print, so you do not need to be limited to Petrie's manual.

In addition to books guiding the Georgians on etiquette and manners, there were also books on elocution. This means that as well as knowing how the 18th-century people wanted to behave, you can also recreate how they may have sounded! Elocution developed into an accepted discipline in the middle of this century thanks to the work of the great actor Thomas Sheridan, who lectured on the subject and published his work in a collection, *Lectures on Elocution*, in 1762. While his approach was to improve pronunciation when reading aloud, a popular entertainment in drawing rooms, John Walker's *Elements of Elocution* (1781) provided more details that would be useful in conversation, such as voice control and accompanying gestures to make. Conversation manuals were published and actors ran elocution classes in major cities of Britain. Sheridan went on to publish *A General Dictionary of the English Language* in 1780 outlining pronunciation, and Walker followed suit in 1791 with *A Critical Pronouncing Dictionary*, two pages of which can be seen at the British Library's website, but there are also reprints of the works of both Sheridan and Walker available if you want to see more. In my approach to costumed interpretation, I do not advocate that old styles of pronunciation should be used during interaction with visitors, as the aim is to make the past accessible and interpret it, not make it even more complicated to understand, as the use of long-forgotten words can do – more of this later in Chapter 5. However, it is possible to run "lessons" on "how to speak" and incorporate some amusing phrases and words that were once "the thing" to say, and for this these books are invaluable.

It is now common to refer to the "long 18th century", as some historians feel that the 19th century did not begin until the reign of Queen Victoria. As with the previous centuries, etiquette and manners were important, and there are many books providing information on just how one should behave in all kinds of circumstances. It was not until the death of Prince Albert at the end of 1861 that the craze for mourning etiquette began. Wearing black as a mark of respect at a funeral and for a short while afterwards was common, but the prolonged wearing of this colour and the various stages of mourning became more pronounced and inflexible after the death of the prince and his wife's endless mourning. There are many sites online offering information on 19th-century etiquette and manners but my advice is to stick to books of the period rather than blogs or other internet sources as the information on this period can be very confusing. There are several including *The Ladies' Book of Etiquette, And Manual of Politeness*, the gentleman's version, *The Gentlemen's Book of Etiquette, And Manual of Politeness* and *The Handbook of Etiquette, A Complete Guide to the Usages Of Polite Society*. I also caution you to be wary of 19th-century American books on this subject, as there is a distinct difference between what was seen as acceptable in this period in Britain and what one could do in the United States. Equally, if you are in the USA, beware of using British etiquette books.

The 20th century is more difficult to navigate when it comes to finding books on etiquette and manners. The Edwardian period was short (1901–1909) but was distinctly different from the Victorian period and often seen as less strict, but even this period had its rules on how to behave, though they are less easy to find. *A Book of Edwardian Etiquette* was published in 1902 and is available as a reprint. It is the book most referenced for the portrayal of Edwardians and also the run-up to the First World War under George V. The emphasis on etiquette and manners changed dramatically after the First World War, with a much more relaxed approach to behaviour compared to the past. When looking online for guidance on manners in this period, it is very difficult to find anything at all, and it is often from fiction of the time that you can gain information. *The Enchanted April* by Elizabeth von Arnim, published in 1923, helps you to understand the changes taking place at the time. The Mapp and Lucia series by E F Benson satirises the manners of the middle and upper classes and takes you right through the period from 1920 to 1939. These are just two examples of fiction reflecting the inter-war period which are excellent resources; there are many others.

So far I have made no reference to *Debrett's*, even though they have been in existence since 1769. This is because it was not until the middle of the 20th century that they produced their first books on various aspects of British etiquette and manners and their well-known *A-Z of Modern Manners* was not published until 2008, with a new edition in 2019. Prior to that, their focus was the peerage, in effect creating a database which is still updated annually.

All of these – courtesy books, etiquette guides, manners and deportment handbooks, elocution manuals – are very useful tools to "get inside the head", so to speak, of what it might have been like to live in various periods of history, showing you what was acceptable behaviour and how you might speak. It is, of course, how one would live in an ideal world, as no one ever follows such guidance to the letter. However, the fact that there were so many (I have only chosen those I have used over the years which are easily accessible or still available in print) means that they were important. For your personal realm, you must consider how you perceive your position in society, both as it is and how you might like it to be, and these sources are the way to find out.

While using these books to create your character, you will also find them useful when interacting with visitors. How people behaved, or at least were purported to have behaved, is fascinating to others, and you can incorporate aspects of mannerly behaviour appropriate to the etiquette of the period you inhabit.

There remains the question of how to portray lower-status/working-class characters, as these books are focussed on the middle and upper classes. They are, however, a remarkably accurate insight into all classes. Servants learnt their manners from those who employed them, particularly those who worked in the mansions and estates of the upper class. As the middle class emerged, they wanted to distinguish themselves from their working-class origins, and with that appeared changed ways of behaving. For example, putting milk into tea after it was poured was regarded, historically, by the middle class as a very working-class practice. Yet it was the upper class who did this and their working-class servants who copied them! Another excellent example of this can be found in the invention of soup spoons and fish knives and forks by the Victorian middle class. Meals of several courses were a great way of showing off wealth. The middle class were rarely invited to upper-class dinners, and when they were, they found that soup was taken with dessert spoons and fish was eaten with two forks. Here was an opportunity to show off their inventing skills and equally their wealth by providing new cutlery for dining. The upper classes stuck to their two forks and dessert/pudding spoons. Fish knives and forks remained popular wedding presents for those seeking to climb the social scale right into the middle of the 20th century.

Newspapers of the past are extremely useful sources of information, as they give a real feel for a particular period, providing snippets of information that are good to drop into a conversation with a visitor. Even if your character would not have read a newspaper, they may well have known some information that was reported on by the late 18th century, such as the arrival times of stagecoaches into the town, as mentioned before. The National Archives provide excellent guidance on how to find newspaper collections, and I thoroughly recommend this as your starting point. If your research is of an early historical period and requires you to read Old English or Latin, it is best to stick to history books by authors recognised for their research and accuracy. This is also true for any period that you are studying. This does not mean they must be academic books of a university standard, but these secondary sources do need to provide reliable information and detail by authors who have studied the period of interest to you.

It is also useful to invest in some history books which give you a good idea of what is happening, as you will need some of this information to inform your character. This is particularly true of real people, as they are most likely to be in the history books, though not always. It is best to stick to history books that have been written recently. As is often pointed out history does not change, and while this is true, what does change are methods of historical analysis based on the evidence and, crucially, whose stories we choose to tell.

As you use a variety of sources, your research will gradually come together to enable you to create your realms. The information contained in them is a distillation of all your investigative research and provides a quick reference point for you to check key details. Importantly, your realms are *not* lists of every fact you have discovered about the history of the period or your character in your investigation, but one will inform the other. This method of character creation enables you to see everything coming together. Whoever you are about to be is taking shape; you are creating a personality for your character that will make you more believable in the context you must inhabit and will greatly aid you in reaching your target audience for the project along with telling the stories required of your persona.

3 Who Am I? The Realms

The realms that I have created for the characters within this chapter demonstrate the level of detail that it is possible to create. It may at first seem rather daunting, but once you have done this a few times, it becomes second nature. Equally, I must emphasise that doing this groundwork really does pay off when you are standing before your visitors and know exactly who you are! You know you have everything you need to provide an engaging encounter.

Real People

1 Royalty – King and Queens

As a costumed interpreter you are very likely, at some point in your career, to take on the character of a monarch. The further you advance through time, the easier it is to find the required information for your research, particularly primary sources, on the web. If, for example, you are called upon to become Queen Victoria, there is a wealth of information that has been made available online since 2012, when the Royal Family provided access to her journals as well as some of her scrapbooks. It may be that you are to take on the character of a monarch further back in history; this can often be more challenging. For my portrayal of Mary, Queen of Scots during my career, I have had to use secondary sources, as I am unable to read 16th-century French, thus excluding me from any primary source material. I use both histories and biographies of this queen, which provide different viewpoints on her contribution to history, thus enabling me to offer varying interpretations of her depending on what is required by the client and the audience to whom it is to be delivered. As with Queen Victoria, there is information about Mary, Queen of Scots on the Royal Family website. Other online sources include National Museums Scotland, Blairs Museum, Historic Environment Scotland and the National Trust for Scotland which relate her story to the objects they hold connected to her and their properties. Other places that have a connection with the queen also have information on their websites such as The Mary, Queen of Scots House in Jedburgh and Traquair House outside Innerleithen.

DOI: 10.4324/9781003260226-4

For the first example on how to create the realms I am using Mary, Queen of Scots to demonstrate how to construct the character of a well-known royal figure in history. While the known facts of her life remain the same, knowledge of the end product informs what is included in your realms. On this occasion (2011), this set of realms was created for a guided walk for families in the company of Mary, Queen of Scots around St Andrews, a town she visited every year from 1561 to 1565. The key messages that the Museum of the University of St Andrews wanted the tour to convey to those on the walk were the significance of the town in the queen's story and a sense of the St Andrews she would have known. Access was to be granted to some buildings associated with the queen that were rarely open to the public. A copy of a map of the town from the 16th century was provided to those attending the walk, which showed that the layout of the core of St Andrews had hardly changed at all. The groups were to be met by the queen outside the Museum on The Scores.

The Personal Realm

It is best to start with the personal realm, as this is what people will expect you to know about yourself. As I have said before, it is impossible to remember everything, as even in our daily lives, we forget things about our past and our family. However, it is amazing how much you will find that you can, in fact, recall. Another reason for providing this level of detail is that it helps to create the identity that you are to portray – it gives you the measure of the persona.

Personal Realm Mary, Queen of Scots up to 1565

Date of birth: 8th December 1542

Name: Mary Stuart

Place of Birth: Linlithgow Palace

Immediate family:

- Father – James V of Scotland, died 14th December 1542
- Mother – Mary of Guise, French noblewoman and 2nd wife of James V; she died 11th June 1560.
- Half-brother – the Earl of Moray, usually referred to as Moray (father is James V)

Note: Though not members of her family, she was accompanied from her departure to France by the "Four Marys" who are with her for most of her life.

Religion: Roman Catholic

Where Mary grew up: Scotland and France:

- From age of 5 she is betrothed to Francis, Dauphin of France, heir to the French throne – hence the move to France, also safer because of English attacks on Scotland.

- Henry II and Catherine de Medici are the parents of Francis, and they decide on Mary's education and upbringing when she is with them.

Where she lived:

Scotland

- Stirling Castle – July 1543 she arrived here from Linlithgow Palace – and this is where she lives for most of her childhood in Scotland. Visits here on her various progresses around Scotland from 1561.
- Inchmahome Priory for 3 weeks in the autumn of 1547 for the safety of the young queen and her mother – Mary is 4 years old. She's not 5 till December. Then it is back to Stirling Castle.
- Dumbarton Castle – from here she sailed to France in 1548 for her safety and to grow up in the French Court with her betrothed, the future Francis II.
- Palace of Holyroodhouse – main residence from 1561
- Falkland Palace – favoured "holiday" home

Note: Edinburgh Castle – her son James is born there 1566 and Loch Leven Castle – imprisoned here from abdication until her escape. Both are beyond period of presentation.

France

- The Louvre and Palace of the Tournelles – Paris residences
- The Palace of Fontainebleau (thirty-four miles southeast of Paris) – a favourite place of the French royal family and Mary, famed for its beautiful gardens and works of art
- Château d'Amboise (Loire) – known as the royal nursery and where Mary came when she first arrived in France
- Saint-Germain-en-Laye – north-central France
- Villers-Cotterêts – north of France
- Château de Blois (Loire)
- Château de Chambord (Loire) – favourite hunting lodge of Francis

Note: A "Château" of the Loire valley was like a cross between a palace and a country house.

The French royal family progressed around these principal residences (as well as homes of the nobility) throughout the year, not necessarily in this order. They stayed about 3 months at each place. When the royal family moved, it took with it another 18,000 people made up of courtiers and servants to ensure a comfortable stay and the smooth running of government. The accompanying soldiers for security were in addition to the 18,000.

Education:

Mary was educated with the other royal children and in the same subjects as Francis which was very unusual for a girl.

Learning was concentrated on:

- languages – Latin, Greek, Italian, Spanish, English and French (the last two she could speak as her mother was French and she had taught her the language in Scotland)
- rhetoric
- history
- geography
- poetry

Note: Texts were chosen to help both her and Francis understand the process of government and its administration.

Leisure time:

- embroidery
- music
- dancing
- singing
- listening to poetry
- hunting
- falconry
- playing cards
- board games – backgammon and chess
- golf – only reference to this is when she is back in Scotland after 1861
- royal tennis – Falkland Palace has surviving royal tennis court.

Note: She also loved having pets – small dogs, ponies and horses were her favourites

Relationship with her mother:

- Mary and her mother wrote to one another constantly after her move to France.
- Autumn 1550 – Mary of Guise came to France and spent about a year at the French Court with her daughter.
- Mary was broken-hearted when she learned of her mother's death in 1560.

What Mary, Queen of Scots wore: She loved luxurious clothes and was aware that clothes provided a statement about who you were. In 1562 Mary instructed her French valet-de-chambre, Servais de Condé, to draw up a detailed inventory of the principal garments in her wardrobe. He came with her to Scotland and kept this list up to date until May 1567. The list includes:

- 35 petticoats, being of "rich fabric", "crimson", "black", "orange", "cloth of gold", trimmed with "gold fringes".

- 59 gowns made from such fabrics as "cloth of gold", silks, velvet and satin.
- 14 cloaks with one being of purple velvet trimmed with ermine.
- 180 entries reference her jewels. For example, a gold cross set with rubies and diamonds and several sets of Scottish pearls.
- She wears jewels in her hair.

Note: She likes to glitter and clearly understands the power of what she wears.
Married:

- Francis, Dauphin of France, at Notre Dame Cathedral in Paris, April 24th 1558 until his death on 5th November 1560
- Lord Darnley, at Mary's private chapel in Holyrood Palace, Edinburgh, 29th July 1565

Note: She marries Bothwell in May 1567, which is out with the period.
Work:

- Queen of France by virtue of being married to Francis who became King Francis II on 10th July 1559 with the unexpected death of his father.
- Though technically Queen of Scotland from the death of her father, Mary does not rule Scotland as Queen of Scots until her return in 1561.
- Rules Scotland from 1561 till her abdication in July 1567 which is beyond the period for the walk.

Life in general:

- In Scotland she is a small child whose life is in constant danger, but she seems relatively unaware of this.
- In France, she is brought up in great luxury, being trained to be the future Queen of France and wife of Francis. Life is very comfortable.
- Becomes Queen of France in 1559.
- Mary of Guise dies June 1560.
- Scotland becomes Protestant in August 1560.
- Francis dies in November 1560.
- August 1561 returns to Scotland as queen because she is now a widow and has no part to play at the French court.

Note: James born in June 1566 – out with the period covered by the walk.

The Local Realm

The local realm of Mary, Queen of Scots for this event is focussed on her visit to St Andrews. It sets out the dates she was in St Andrews and what she did or may have done while there as well as where she stayed or might have from the evidence provided by the museum and other sources. Learning the dates is not essential, but you do need to know the order in which things have happened. In this realm, it is useful to list the stops that will be made on the walking tour around the town. What you decide to put into the local and wider realms is ultimately dictated by what you need to know for the event in which you are portraying the character.

The Local Realm of Mary, Queen of Scots up to 1565

Note: Mary, Queen of Scots visited St Andrews six times, but the references to where she stayed on each visit are vague. The museum have provided some helpful suggestions of where she might have been.

1561 – September as part of her Royal Progress around Scotland she comes to St Andrews, therefore, an official visit.

- She is here for a week.
- Two possible locations for her to have stayed in:
    - the New Inns, built by James V in the grounds of St Leonard's. Her mother stayed here with James when she arrived in Scotland. (James VI stayed here in 1580 so clearly sufficiently royal.) Only the New Inns' gate is visible now.
    - the Prior's House in the grounds of the cathedral where her half-brother, Earl of Moray lived when in the town.

1562 – early spring – a leisure visit

- There is a house in St Andrews known as Queen Mary's House and it is here she may have stayed on this visit. (House now part of St Leonard's School and being opened specially for this tour).
- At this time the house is owned by Orme who is Chamberlain to the Earl of Moray. He owns a lot of land in St Andrews and is regarded as important within the town.
- During this visit to the town, it is recorded by the English ambassador, Randolph, that the queen read every day after dinner and that she was studying the Roman histories of Livy with George Buchanan.
- Randolph is invited to watch Mary and the Earl of Moray "Shoot at the butts" (archery) in the Privy Garden. (Privy means private – and this house had, and still has, a garden hidden from public view).

1563 – February/March – a leisure visit

Mary is known to have come to St Andrews after Châtelard, a French poet, was found hiding in her private bedchamber in Holyrood. He follows her to St Andrews where he accosts her again in her private bedchamber. He is taken to dungeons, though it is not specified where these dungeons are, and later tried for treason, found guilty and executed.

- 22nd February – the execution of Châtelard in the Market Square of the town. It is unclear whether the queen witnessed the execution or not.
- Still in St Andrews on 15th March when she is informed of the murder of her uncle, the Duke of Guise, by Huguenots.
- It is thought that the hawthorn tree at St Mary's College was planted by Mary after the death of her uncle. According to Gaelic tradition, this tree is associated with entry to the next world, so its planting as a memorial would be appropriate.
- She leaves St Andrews and goes to Falkland Palace.

1564 – April – leisure visit

- Mary visits her half-brother's wife, Lady Moray, who is expecting a baby.
- No mention of whether she stays with her or somewhere else in the town.

1565 – January and then September
January – leisure visit

- Talks of being lodged in a merchant's house.
- Randolph, the English ambassador, is invited to dine with her on three successive days. She talks to him of living as a "bourgeois wife . . . with my little troop", as well as her anger with Elizabeth trying to make her marry Dudley.

13th September – official visit

- Mary arrives with her new husband, Lord Darnley, and the court and there is mention of them using Moray's furniture wherever it is they are staying. This is quite possibly the Prior's House. Mary makes an important announcement regarding Moray and his supporters who oppose her marriage.

Route and sites (and connections) associated with the story of Mary, Queen of Scots around St. Andrews that will be the stops on the guided walk

- Start at the museum
- St Andrews Castle – Knox
- St Andrews Cathedral – the Prior's House – Moray and Knox; her mother and father
- Deans Court – dates from the 12th century; would have been there at the time of the queen's visits to St Andrews. She could have stayed here too. Access granted on the tour by University.
- The Pends – reference to the New Inns – James V & Mary of Guise
- Queen Mary's House and garden – access granted on the tour by St Leonard's School
- St Leonard's Chapel – James V – access granted by the University

- St Mary's College and the tree – Duke of Guise – access granted by the University
- Holy Trinity Church – Knox
- Market Square – Châtelard's execution – Knox's view.
- Butt's Wynd – archery
- Back to the museum – end of tour

Wider-World Realm

As these realms are being created for a costumed guided walk, the essential thing to remember is it must not turn into a potted history of the life of Mary, Queen of Scots. You are there to outline her significance to St Andrews, and while your research will provide you with an overview of her life up to 1565, it is important to remember that for this walk, St Andrews is your focus, as are the other historical personalities who have associations with the town and her story. You do not need to learn the dates relating to Knox, but chronological order helps you to work out what happened when in your mind.

The Wider-World Realm of Mary, Queen of Scots up to 1565

1536: John Knox graduates from St Andrews University. He then becomes a priest as well as being a notary (lawyer in civil law) and a tutor. He is influenced by a fellow priest called George Wishart around 1538 who advocates a new religion and in 1543 Knox converts to what is called the Reformed Faith which we now call Protestantism. (Remember Mary, Queen of Scots is born in December 1542.)

1546 – Wishart burnt at the stake for his heresy on the orders of Cardinal Beaton outside St Andrews Castle (stop on the walk). Beaton is later murdered and the castle taken over by the "reformers".

Knox goes into hiding but reappears in 1547 to join the reformers who still hold St Andrews Castle. In July of that year Mary of Guise and the French fleet win back the Castle and Knox is among those captured and sent to be galley slaves to the French. When freed he spends time in Switzerland where he is influenced by Calvin's Protestant teaching.

1558 – he made public his views on women ruling in his publication *The First Blast of The Trumpet against the Monstrous Regiment of Women* which was aimed at Mary of Guise and Mary Tudor rather than Mary, Queen of Scots, though this reference is often mistakenly seen as being against the latter.

1559 – John Knox returns to Scotland with a mission to convert the country to Protestantism. He heads back to St Andrews where he preaches at the parish church of St Andrews (Holy Trinity Church stop on the walk) and incites the congregation to ransack St Andrews Cathedral (stop on the walk).

1560 – The marking point of the Scottish Reformation – Parliament rejects the rule of Rome and forbids the celebration of Mass in a series of Acts in August.

1561–19 August, return of Mary to Scotland which is now a Protestant country. She is permitted to be a Catholic provided she practises her religion in private. Even though it is in her private chapel, Knox is not happy about it.

25 August – royal proclamation that Mary will respect that the religion of Scotland is Protestant if she can worship in private – very pragmatic approach, and unexpected too.

4 September – first meeting with Knox. He makes it clear he is not happy with her rule or her religion. She makes it clear she is not changing her religion but is happy for the rest of Scotland to be Protestant. Knox realises that Mary is clever.

The week after her meeting with Knox, Mary undertakes a royal progress to Stirling, Perthshire and Fife. Her final stop is St Andrews – she is there by 21 Sept – where she stays for a week and is back at Holyrood by 29th September. The progress is seen as a success as she is well received at the various places she visits.

During 1561, Mary begins overtures of friendship to Elizabeth in the hope she will name her as her successor. This is important because the English Ambassador comes to St Andrews with Mary. Wonder where he stayed?

1562 – Mary is still interested in what is happening in France. The two major events are:

- January – Catherine de Medici (Regent for the French King) issues the Edict of Saint-Germaine granting limited tolerance to the worship of French Protestants (Huguenots).
- Massacre of Huguenots at Vassy under the command of Mary's uncle, the Duke of Guise, sparks of the Wars of Religion in France. This is of note for what happens in 1563.

In Scotland, Mary tries hard to achieve a meeting between herself and Elizabeth, believing that if they could speak personally Elizabeth would see her as a worthy successor. This may be why she invites Randolph, the English Ambassador, to join her in St Andrews and impresses him with her studious behaviour. Early spring visit to St Andrews is not an official visit but one for rest and relaxation – may have stayed in the house owned by Orme (stop on walk).

Note: a visit for a rest – yet she invites the English ambassador to join her in the town! Clearly trying to make a good impression.

1563 – this year the search for a suitable husband for Mary begins in earnest. She is now 21 years old and is aware her duty is to provide an heir to the Scottish throne and therefore secure Scotland's future. Don Carlos, son of Philip II of Spain, is the main candidate. As he is a Catholic he is not a popular choice with either Knox or Cousin Elizabeth.

February – the poet Châtelard is found hiding under the queen's bed in Holyrood. Mary banishes him from court. He then follows her to St Andrews where he bursts in on her in her private chambers and makes advances towards her. Moray comes to her rescue and the poet is sent to the dungeons. He is publicly tried and sentenced to death in the market square (stop on the walk). It is not known if Mary witnessed his death, but she is still in St Andrews. Knox later accuses Mary of encouraging the poet to believe she was in love with him – not the case at all.

Mary remains in St Andrews and is informed of the death of her uncle, the Duke of Guise. He has been assassinated by a Huguenot – planting of hawthorn (hawthorn tree is a symbol of love) at St Mary's College, St Andrews University (stop on the walk) in memory of her uncle. (Remember he is responsible for killing a lot of Huguenots – see 1562)

Note: could it be that these incidents heighten her sense of needing a husband?

1564 – Mary begins the year by trying again to establish a relationship with Elizabeth with a view to her agreeing with her choice of husband and naming her as her successor.

March – Randolph informs Mary, that Elizabeth would like her to marry Robert Dudley, Earl of Leicester. It is also suggested that if she marry an English noble Elizabeth might just name them as her successors. Mary is very angry but she does not refuse, nor does she accept! She realises that she will never please anyone with her choice of husband.

She is in St Andrews in April to visit the wife of her half-brother, Moray, who is expecting a baby.

Mary sets up the process for the return of Darnley to Scotland.

1565, early February – Mary is in St Andrews and Randolph is there too, ostensibly trying to find out whether she will accept Dudley as her husband. They talk together and she makes it clear that she is fed up with Elizabeth's hollow promises and makes the point that they are just words with no meaning.

Her reference to living as a "bourgeois wife" – could she be teasing him or just annoying him?

17 February – Mary meets Darnley for the first time on her way back to Edinburgh from St Andrews at Wemyss.

29 July – Mary and Darnley marry.

Moray and other Protestant lords oppose the marriage leading to the "Chase-about Raid" in August against Moray and his supporters.

13th September – in St Andrews, Mary issues a statement against those who dislike her husband on the basis of his religion and suggested that this might be because they wanted to rule. Clearly directed at Moray. She may have stayed in the area around the Cathedral (stop on walk).

There is no record of another visit to St Andrews after this one.

Sources

Always list your sources at the end of your realms. It is very easy to forget where you have found your information, and you may well want to go back and check some detail. This is only for you, so a simple list is all you need. No one else is going to see it. While the work for the guided walk is particular to St Andrews, the information you have gained will come in useful if you interpret this queen again, and you will be glad that you have a list of sources to look back on. For this particular project I used:

- *My Heart Is My Own, the Life of Mary, Queen of Scots* by Guy (2004)
- *Mary, Queen of Scots* by Fraser (1970)

- *Mary, Queen of* Scots by Watkins (2001)
- *Maria R* by Hamilton (1991)

Some additional information was supplied by the Museum of the University of St Andrews based on their collection.

Having read through this set of realms, you may be overwhelmed with the amount of information I have provided. It is very unlikely that you will need to memorise dates, but you do need to know the order in which things have happened, which is why I have included them within the realms. The likelihood is that if you have been asked to portray Mary, Queen of Scots for this walk, you will do so again or have already done so; therefore, all the information within the personal realm may be useful again in the future or act as a reminder of what you already know. For a walk, it is less likely you will get asked much about her personal realm, as where the queen spent her childhood in France, what subjects she learned and what leisure activities she enjoyed are not really relevant to the walk. However, just having a look at some of the places where she lived while in France gives you a sense of the culture shock her return to Scotland must have been or knowing what she learnt in her lessons or liked to do for fun gives you a greater understanding of her as a person. The local realm is the core of your walk; therefore, you must know this. The wider realm provides what would have been happening around her and the people with whom she had to deal. Knox, for example, is very significant in her story, and it is essential to have an understanding of his life to appreciate what he thought of Mary. Remember, the dates are only there to show the chronological order of events, not to be learned off by heart.

The realms provided here for my guided walk as the queen enabled me to give life to my interpretation. I knew the various times that she was in St Andrews, her likely state of mind at the particular times she was there because of what was happening in Scotland overall, the historical personalities that were affecting her life and their links to St Andrews. All of this brought together transformed me into Mary, Queen of Scots for the day.

2 "Ordinary" People

It is just as likely that you will be asked to interpret the life of someone who is not famous and, to all intents and purposes, seems very "ordinary". This of course is rarely the case, because once you start your research, you nearly always find that these "ordinary" people have led very interesting lives in their own quiet ways and often made important contributions and met some rather remarkable people too.

For this set of realms, I have chosen an "ordinary" character from the 20th century. In this case, all the information has come from the family of Alec Coltman, an original resident of the new town of Welwyn Garden City, which celebrated its centenary in 2020. Alec was my husband, Dr Chris Lee's, maternal grandfather and the family have kept a meticulous record of his life and granted me access to this for the creation of this set of realms. Providing costumed interpretation of a fairly recent character is not at all easy. With regards to costume, it is often hard to distinguish what is worn nowadays, particularly as vintage fashion is so popular, with what is being worn by the interpreter. A late-20th-century character does not have the luxury of being out with living memory. The audience at whom the event is aimed may have contributions they can make about the person – these can be very positive, but they can also be negative. The interpreter has to be prepared for such occasions. Equally, family may visit to see their beloved relative brought to life and may not agree with how he/she is being represented. My advice, should you be in the position of interpreting a 20th-century character within living memory, is to be sensitive to the material available on which you are basing the realms. This is not an attempt to impersonate the individual, but equally you are trying to be as authentic as possible in interpreting their story as it relates to key messages selected by the organisation that has hired you.

For this character, the focus is an imaginary summer family event organised in the planned town of Welwyn Garden City to celebrate the experiences of the town's first residents in the interwar period. The key messages to convey to visitors are the significance of the Garden City as a symbol of renewal, promise and hope after the 1914–18 war and the enthusiasm of the first residents. There will be guided walks, a drama production and an exhibition. Several local figures have been identified and researched to give the event a cohesive and diverse focus. Those selected include Alec Coltman, an electrician and a well-known figure in the town, who died in 1971. His family have recently granted access to a collection of archives, photographs and objects which tell the story of this ordinary man and his family, living and working in a progressive town-planning experiment. Family members have also been diligent in recording Alec chatting about his time living here and have also allowed access to these recordings. An exhibition built around this material has opened in the town centre. It is called "The Lights Have Fused, Mr Coltman". We meet Alec in June 1957 on his sixtieth birthday, awaiting the arrival of his family and grandchildren who are joining him and his wife, Margaret, for the celebrations; he is looking back on his life and is happy to have a chat with you.

Personal Realm of Alec Coltman

Date of birth: 24th June 1895

Name: Alec Coltman

Place of Birth: Burton upon Trent, Staffordshire

Immediate family:

- Father – Frederick Coltman, a coppersmith at Marston's Brewery; died 29th November 1943, aged 72.

  Alec describes him as "a not very nice man, a real Victorian. He used to beat my brother, Arthur, and I with a Malacca cane". He was a big man with snowy hair.
- Mother – Lucy Bright, a trained dressmaker; died 22nd July 1956, aged 85.

  Alec recalls her as "dainty, refined and gentle with wispy hair"

- Brother – Arthur, born 1894

  Emigrated to Canada in 1913 to work on a farm in Ontario because he did not get on with his father. Joined the Canadian Infantry when war was declared in 1914 and was killed near Ypres in 1916.

  Alec never talks about him and just says "poor Arthur" if his name is mentioned.
- Sister – Mabel, born 1892 and is a trained tailoress.

  Alec says that his sister was "spoiled" as a child and was the "favourite of his father". He also makes the point that "she has never gone out to work but she makes all her own clothes. She made a lovely coat for my daughter, Kath".

Alec also remembers his mother and sister were obsessed with housework. "You could see your face in the floor, and they were always polishing, the furniture. Still, they had nothing else to do I suppose".

Note: Mabel died in 1982, but this event is set in 1957.

Education:

- Winshill Boys School, Burton upon Trent. He won a prize for perfect attendance in 1904. He still has the book *Red Dickon the Outlaw*, written in 1904 by Tom Bevan, a teacher and prolific author of boys' adventure stories.
- He paints and draws well. He has a drawing he did of a nurse at the bottom of his hospital bed in the First World War that is in the hall of his house.
- He is interested in nature, particularly trees and birds, and often says "Isn't nature marvelous?"
- He likes the story of *Ivanhoe* by Sir Walter Scott and has a copy of this book that belonged to his Aunt Harriet

Note: Both books are part of the family's collection

Work before First World War

- When he left school he first worked at a garage in Burton upon Trent.
- He then moved to Marston Breweries where his father worked.
- He learnt his trade as an electrician in the trenches in First World War, where he was "In signals", often working under fire.

First World War:

- Enlists on 8 September 1914.
- In the 2/6th North Staffs. He still knows his regimental number off by heart – 240649.
- He becomes a Corporal.
- He is "In signals", often working under fire.

- He was in the second battle of Ypres between 23 and 30 September 1917. His regiment was heavily engaged in the battle for Polygon Wood on 27th–28th September.
- He is mentioned in "Dispatches" for his bravery and receives a Divisional Commander Commendation.
- He is invalided out of the war and is fully discharged 30th July 1918.
- He dislikes talking about the war.

Work after the First World War

- After the war he works for The Electricity Supply Company laying cables for the new town of Welwyn Garden City. Famously, he helped put up the lights on one of the town's significant landmarks, the silos at the Shredded Wheat factory.
- He then sets up on his own with a little electrical shop in Lemsford, where he bases his business. He sells new wireless sets and makes repairs to old ones, as well as being an electrician on call to make domestic repairs. He closes the shop with the outbreak of war.

Work during Second World War

- He now works from a large shed in the garden mainly doing domestic electrical repair work and is often called out at night. The call usually starts with "The lights have fused, Mr Coltman". He still repairs radios as well.
- He has apprentices who get 7/6 a week.
- He is not a greedy man. He is happy to do a good job, with "just a little bit of profit".

Note: In the Second World War he could have made a lot of money on the "black market". Some of the other interviewees on this project knew him and said they would have paid anything he asked. One customer, an amateur artist, could not afford to pay him in cash so paid with landscapes! He still has two of these pictures in his sitting room.

Note: these are part of the collection from the family.

Married – twice

First Marriage: Alec married Kathleen Fisher, known as Kitty to the family.

- Kitty was born in 1897 and came from Harpenden.
- Alec met her on Harpenden Common when his regiment was stationed nearby at the beginning of the First World War.
- After the war he cycled to Harpenden from Burton upon Trent to court Kitty.
- They were married in 1921 at St Nicholas's Church.
- Alec had applied for a council house in Welwyn Garden City. It was not ready when they first got married, therefore they lived with Kitty's sister,

Rose, and husband Tom until they could move into Elm Gardens, where Alec still lives.
- Kitty died very suddenly on 10th January 1947.

Children: Alec and Kitty had four children:

- Kathleen Olive, 1922, known in the family as Kath
- Eileen Norah, 1924
- Brian Arthur, 1927, known in the family as Bob
- Doreen Margaret, 1929, known as "young Marg".

Alec loves his family – he plays games with his children, lets them have pets – a dog, cats and rabbits – and looks forward to the family holiday at the seaside every year, up to the outbreak of war in 1939.

Note: by 1957, all his children are married and have their own children – he now has nine grandchildren.

Second Marriage: Alec married Margaret Connolly

- He does not like being on his own, even though he is quite practical and his family (with the exception of his daughter Eileen who has gone to Canada as a wartime bride) keep an eye on him, especially Kath who lives in Welwyn Garden City with her husband and family.
- He is introduced to Margaret by a friend.
- Margaret is from Ireland where she was matron in a boys' school. She was born in 1899.
- They marry in 1949. She is 50 and he is 54.
- They continue to live at Elm Gardens.
- His children find their stepmother difficult to get on with.
- She is a rather strict step-grandmother.

Religion: no religious belief – "How could you after the trenches?" he says.

Dress:

- A collar and tie, and V-necked pullover and jacket and smart trousers
- Wears a tie pin and elasticated arm bands to hold up his shirt sleeves
- He does have a slightly jaunty scarf with a paisley pattern and tassel ends.

How he perceives his position in society:

- Working class
- Aware that he is highly regarded and seen as reliable and dependable

Friends:

- Knows everyone from the neighbours to the Company Secretary of Welwyn Garden City Ltd

- Meets his male friends in the pub.
- Mr and Mrs Coggins are particular friends in Luton and he drives the family over to see them regularly.
- His life, however, is very centred around his family.
- Margaret and Alec enjoy travelling abroad. This is resented by the family as their mother never had this opportunity.

The Local Realm of Alec Coltman

Welwyn Garden City

- During the Second World War, Alec is a civilian volunteer in The Royal Observer Corps from 1941 as well as running his electrical repair business.
- He is Head Observer in charge of the post known as Baker 2, which was located in the area now known as Knightsfield.
- The Ministry of Information make a film about the Observer Corps in which he features as does "young Marg" who hands a gas mask to one of the team.

Note: The film is in the Imperial War Museum.

- Alec takes part in the Victory Parade through the town.
- The part Alec has played during the war enhances his feelings of pride for Welwyn Garden City and the part he has played in it from its beginnings, from the silos of the Shredded Wheat Factory to having his own business with some very famous clients:
    - Lisa Sheridan, royal photographer of *Studio Lisa* fame
    - James Leslie Mitchell, better known as Lewis Grassic Gibbon, writer
    - Flora Robson, actress (not a Dame till 1960)
    - George Bernard Shaw, playwright
    - Mrs Rose of *Rose's Lime Marmalade*
    - Dame Myra Hess, the pianist famous for her lunchtime concerts in the National Gallery during the Second World War who played for Alec while he did his repairs.

How others see Alec

- He is well respected.
- He and his wife are addressed as Mr And Mrs Coltman, unless given permission to call them by their names. "Best to be formal first" is his view.

Getting About

- Alec has always had a car for his work. It is more practical to him than a van because he can use it for family outings too. He likes Austins and Vauxhalls.
- There is an annual seaside family holiday until 1939.

- Alec goes on two cruises, one to Spain and the other to Portugal, organised by the Philco Company. Wives and children are not invited but he brings gifts home. He feels going on these helps his business.
- He and Kitty have few holidays together but he takes her over to see her family regularly.
- He travels abroad with his second wife several times.

The World Realm of Alec Coltman

Reigning monarch: Elizabeth II

World events:

- Although he was little, he remembers his parents talking about the death of Queen Victoria (1901)
- Served in the First World War
- Remembers the Abdication crisis
- Served in the Observer Corps in the Second World War
- Remembers the death of George VI and the return of the young princess Elizabeth, now queen.
- Coronation of Elizabeth II – watched it on the family television
- The Geneva Summit 1955 – his daughter, Margaret, was working as an air stewardess for BEA and was on the flight that brought Harold Macmillan, the Foreign Secretary, back to London.
- The Suez Crisis 1956

Government in 1957: Conservative government since 1955, under Eden.

He resigns as Prime Minister because of the Suez Crisis and Harold Macmillan becomes Prime Minister and leader of the Conservative Party on 10th January.

Sources

- Archives, photographs, objects and recordings of Alec: access granted by his family
- *Welwyn Garden City* by Angela Eserin (1995)
- *A History of Welwyn Garden City* by Roger Filler (1985)

On this occasion, you have recordings of what Alec sounds like – do you try to replicate his accent? My advice is that you should not. Once again, I emphasise that this is not an impersonation; you are not pretending to be the person; you are taking their story and using it to make some aspect of history clear and understandable through the experiences they have had.

The Generic Character

Over the years, I have portrayed many generic characters that are constructed to serve a particular purpose. Such characters are designed specifically to convey a distinct set of interpretive messages at a site or museum.

Let us imagine that you have been asked to present a lesson on Georgian etiquette and manners in a country house just outside Edinburgh over a weekend. The management have decided it is to be set in 1791, the year the building of the house was completed. The house belonged to a family with close ties to the city of Edinburgh. There are to be four "lessons" a day. In between these set sessions, you are asked to move between the hall and the drawing room, interacting with visitors through conversational encounters. The house management are keen to show off their collection of Georgian caricatures, many of which make fun of some of the ridiculous aspects of fashion and behaviour of that time, and silhouettes of the family who had the house built. Given that this is to be a light-hearted event, the organisation has asked that your character be called Mrs Lydia Bole. They are also keen that you include the language of the fan. The management hope that by the end of the day, visitors will have a greater understanding of how important it was for the well-to-do Georgians of Edinburgh and its surroundings to learn their manners and adhere to the etiquette of the time – the key message of this event.

The realms of Lydia Bole provided here give sufficient detail for the presentations and also for the informal conversational engagements. Within the personal realm, what you decide to include is really up to you. You need to create a "backstory" that is believable for this made-up person and one that you feel you can own and remember. With regards to information such as date of birth, I usually choose a date that is already important to me, like my own birthday; it is then easy to remember. As to the year of birth, it is best to pick a year that reflects the age you are portraying and which also echoes the age you look. There is no point trying to be a coquettish twenty-year-old if you look forty! When deciding on who your immediate family are to be, keep it simple. If it is appropriate, give the character some education. In the case of Lydia being lower middle class, she would have attended a dame school and learnt very basic skills to equip her to go into service in a large house. The marriage that I have given the character was not impossible in 18th-century Britain and provides an excellent means for her to think herself able to teach others seeking to rise up the social scale how to behave. In terms of where she and Mr Bole live, it has to be Edinburgh because of the location in which the event is to take place. This then enables you to provide all the relevant information you have discovered in your research.

Some information for the local and wider-world realms that is provided is beyond the period that is being interpreted or includes modern terms such as the Scottish Enlightenment. This is because, as I have mentioned before, you have to know some things that are in the "future" so that you can answer questions. I will deal with this more thoroughly in Chapter 5, but as an example, it could be that someone may comment to Lydia about Pitt, "the Younger", being an interesting and clever prime minister. Pitt was, of course, not called prime minister until 1801, nor was he referred to as "the Younger" in his lifetime. Lydia could reply, "Prime minister – what a wonderful title, because that is exactly what he is. I must mention it to Mr Bole. And as for "the Younger", he's that too". This way, the visitor gets an answer, and Lydia stays in character. My reason for referring to her husband as Mr Bole is because 18th-century etiquette dictated that husbands and wives did not use each other's first names in public.

The realms for a generic character sometimes require a bit more detail, as you are creating this persona for a particular job. As you will see here, you can construct a rounded individual who is completely fictitious yet with enough information to be believable.

The Personal Realm of Lydia Bole

Date of Birth: 5th September 1750

Maiden name: Lydia MacLeod

Married name: Lydia Bole

Place of Birth: Leith

Where Lydia grew up: Moffat, a spa town in Southwest Scotland as her father was lost at sea when she was still a baby. Her mother was originally from Moffat, hence the return after her father's death.

Moffat:

- Important centre of the wool industry
- In 1633 a mineral spring was discovered and the sulphurous water from it was taken as a cure to many ills. Moffat became a spa town as a result.
- In 1748 a second spring was opened, thus increasing the town's popularity.
- 1760: two new hotels open in Moffat
    - The Buccleuch Arms Hotel – a coaching inn for stagecoaches
    - The King's Arms Hotel, also a coaching inn but in 1786 took on the mail coach service from London to Edinburgh. In 1788 it also provided for a new London-to-Glasgow mail coach. Mail coaches could take four inside passengers and several outside.

Note: This means Moffat had good transport links by 18th-century standards.

- 1762: The Earl of Hopetoun has Moffat House built. The architect is John Adam, brother of Robert Adam.
- The mineral waters increased the town's prosperity and made it fashionable to visit.

Immediate family:

- Mother is a widow who runs a haberdashery shop in Moffat.
- Father was captain of a merchant ship and he was lost at sea.
- Older brother, Tom, is a Midshipman in the Royal Navy.

Education: Lydia attended a Dame School in Moffat run by Miss McSporran where she had learnt to read, sew and cook but not write as this was seen as unnecessary for girls.

Her mother taught her to sing.

Work: An elderly widow, Mrs May Bole, living just outside Moffat employed Lydia at the age of 16 as a companion. It amused Mrs Bole to teach Lydia how to be a lady. Thanks to her employer, Lydia has learnt:

- Embroidery – as this is a skill that is decorative and has no real use, it is the mark of a lady.
- Reading poetry – Mrs Bole enjoyed poetry but her eyesight was failing so she encouraged Lydia to read. She particularly liked the works of James Macpherson.
- The spinet – a musical instrument thought to be very suited to young ladies. Women were not permitted to play wind instruments, the violin, viola or cello as these were considered crude. Mrs Bole provided a music teacher for Lydia and when guests visited she played for them as well as singing too as she already had a lovely voice.
- The art of tea drinking – she learns how to make tea in front of guests and how to drink elegantly from fine porcelain cups.
- The art of conversation – she learns:
    - how to sit when listening to others talking
    - how to show awe and wonder
    - polite things to talk about in company
    - how to use her fan to communicate with others around the room.

Characteristics: Lydia is known for her charming manners and politeness. Over the years her accent has become affected and her speech reflects this.

Married: in 1771, aged 21, to James Bole, nephew of Mrs Bole, whom she met when he visited his elderly aunt. It was love at first sight and they corresponded for several months before eloping to Gretna Green and marrying, much to the annoyance of his aunt. They have no children and now live in the New Town of Edinburgh.

Their home when first married: Lydia and her husband have lived in Edinburgh all their married life. Their first home was in the Canongate in a land (Scottish term for a flat), which was removed from the hustle and bustle of the city. While their home was on the first floor and large, they had to share the stair to it with all who lived there, including a rather unsavoury man who worked in the theatre and was often drunk.

By the 1780s, James is a successful and wealthy tea merchant in Edinburgh looking to move to the New Town to keep his wife happy as well as to demonstrate his considerable wealth.

Their home from 1791: a three-storey house in Hanover Street in the New Town.

Religion: Church of Scotland. She and her husband attended the Canongate Church in the Old Town and now go to St Andrew's Church in George Street.

The main activity of the city: this is centred around the Luckenbooths (small shops) beside the Cathedral with the Courts nearby as well as the Mercat Cross and the Royal Exchange – all situated at the far end of the Royal Mile near the Castle.

It is here Lydia goes for her shopping even though they have moved to the New Town because there are no real facilities there for shopping.

- She still does this herself although they have servants.
- She usually takes a servant with her to carry what has been bought.
- It is a way to find out what is going on as the Old Town is still the heart of the city.
- While their house is beautiful, the New Town is a muddy building site.

Social life:

- The Assembly Rooms are now open in George Street. They opened in January 1787 funded by public subscription – Mr Bole contributed £20 (Today that is over £1,000).
- They attend balls and concerts.
- Lydia enjoys balls more than anything – she is well versed in the language of the fan and is always on the look-out for who is flirting with who. Even she occasionally catches an eye!
- Lydia is so pleased she no longer has to go to the Old Town Assembly Rooms which were so small.

The Assembly Rooms are still incomplete – there are no chandeliers and a lack of decoration expected of such a building. Further subscriptions are sought – Mr Bole has not given any more.

Note: The chandeliers were added in 1796 and work continued on it till the beginning of the 19th century.

- Their New Town home is large enough for Lydia to invite friends and acquaintances for tea in the day while her husband is at the Coffee House and at business. Ladies always drink tea – coffee is considered far too strong for a feminine palate. In the evening, there are soirées and conversations.
- They like to go to the theatre and were fortunate to see Sarah Siddons when she performed in June 1784 at the Theatre Royal as Lady Randolph, in John Home's tragedy, "Douglas".

Position in society: middle class

How Lydia perceives her position in society: She regards herself much further up the social scale than she is. She realises she will never be among the real nobility as they number only about 350 families in Britain out of 18million people. One can, however, be ready if the call comes.

Dress: Mr Bole can afford to dress his wife in whatever is fashionable.

Note: By 1790 the emphasis has moved away from the panniers which accentuate the hips. Support at the waist almost gives the hint of a bustle. The bodice remains tight while the skirt of the gown is fuller.

Politics: she appears to know very little of politics as it is not seen as polite for ladies to do so.

Local Realm of Lydia Bole

Expansion of Edinburgh:

- It was clear that Edinburgh had to expand to secure its future. The city centred around the Royal Mile was overcrowded and dirty; not an attractive place to be.
- The Town Council of Edinburgh held a competition in 1766 in the hope someone would come up with a plan for a new Edinburgh.
- James Craig's plan wins – his idea is for a simple grid with wide streets and a garden square at each end of the main street one of which is to be called after the King. It is to be built on land already purchased by the Council to the north of the Nor Loch which is also to be drained to create gardens.
- Building begins in 1767 at the St Andrews Square end of George Street (the east end) because North Bridge was already built to improve access to Leith, which is Edinburgh's port.

Charlotte Square:

- St. Andrews Square is at the east end of George Street and the square at the west end is now to be called Charlotte Square not George Square as there is already one in the old part of the town.
- Robert Adam, appointed by the Town Council, has drawn up plans by the end of 1791 for the front elevations of Charlotte Square, thus creating a façade behind which the houses will be built. There is some concern that the original intention to produce elegant buildings has not happened. As Cosh puts it "Uniform height and monotonous plainness had hitherto been the order of the day" (Cosh, 2003).

Note: The development of the New Town of Edinburgh is part of what we now call the Scottish Enlightenment, which is a 20th-century term. There is nothing that really suggests that the people of this period knew what was happening, intellectually or culturally. However, given the number of developments in thinking, science, industry and culture taking place, there must have been a feeling that society was progressing and this was a good thing.

It is probable that someone like Lydia would sense that life had improved from the time of her mother and that a lot was going on.

People in Edinburgh in the 1780s/90s

The following people were in Edinburgh but it is more likely that Lydia's husband would meet them than her, though it is not impossible:

- Robert Adam, architect
- Robert Burns, poet from Ayrshire who visits Edinburgh in November 1786
- James Boswell, lawyer and biographer
- Henry Dundas: senior political figure in Scotland
    - o When the New Town is in an early stage of development Dundas bought the prime site looking straight down George Street. Craig's plan had

suggested a church here. A grand villa was built instead called Dundas House.
    - Lord Advocate 1775–1783
    - MP for Edinburgh 1790–1802
    - Home Secretary in 1791–94

- David Hume, philosopher
- Henry Cockburn, lawyer and writer for the *Edinburgh Review*, an intellectual magazine
- Adam Smith, political economist
- Walter Scott, lawyer
- Sir James Stirling, Lord Provost of Edinburgh 1790–1800
- Rev. Robert Small, Moderator of the General Assembly of Scotland, 1791, also a founder member of the Royal Society of Edinburgh established in 1783 which focussed on science, philosophy and the arts.

Note: 1778: Joseph Knight wins his case in the Court of Session to be freed from slavery in Scotland. This ruling effectively means that any plantation owners who bring slaves back to Scotland have to employ them as free men and pay a wage. This case receives a lot of attention in the newspapers of the day and in conversation around Edinburgh and beyond. Lydia and James would know about this event.

Knight had been brought from Jamaica by Sir John Wedderburn to Perth. Here he had met and married a servant girl who had his child. He asked permission to leave and be with his wife. This was refused; he left anyway to be with his family. Wedderburn had him arrested. Knight was found guilty but appealed on the grounds that slavery was not recognised in Scotland. He won his case and was therefore free.

Wider World

While not that interested in politics, Lydia will know something of what is going on through what she hears her husband talk about and because she has a brother in the Royal Navy who will have been involved with the American colonists.

- 1738–1820: George III is king.
- 1775–83: The American Revolutionary War, known today as the American War of Independence – the colonists won against the British forces. Her brother, Tom, has been involved.
- 1783: William Pitt ("The Younger") becomes the Head of the Government as well as Chancellor of the Exchequer. He is 24 years old and the youngest man to take on such high office. (He is now known as "The Younger" in order that he is not confused with his father who also held high office and is usually referred to as Pitt, "the Elder". These are more modern terms. To distinguish him from his father in his own time, he was known as the 'schoolboy'.)

Note: In 1801 Pitt is given the title of Prime Minister but not until then.

All the talk is of this very young politician called Pitt.

- 1787: Committee for the Abolition of the Slave Trade is established with the MP William Wilberforce representing the Committee in Parliament.
- This kickstarts campaigns in favour of abolishing the slave trade.

Since the case of Joseph Knight in 1778, more people in Scotland and particularly Edinburgh are aware of the issue of the slave trade.

Note: it is not until 1807 that abolition of the slave trade is achieved.

- 1789: French Revolution – is not initially seen as any great threat to Britain. The early actions of the Revolution which sees the re-establishment of the States-General (the French version of Parliament) is viewed as an end of absolute rule by the French monarchy.
- 1790: Edmund Burke published *Reflections of the Revolution in France* in which he criticises what has happened in France and predicts it will result in chaos and anarchy. It is this publication that gradually makes British people think that perhaps a Revolution so close to Britain is not good at all.
- 1791: Thomas Paine publishes *The Rights of Man, Part 1* more supportive of the revolution and advocates democracy.

Note: *The Rights of Man, Part 2* is published in 1792 and is more radical, demanding a republic. Paine has to leave Britain as he faces prosecution by the government. He escapes to France. This is beyond the period portrayed by Lydia.

Through 1770–91 there is growing tension in Britain about the influence that the Revolutionaries' republican doctrines could have on the British working class. Political societies are beginning to emerge in Britain run by working men who debate and discuss issues like votes for all men.

Note: The French set up their Republic in 1792 and there was an escalation of violence in France itself. To cut a long story short continuing tension between royalists and republicans led to the execution of the French king in January 1793 which in turn was a catalyst to Britain declaring war on France using the execution and condemnation of the Revolution's doctrines as two of the many reasons for this action. Once again, this is beyond your period but important to be aware of.

Sources

For a generic character, it is likely that you will have used quite a lot of sources from which to build a rounded character. It is improbable that you will have had to read all of every book. You will see that I have used John Galt's *Annals of the Parish*, which is a very useful early-19th-century novel set at the end of the 18th century that describes life in a small Scottish village, and it is from here that I have drawn much of my inspiration for the local realm of Lydia. Remember that this is a list of books just for you to remind you what you have used in case you need to go back and check some details.

Gender and Enlightenment Culture in Eighteenth-Century Scotland by Carr (2014)
Edinburgh in the Golden Age by Cosh (2003)
Annals of the Parish by Galt (2009)
The Social Life of Scotland in the Eighteenth Century by Graham (1961)
The Rules of Good Deportment by Petrie (2010)
The Accomplished Lady, A History of Genteel Pursuits c1660–1860 by Riley (2017)

The Language of the Fan – Did It Exist?

In this imaginary programme, the costumed interpreter has been asked to include the language of the fan. This is a popular activity often requested for events focussing on 18th-century manners, and I have used it on many occasions to the delight of those taking part. The strange thing about this so-called language is that many people deny it ever existed.

There are others who say that it was invented by fan makers to boost sales. In the British Museum, there is a fan of 1797 which displays on its leaves instructions on how to spell out words, and it is called "Fanology". In 1827, Duvelleroy, a fan maker in Paris, produced a list of various poses and movements that could be made with a fan, and even though it is from the 19th century, it comes within the time frame of the long 18th century, which ends with the accession of Queen Victoria. This certainly provides evidence that those making fans were keen to boost sales!

However, from my research over the years for events that wish to run the "language of the fan", there is evidence to suggest that using fans as some form of communication was well underway in the early part of the 18th century before there were printed instructions from fan makers provided to those who purchased the fans. There are too many references to ladies using fans in some form of communication for it not to be real. It must, however, be emphasised that the women using these fans are all middle or upper class.

Joseph Addison, the famous essayist of *The Spectator*, a periodical which provided a satirical view of society in the early part of the 18th century and was published daily except Sundays from 1711 to 1712. In this publication, he wrote an essay on fans in edition No. 102, 27th June 1711. It is written as a letter from the owner of a "fan academy" that teaches young ladies how to use their fans in a similar fashion to how gentlemen learnt to use swords. His style is satirical, but the fact that it is a subject at all suggests very strongly that fans were very much part of women's arsenal in pursuit of a husband:

> there is scarce any Emotion in the Mind which does not produce a suitable Agitation in the Fan.
>
> (Addison, 1711/1816)

In 1729, Soame Jenyns wrote *The Art of Dancing, A Poem in Three Cantos*, referencing the use of the fan within the poem:

> What daring Bard shall e'er attempt to tell
> The Pow'rs that in this little Engine dwell?
> What Verse can e'er explain its various Parts
> Its numerous Uses, Motions, Charms, and Arts?"
>
> (Jenyns, 1729)

Jonathan Swift, another of the great satirical writers of 18th-century Britain, also makes mention of ladies and their fans in the introduction of his witty piece, *A Complete Collection of Genteel and Ingenious Conversation*, published in 1738. Within this piece, he laments the dilemma of ladies engaged in conversation having to cope with so many things. Not only must they pour the tea, be good listeners and smile and frown in the right places, but they must also cope with "the whole military management of the fan" (Swift, 1738/2007).

And this was not happening just in Britain. Fans were being used across Europe; portraiture of women in the 18th century shows that nearly all of them have a fan in their hands, sometimes closed, sometimes half open. For example, Louis de Silvestre painted Barbara Katarzyna Branika, a Polish lady, in 1728, a portrait which now hangs in the National Museum of Warsaw with her fan open. Getty Museums has the Pietro Antonio Rotari portrait of a *Young Woman With a Fan*, dating probably to the 1750s, with the fan closed but pressed against her forehead. In the Gallery of Fashion series of costume plates by Nicolaus Heideloff for the years 1794–95, many of his images feature women holding fans in various stages of being opened or closed. These are now in The Metropolitan Museum of Art, New York.

Fans, therefore, clearly had a role to play in the communication process of women across Europe and in Britain. From my research, I have concluded that it was more about expressing a feeling such as modesty, virtue and, in some cases, anger rather than an actual language. Clearly, fans could also be used for keeping cool. Most "language of the fan" sessions requested by organisations are based around the French printed instructions. Lists of meanings can be found on the internet.

This Is NOT My Story!

In this chapter, we have looked in detail at developing the character of a 16th-century queen, a 20th-century electrician and a generic 18th-century woman, all representing different classes and time periods. I would be the first to admit to the lack of diversity in the widest sense. Issues of race, sexuality and gender have not generally been well explored or represented by costumed interpretation. Nothing would delight me more than Artemis Scotland being approached by an organisation to provide a character that did not fit the typical heterosexual white model of the characters we have provided over the years. I do see signs of change with the representation of diverse groups beginning to be addressed, which offers a whole range of exciting possibilities in the future.

As early as 2008, at the Performing Heritage Conference at Manchester University, which I attended, there were examples of costumed characters who provided an insight into other cultural identities. We were introduced to "Gabrielle", a woman originally from St Kitts but now living in Manchester and looking back on what it was like to be an immigrant. This had been part of the education programme run at that time for the People's History Museum in the city and was done as a presentation in which Gabrielle, as an older woman, sat in her sitting room and reminisced about her life, inviting those round her to ask her questions, the same format that was used with the schoolchildren in "Seeing It For Real" that I highlighted in Chapter 1. We then took part in a promenade performance called "This Accursed Thing" through various galleries at Manchester Museum, which held objects related to slavery and the slave trade. The performance brought to life elements of the slave trade, such as the negotiations between a black African slave trader and his white equivalent and being on board a slave ship with one of the captives, as well as portraying the campaign which led to the Abolition of the Slave Trade in 1807. Both of these events demonstrated most powerfully how possible it was, within a museum context, to provide ethnically diverse voices through the medium of costumed interpretation and museum theatre. It reinforced that while historical facts do not change, how we interpret history does, which is a mark of how far we have come in understanding our role in the past, particularly as the Western world faces up to its colonial past.

In 2019, the People's History Museum in Manchester provided a museum theatre piece titled "No Bed of Roses", in which the central character was a woman of the Windrush generation reflecting on what it was like to look for somewhere to live and work and the reactions of local people to her, very similar to the schools' activity of 2008. The play was aimed at those who were of the Windrush Generation or were related to those who arrived then and included a discussion at the end of the performance.

The *Cutty Sark*, part of Royal Museums Greenwich, tells the story of 19th-century men working at the London docks and reflects that this was a place where immigrants could find work. Currently, this museum has as one of the characters that you can meet on board Raj Fernandes, a docker from 1895, who explains what his working life is like. There is very little evidence of costumed interpretation being used to bring to life culturally diverse stories here in Britain. These stories are being told, but as reflected here not many are using costumed interpretation to do so.

During my visit to Colonial Williamsburg in 2010, I was able to have a discussion with two Black costumed interpreters who played the part of slaves. Both confirmed that portraying the role of slaves on site was tricky and not without its problems. Some visitors were not willing to accept that in the 18th-century world that this site presented, more than half of the population was Black. To sustain the lifestyle of the white people, every household needed several slaves working there. They also found that people often spoke to them in a less polite way than they did to their white counter-parts – it was almost as if the visitors thought they were still slaves. They added that there were not enough of their "own people", as they put it, coming along to visit sites like these because their story was so under-represented. What they said was so true; the visitors I saw there were predominantly white, and the advertising material for the site was the same. Their parting comment was that at least something was now being done to tell the story of slavery and the Black population of Colonial Williamsburg, and they hoped more would follow.

In my quest to discover if more was being done to tell culturally diverse stories, I came across an article in the *National Geographic* from 25 September 2020 published in their Travel Section on "Race in America" – the article is entitled "Historical interpreters share their sides of the story"; it is by Jennifer Barger and Heather Greenwood Davis. This interesting piece introduced me to Cheyney McKnight, an historical interpreter. Unhappy with the inaccurate portrayal of enslavement and the subsequent freedom of Black Americans after the Civil War, she felt compelled to set the record straight and tell the story of her ancestors and has created "Not Your Momma's History" as a vehicle to explore aspects of history that are still ignored. Cheyney has developed a variety of workshop-type sessions, of which one is the "Let's Talk About Slavery Table", which can be set up anywhere with objects, images and documents related to slavery. Cheyney, in the costume of a slave, is there to discuss the objects and answer questions and does so in third-person rather than first, as she feels this enables her to explain challenging topics that arise from discussion. While the stories of enslavement are her main concern, Cheyney helps to tell the stories of other ethnic groups, as in the case of a living history programme she has been involved with at the New York Historical Society Museum. Here, they ran an event called "Stepping into the China Trade" that highlighted the trading connection between China and America in the 18th century and the role that women played in this business in New York of that period. In my online visit to this museum, I found that they run regular events for families that reflect the stories of diverse cultural backgrounds, using costumed interpreters. For example:

- A session on domestic service in the large houses of wealthy New Yorkers in the 19th century emphasised that their servants' position and duties depended on their ethnicity.
- "What is the Juneteenth?" featured costumed interpreters as newly freed slaves on 19th June 1865 – the date that American chattel slavery ended – who tell their stories of their newly won freedom.
- The Black Women's Club Movement, a 20th-century story about the national network of clubs set up by Black women to fight for the right to vote and features Ida B Wells, an early activist in the civil rights movement.

The article also features Anneliese Meck, a Chinese-American, who is the historical interpretation and programme manager of Genesee Country Village and Museum in Rochester, New York, who also takes part in on-site delivery. She finds that people are aghast to discover how long Chinese people have been part of the story of America, the assumption being that it is a white story. She used the tour to emphasise that many ethnic groups have contributed to the history of the country and tells them, "This is also my history" (Barger & Greenwood Davie, 2020).

Within the article, there is also mention that at Colonial Williamsburg, out of thirty-six first-person costumed interpreters now employed on site, only fourteen are Black, and the problems encountered by the two interpreters I spoke to in 2010 are still there. They are, in fact, worse, with some visitors refusing to believe the stories of the treatment of the enslaved and becoming aggressive towards the interpreters. Further investigation led me to an article by Christine Fernando of the Associated Press in which she points out that while Colonial Williamsburg has taken on the challenge to tell the difficult stories associated with slavery, this has not only led to abuse of their interpreters, but having to portray the slaves' stories has also taken a toll on their health. The site management have acknowledged that this is unacceptable and, when it is required, pay for therapy sessions for their staff who encounter such abuse.

I have found several articles online that cover this topic, and what is remarkable in all of these is the strength of the interpreters of colour who are determined to tell their various stories regardless of the effect it has on them. From my search online, it appears America is leading the way in using ethnically diverse costumed interpreters, and while they all admit they have a long way to go, it is a start. The few examples I found in the UK lead me to hope there will be many more examples of such diversity in the future here and farther afield. I have yet to find examples of costumed interpreters taking up the challenge of portraying gender diversity or queer history, but I feel sure that this will happen and may well be happening already.

4 The WOW Factor – The Importance of Costume and Props

The Role of Costume

The information that you put together for your character is of course essential to your interpretation. Another element is equally important – the costume itself. You can learn all that there is to know, but without a costume that immediately conveys who you are to the visitors, then all your hard work is for nothing. In many cases the visitors will see you in costume before they meet you in person. From a distance, the costume should immediately express the character's status and the time period. It is therefore crucial to get it right.

It really is the WOW factor in your presentation, and the WOW factor is central in the communication process of costumed interpretation. It may well be that the visitors are saying, "Wow, look at that beautiful costume. It's really striking. I can see that she/he is really important. I wonder what it's like to wear that? Be interesting to try something like that on. Let's go and see and have a chat". Equally, they may be saying "Wow, look at that dowdy costume. Imagine having to do a day's work in that! Let's go over and have a chat and find out what it's like to be him/her". Either way, the costume has made an impression and enticed the visitors to investigate further, and that is precisely what it is supposed to do.

If the costume is doing its work and making people talk, it moves away from the idea that it is "just dressing up". It takes on the role of being a significant part of the interpretation, not just a person wearing odd clothes. At a heritage site, it reminds visitors that a particular time period has had special significance and that the person in these clothes is going to help you understand that importance. It is much easier to understand why Georgians favoured wide doorways in their houses when you see a woman in the wide skirts of the period sweep through the space. An understanding of why an object like the 1766 map of Edinburgh New Town was so revolutionary with its wide, straight streets is apparent when you see someone, male or female, in the elaborate costume of the time (that was as much to show off one's style and elegance as one's wealth) walk along those streets in the reality of today. Equally, the costume of 18th-century servants is plainer and well suited to the narrow service streets between the wide streets of Edinburgh's New Town. All this is conveyed by what is being worn before conversation has even begun.

DOI: 10.4324/9781003260226-5

While the costume is doing all this work to encourage visitor engagement with the interpreter, it is also helping the interpreter get into character. As soon as a costume is put on, it changes you in so many ways – it affects movement, posture and, of course, how you look and thus prepares you for your appearance before the public. The costume is as much part of the communication process of heritage interpretation as what is said.

Costume Research

Along with the research that has been done for character creation, you must not lose sight of the fact that you need a costume. Part of your investigation into the character to be portrayed should include looking at images of the period to help you work out what you need to wear and what jewellery you might also want to add. The internet is full of images covering most historical periods, but it is best to be very wary of many of the pictures you find, particularly of earlier times. If, for example, you type "medieval costume" into Google, the images you will be shown are extremely confusing, as 16th-century garments are shown as well as outfits more typical of the early medieval period. Even typing in "original images of medieval costume" does not produce much that is of use. Galleries are good places to look at costumes, but not everyone lives near such places and must use the internet instead. Most national museums and galleries around the world provide opportunities to explore parts of their collections online, and these are valuable tools to use when trying to find costume images. Portrait galleries are particularly worthwhile. However, keep to images of the period that is to be interpreted rather than later portrayals of the particular point in time that interests you, as artists that are from different times, without the knowledge of what was worn, often portray clothes of the past very differently to what they looked like.

A good example of how clothes worn can be changed by their depiction in art is seen in the representation of the Stuart court of Mary, Queen of Scots. The tendency for those looking for a 16th-century costume of this period is to assume everyone in Britain dressed like the Tudors. This, however, is completely wrong, because Mary, Queen of Scots was influenced by her French mother, Mary of Guise, and her time spent in France from the age of five till she was eighteen. The Queen of Scots wore a very different style of clothes to that worn by her Tudor cousins and their courts, which can be seen from examination of the few portraits completed during her time as queen – the distinct difference being the lack of a full-sized ruff. There is an indication of frills (and these are not ruffs) in the image of her on coins of the time, but in her portraits, she wears high collars similar to what were called Medici collars, but without the ruff that typified the English court. Clearly Mary, Queen of Scots was creating her own style.

The only portrayal of her in a large ruff was made in England when she was in captivity. As a queen, she was still allowed to hold her court while in custody, and therefore, the clothes she had made were probably influenced by what was being worn in England; hence the ruff. Her death fuelled interest and fascination in her that has lasted down the centuries, and this, in turn, has resulted in artistic representations of this queen, drawing on fashion influences far removed from the

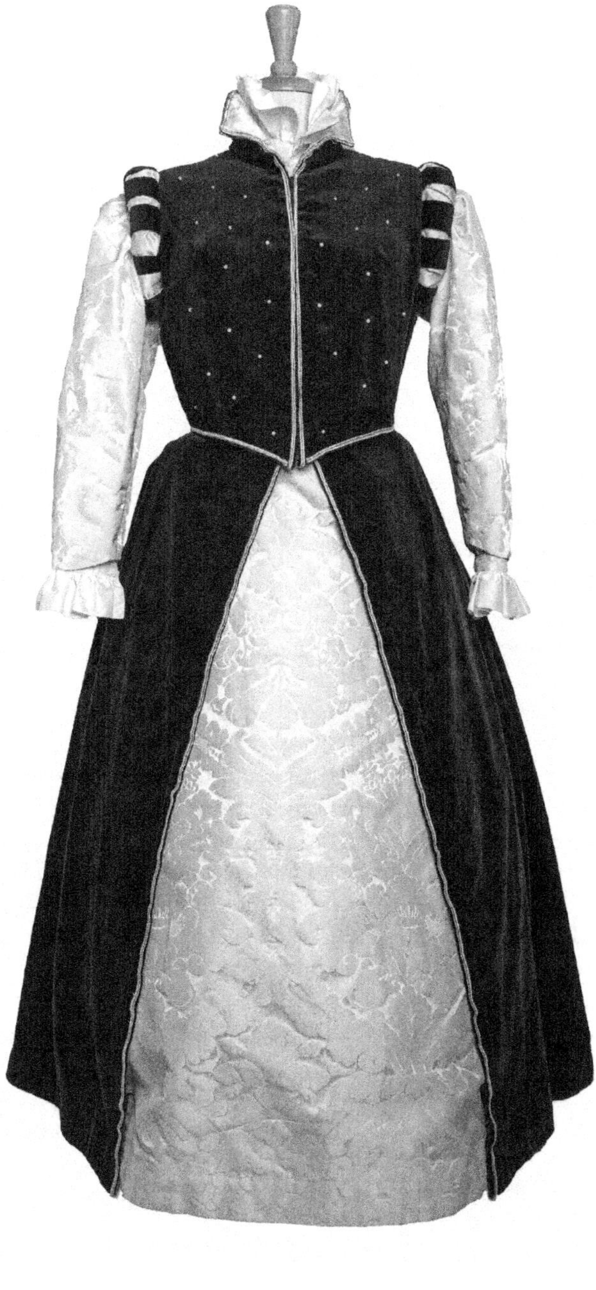

Figure 4.1 Note the frill at the neck and cuffs which provides decoration on this costume for Mary, Queen of Scots.

Source: © Keith Shaw Buckley/costume from the collection of Artemis Scotland

Scottish court. The marble effigy of Mary on her tomb in Westminster Abbey, in which she was interred in 1612, twenty-five years after her death, by her son King James VI and I, again depicts her in the clothes that are not of her time and has her wearing a ruff.

This form of portrayal has continued down the years, reaching a peak in the 19th century with a renewed fascination brought on by Schiller's play and Donizetti's opera about her. Many of the images of Mary, Queen of Scots that we are familiar with today come from the romantic representation of key moments in this queen's life by artists of the mid to late 19th century, heavily influenced by the romantic movement showing her in costume that is more Victorian than 16th century. Even in modern times, her depiction has shown her in clothes that are more Tudor than Stuart. Katherine Hepburn plays the queen on screen in 1936 wearing a ruff, as does Vanessa Redgrave in the 1970s film. In 2015, a statue was erected of Mary outside Linlithgow Palace, where she was born, and again has her wearing a ruff. The most recent film interpretation of her in 2018 does not have her in ruffs, nor does it have her in a costume of her time. These examples of how perception of costume changes through time make it very important that you check your sources for accurate images and be careful not to make assumptions about what people wore in the past.

Costume colour is also an important consideration in your research. From as early as the time of Greece and Rome and reaching as far as China and Japan, sumptuary laws existed to control consumption of goods. In essence, these laws were created to reinforce a hierarchical society, keeping people in what those at the top end of society saw as their station in life. Sumptuary laws have come to be associated in the Western mind with the colour and type of fabric used to make clothes, as they set out exactly what each socio-economic group could buy and wear. These laws took on more significance during the Renaissance, as prior to this period, social distinctions were more clear-cut. There was the monarch, the nobility, the clergy and the peasants. The Renaissance resulted in a growing number of wealthy merchants who sought to improve their social standing and that of their family. Wealth could be easily displayed through what was worn through the fabric-type and colour. Those at the top of society felt their position threatened and saw sumptuary laws as a way of controlling the new merchant class. Velvet, satin brocade and silk coloured gold, purple, royal blue, crimson or dark red were for nobility only in most European countries. In some cases, purple textiles were only worn by royalty. Banned from certain colours and fabrics, the merchants began to decorate their clothes as a way of displaying their wealth, and that then led to the embellishment of clothes, with embroidery, beads and jewels becoming part of these laws. The upper echelons of society were, of course, allowed the most adornment of their garments. Fines were imposed on those who disobeyed. Without this becoming too complicated, it is always worth noting the colour of textiles used in period portraits, as it denotes rank and reflects the society of the time.

On the subject of colour, there is a tendency to think that because people are dressed in black they are in mourning, and while this colour has had an association with death, funerals and grieving since the Romans, portraits of their sitters in black garments do not necessarily mean that a death has taken place in the family. Black is also the colour of power and dignity. This is particularly true of the latter part of the Renaissance, when monarchs and nobility throughout Europe were often depicted in black clothes. The Spanish courts of Charles V and Phillip II demonstrate this, as do portraits of Henry II of France and his wife, Catherine de Medici, Elizabeth I and Mary, Queen of Scots. Apart from demonstrating power, black also showed wealth. To dye fabric a black that would not wash out if you were caught in the rain was a long, labour-intensive process, making it very expensive. At the end of the process, there was a lustre and shimmer to the fabric that was absent from mourning garments, and the design of the garments for the monarchy and upper levels of society was elegant and stylish. It was also possible to create black using tree bark, but it was not so lasting or rich looking in its appearance. However, it did mean that those of lower status could wear black, too, and there were no sumptuary laws to stop them from doing so. It was also a very practical colour for the poorer people as it did not show the dirt.

Black has gone on to be the colour associated with many professions because of the dignity it brings and is still in use on a daily basis today in courts of laws and by some Western religious clerics. Many orchestras still have their members wear this colour. Equally, for quite some time, black has been used for staff uniforms, particularly those in domestic service. And of course, black made an important transition to *the* must-have colour of high fashion when Coco Chanel produced "the little black dress" in 1926, the staple of many women's wardrobes for any occasion.

Useful Sources for Costume Research

It is useful to build up a collection of sources on costume for your research. The internet can be unreliable, as I have already highlighted. Therefore, until you have the confidence to trust certain sources and be able to recognise those that are not quite right, it is better to stick to publications that are tried and tested by others. I have referred to all of the books that I am listing here at some point in my career.

Textiles and Clothing 1150–1450 by Elisabeth Crowfoot, Frances Pritchard and Kay Staniland (2006) is easy to read and is based on finds from archaeological digs in London. It gives an insight into the fabrics worn and their colour, as well as providing the history of clothing over this time period. This is particularly helpful, as the medieval period, or Middle Ages, as it is also called, spans such a considerable number of years that it can be quite daunting to figure out which garment belongs to which period. Surprisingly, a book published in the 19th century is still a good source of information, and this is *The Costume History from Ancient Times to the 19th Century* by Auguste Racinet (2006). It is a useful starting point, spanning a huge period – early times up to 1888 – and is full of images. Even with the limitation of its coverage coming to an end in 1888, it is still regularly referred to as "the bible" for costume inspiration, and it is worth having a copy of it now that it has been reprinted in one book rather than the original six volumes.

How to Read a Dress: A Guide to Changing Fashion from the 16th Century to the 20th Century by Lydia Edwards (2017) is a great guide to fashion history and is important because it includes the 20th century. It is well illustrated and easy to read. There is a companion volume, *How to Read a Suit: A Guide to Changing Men's Fashion from the 17th to the 20th Century* (2020), which is as valuable as the one on dresses.

For those of you able to make costumes, there are also books on the market that provide patterns. *Creating Historical Clothes: Pattern Cutting from Tudor to Victorian Times* by Elizabeth Friendship (2013) only features women's clothes, which is a drawback. However, it is generally agreed that this is a great book for beginners, as it highlights the equipment required and how to make patterns for period garments and provides lots of instruction on the process, though many who use it feel more illustrations would be useful. There is a series of books covering the Tudor period, the first of which is *The Tudor Tailor, Reconstructing Sixteenth-Century Dress* by Jane Malcolm-Davies and Ninya Mikhaila (2006), which is full of details on how to make costumes for men and women. It is well illustrated with images of garments made by the authors. It also provides a lot of historical information on clothes of 16th-century England. Some of the details in the book were used by my costume maker, Karen Ashfield, when I required a gown for Elizabeth I. She did highlight that while she found it helpful, she felt it was aimed at those who already had some sewing experience.

As companions to this book, *The King's Servants: Men's Dress at the Accession of Henry VIII, The Queen's Servants: Gentlewoman's Dress at the Accession of Henry VIII* and *The Tudor Child: Clothing and Culture 1485 to 1625* have followed. *The King's Servants* and later *The Queen's Servants* are both by Caroline Johnstone. The second editions of both of these books contain helpful glossaries of terms used and take the form of case studies, dwelling less on patterns and sewing instructions, though these are still there, and more on the textiles, colours and styling of the early period of Tudor costume. *The Tudor Child* by Jane Huggett and Ninya Mikhaila also contains diagrams and is again backed by excellent research that examines what children, male and female, wore from infancy to the age of twelve and includes patterns and instructions on how to make the clothes. All four books are great resources for the costume information they provide for the period, even if you are not up to making your own garments. The online Tudor Tailor shop sells individual patterns, fabric and accessories for those who do not require all the information that is included in the books.

To give you a feel of what Renaissance Scotland was like, I suggest you look at *Glory and Honour, The Renaissance in Scotland* by Andrea Thomas (2013). Although this is not a book on costume, there are pictures of the key figures – James IV, James V, Mary of Guise, Mary, Queen of Scots and James VI – which enable you to see the costumes of the period as well as to get a feel of how different the country was from its neighbour, England. It also reinforces that the Stuart monarchs and their courts were not carbon copies of their Tudor counterparts and that they had their own distinctive style. This can also be seen in the extensive research undertaken by Historic Environment Scotland for the re-creation of the court of James V at Stirling Castle. This organisation has published online resources that give insight into how colourful the court was in its dress and highlights the lavish clothes worn by the king.

The excellent publication *Dressing the Scottish Court, 1543–1553, Clothing in the Accounts of the Lord High Treasurer of Scotland* by Melanie Schuessler Bond (2019) provides a detailed picture of what was being worn after the death of James V. The focus of the book is James Hamilton, Earl of Arran, and his family and household. Arran was appointed the Regent of Scotland early in 1543 after the unexpected death of James V in December 1542, his daughter Mary being only six days old. Using the accounts, which itemise the purchases made for him, his family and his servants, Schuessler Bond is able to create an incredibly detailed picture of what Scots were wearing at this time for different occasions, the fabrics used, the colours, the fastenings, the lining materials, the threads used to sew the garments and the footwear of the period. What is particularly interesting is that this book does not just feature the highest levels of society. It also provides information on gifts of clothing made to servants who attended the Earl's family and the lower servants, the quality of the material denoting their status. For example, the Keeper of Arran's Children (this was his rather unusual title) is given travelling clothes made of good-quality wool, with black velvet provided to trim his coat. And Gilbert Ruthven, a servant to Arran's youngest daughter, Anne, is given clothes that suggest a lowly servant, his doublet being made of fustian, a rougher woollen cloth, which is hard wearing. While there are no guides on how to make the clothes, the information on what is being worn makes this book essential to those who are interpreting this period.

The textiles used to make the garments for Mary, Queen of Scots were the finest available – silk, velvet, satin, brocade, taffeta and fine wool. Of fifty-nine gowns listed, the following colours are also recorded:

- two – cloth of gold
- three – cloth of silver
- twenty-one – black
- ten – white
- nine – crimson
- four – yellow
- four – blue
- two – orange
- two – soft grey
- one – carnation pink
- one – green

The Court of Mary, Queen of Scots was clearly anything but dull! Reference is also made to slashing. This is usually at the shoulders of a bodice or jacket where the sleeve begins and is a decorative feature where the main fabric is cut and a contrasting fabric woven through the fabric. It is extremely wasteful of fabric and therefore only something affordable by the very wealthy and royalty.

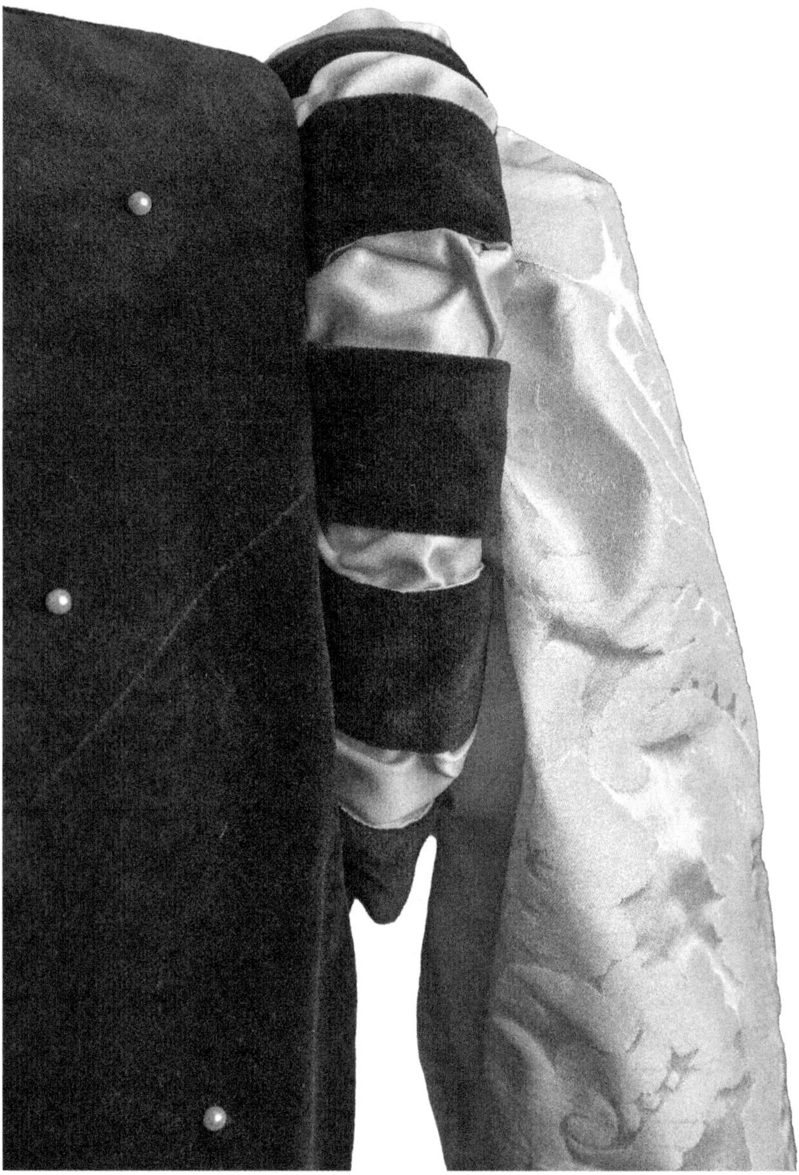

Figure 4.2 The decorative feature known as slashing can be seen at the top of the sleeve on this costume.

Source: © Keith Shaw Buckley/costume from the collection of Artemis Scotland

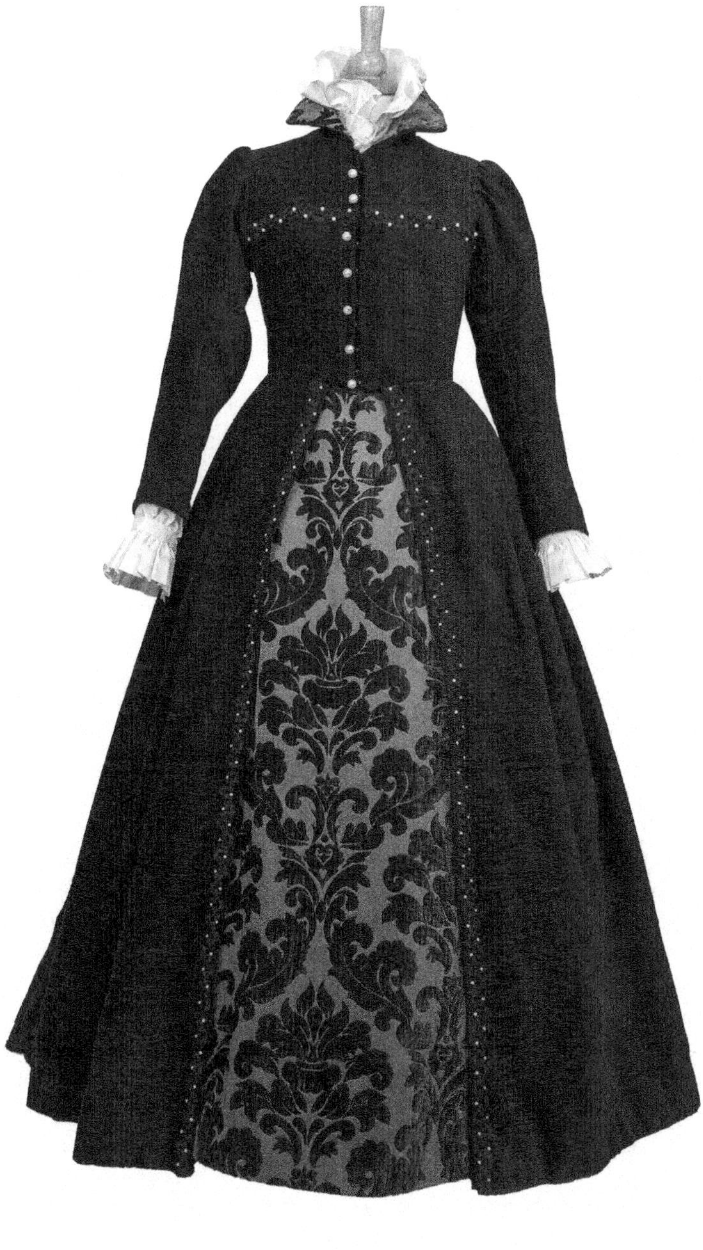

Figure 4.3 Pearls have been used to decorate the bodice and the edges of the overskirt in this costume for Mary, Queen of Scots.

Source: © Keith Shaw Buckley/costume from the collection of Artemis Scotland

There is also mention of the trimmings and decoration on her clothes, such as gold buttons and pearls stitched on to bodices and gowns. Such detail is important when having costumes made for yourself, as these are interesting details to include that add to the story of your character. Again, there are no instructions on how to make any of these costumes, but with the help of an experienced costume maker, these descriptions can be transformed into reality.

For information on what Mary, Queen of Scots wore, the best sources are the inventories she instructed her French valet-de-chambre, Servais de Condé, to make of her principal garments. From February 1562 through to May 1567, Condé diligently kept this list up to date. As with James V and the Earl of Arran, money spent on fabric and accessories for clothes appears in the Accounts of the Lord Treasurer. In 1578, an inventory was made of clothes that had been left at Edinburgh Castle after her abdication and later flight to England. Access to all this material is through the National Archives of Scotland. Books on her clothes are harder to find, but in Susan Watkins's book, *Mary, Queen of Scots* (2001), several useful mentions are made of the queen's wardrobe.

Stuart Style, Dress and the Scottish Male Elite by Maria Hayward (2020) examines the court of James VI when he became King of England in 1603. Here, you will find a considerable amount of information on 17th-century male fashion and how the Scots who went south with James affected what was worn at court. In costume terms, the 17th century is much neglected, as is the study of men's fashion, so this is a most welcome addition to the field. Unfortunately, there are no patterns or construction advice in this book. However, this information can be found in a Victoria and Albert Museum (V&A) publication *17th Century Men's Dress Patterns 1600–1630* by Melanie Braun, Luca Costigliolo, Susan North, Claire Thornton and Jenny Tiramani (2016), which covers a similar period as the new Hayward publication on the Scots at court. The book is well illustrated and has lots of diagrams and helpful hints on costume making.

The V&A have a series of books called *Fashion in Detail* covering the 18th, 19th and 20th centuries. These books really do go into the detail of construction of particular aspects of costume for women and men, such as a neckline or a sleeve, as well as different techniques such as gathering and pleats, but do not actually instruct on how the whole garment is made. The details on which they concentrate are well illustrated but sadly not in the context of the whole garment. However, if you need to know about detail, these books are for you.

There is a remarkable lack of pattern books for clothes of the early part of the 20th century, but then again, the Edwardian period is less represented in costumed interpretation for some reason, and the period around the First World War and thereafter gets more attention. *Vintage Dress Patterns of the 20th Century* by Anne Tyrell (2013) covers from 1911 right up to the 1990s, which is quite unusual. The book also provides guidance on how to accessorise the costumes. It is aimed at those who are experienced sewers and is a rare treat given the lack of provision for this period.

While the style of clothes across Europe has remained very similar because of the influence of Italy and France on design from quite early on, there is a very useful website which I thoroughly recommend – Refashioning the Renaissance (refashioningrenaissance.eu). This site hosts a five-year study of Renaissance fashion in Italy and Scandinavia and provides a wealth of information and new insights into the garments worn at various levels of society.

This is just a small selection of what is available if you search the internet. Some sources are better than others. Those that I have featured here have a proven track record of usefulness within the world of costume interpretation.

Sourcing Costume

It may well be that the organisation you are working for already have a suitable outfit, and if that is the case, it is important to set aside time to try it on and make sure it fits. This may seem such an obvious statement, but it is surprisingly easy to think that because a costume exists it will fit when, in fact, it probably will not. One size does not fit all. And if indeed it does need alteration, you must find out if you are expected to do it or if the organisation will sort it out. Being given the responsibility to make it the right size for yourself is tricky. Firstly, you need to be good with a needle, and secondly, any alteration made by you must be able to be undone, as this ensemble will be returned to the organisation for whoever wears it next. My advice is that alterations to costume should be the responsibility of those who have provided it.

If the commission you have received is short and no costume is to be provided, it is more sensible to hire one, as this can be done at a reasonable cost. There are many options all over the UK. The National Theatre, the Royal Shakespeare Company, Liverpool's Royal Court, Scottish Opera, Welsh National Opera and Manchester's Royal Exchange Theatre all have costume hire departments, as do some smaller theatres like Dumfries' Theatre Royal and Tonbridge's Oast Theatre. Not all require a visit, and costumes can be arranged by email and telephone conversation, but it is much more satisfactory to see and try on the garments before you hire them. If money is no object and you need something very spectacular, then Angels Corporate, boasting the largest collection of costumes in the world, or Cosprop, also with a large selection of excellent costumes, is for you. An internet search shows that there are plenty of opportunities for costume hire across Europe and beyond, though I have no experience of any of the suppliers. In some cases, props can also be hired. The minimum hire period is usually a week, which gives you time to try a garment on and get used to wearing it. There are also many companies online, but be very careful about these, as many of their costumes are more of the "fancy dress" variety rather than historically accurate. I recommend that when you have your hired costume at home, you take photographs of it so that you can prove the condition it was in when you received it. If you find any small repairs are required, such as tightening loose fastenings, hemming or seam sewing, take a photo of the clothing before repair and check that wherever you hired it from is happy for you to repair it. Obviously, this is unlikely if you have hired it in person, but if it has been arranged online, it is best to make a record of how it looks on arrival in case of any questions later by the company providing the costume. Within museum circles, this is known as a condition report. It is also very easy for buttons and fastenings to work lose if the costume is worn over several days, so do check that you are able to fix such occurrences yourself. It is also a good idea to note the state of the costume on departure through the same procedure of photographing it. This way, if there is any question about its return, you have evidence to show to the hirer.

If you are providing a military character, use a company that has proven expertise in their production of uniforms. This is an area in which to get anything wrong is not a good idea, particularly if you are interpreting a modern military interaction. Those who served and their relatives will be well acquainted with the uniforms, and mistakes in costume show a lack of appreciation for those who have served their country. Be wary of online sites that also provide uniforms for fancy dress, as the quality is not always satisfactory.

It may well be that you are able to make your own costume, and if that is the case leave plenty of time to do so. It is hard for me to say how long it will take you, because I have never made a costume as my sewing skills are not good enough. However, when I am having a new costume made, I always allow at least six weeks.

Having a costume custom made is expensive. Nevertheless, if you will be portraying a certain character on a regular basis, it makes sense to have a custom-made outfit, as it will be worn on many occasions and justifies the expense. It is a good idea to find several costume makers who have good reputations and establish relationships with them. When I began my career, it was much harder to find people with the skills required. However, it has become a lot easier to find costume makers. There are now costume-making courses all over the world. Currently, within the UK, there are seventeen practical courses at university level on stage and screen costume design and construction. Most costume makers are freelancers who are happy to take on a project with a single client for a short period. I also find that contacting the university departments running the courses is very beneficial, as sometimes, you can be lucky and find that one of their students is working on a project that fits with your needs. This is particularly useful to you at the beginning of your career, when funds may be an issue. Equally, even further down the line when you are more established, keeping in touch with the course providers and their students means you are likely to be asked to end-of-term shows, where you can spot people you want to work with in the future.

The Process of Getting a Costume Made

Let us imagine that you have decided to go ahead and have a bespoke outfit made because of repeat bookings for a character but are not sure of the process. Here is a step-by-step guide.

1 The Design and Cost

- It is crucial that you establish that in making the costume, the costume maker will use a toile before making the final product. A toile is a mock-up of the required garment(s) made up of bits of other fabrics; it enables the maker to carry out changes during fittings before cutting the fabric being used for the actual costume.

- Give as much detail as possible about the costume required. This should include the purpose for the garment. For example, perhaps it will be worn outside for some of the time, and you will need a cape as part of the outfit, or you might be demonstrating a particular activity in it and need it to be more robust in certain areas. It is also useful to let the costume maker know whether you need to be able to put the costume on by yourself, as this will affect the construction of it. Fairly early in my career as a costumed interpreter, I discovered that a gown which traditionally laces up the back is impossible to put on without assistance! It was not until I was on site that I realised I could not tighten the laces properly, because the bodice construction meant I could not reach the laces, which also meant I could not tie them at the back of my neck. Fortunately, the headdress had a long veil at the back, and it hid the gap at the top of the gown on that particular occasion. There was no one who could help me, as the female member of staff was on her break, and the male member of staff was not at all keen on the idea! For future events, I worked out a technique for loosening the lacing and pinning the ties to the front of the dress over the shoulder so that when the outfit was on, I could reach the laces and pull them tight enough to close the gap, although I still could not tie them. I do not recommend this, as it does rather cause panic before you go out to meet the visitors! However, it was a lesson learnt and not repeated. The situation was resolved by my costume maker, who opened a side seam fastened with hooks and eyes. The back lacing was left permanently tied so that the look was retained.
- It may be possible at this early stage to discuss with the costume maker the fabric that would be suitable for the costume as well as any embellishments that might be required or extras like a hat or cloak. At this point, it is also important to check that every effort is made to ensure that the fabric and trimmings that will be used have been ethically sourced. In the current world situation, it would be unusual to find a costume maker who did not already use fair-trade, ethically sourced goods, but it is important to make sure. It may also be the case that the costume being made requires fur. Faux fur now looks so good that there is no need whatsoever to use the real thing, which makes it possible for costume to look the part without being ethically questionable. Imitation fur is also much easier to sew onto fabric. I have been in many situations in which I have had to explain why I am wearing fur by looking into the future, and I will address this issue more thoroughly in the next chapter when explaining about how to deal with how things have changed over time. It is a good idea to ask that a little extra of the faux fur is ordered, as it is useful to have it available for visitors to handle,

thus proving that no animals have been killed to make your costume look authentic.
- What is really essential at this point is to give as much detail as possible of what you want, thus enabling the maker to provide a realistic price. Remember to tell the maker the date by which you need the completed outfit, something that is easy to forget in the excitement of preparation.
- In the costing, the maker will provide ideas on how the garment will look based on the information you have provided, the fabrics that will be used, what kind of decoration will be needed, how many fittings are required and an estimate of how long it will take to make it.

2 A Completion Date

- While an estimated date has been given, make sure you agree on a completion date once you commission the maker to go ahead. This will avoid any misunderstanding later on. I learnt this the hard way with my first-ever costume as I sat in the maker's studio the day before I needed the garment, watching it being hemmed and buttons sewn on and then driving home late at night! This is not desirable for anyone.

3 Measurements and Agreement on Design and Fabric

- Once the price and completion date are agreed, your measurements are needed for the process to begin. You may be able to provide these yourself, but you will need to meet the costume maker at some point for fittings, so attending personally for a measuring session is a good way to get to know one another a bit better.
- This is also a good opportunity to discuss the design and construction of the required garments as well as the fabric and trimmings to be used and to finalise that you are happy with the suggestions made.
- It is also good to find out at this stage how the fabric used is to be cleaned.

4 Fittings

- It is likely that two or three fittings will be required; it really depends on how complicated the costume is to make.
- After the construction of the toile, measurements will need to be checked with you wearing the garment, and if the changes are considerable, the maker may want another checking session before making the costume in the fabric. It is between you and the costume maker whether you want a fitting of the costume before collection.

5 The Finished Costume

- The day of collection is an exciting day. Now you have your bespoke creation to enjoy wearing at work. Even after over twenty years in the business, I still enjoy seeing the costume fully made and very often say "Wow!" when I see it.

Costume Tips

Over the years of having costumes made, I have found that there are ways of creating "the look" that enable the wearer of the clothes to be more comfortable while equally retaining the correct appearance.

One of the aspects dreaded by most female costume interpreters is that of wearing a corset. I have discovered that this can be circumnavigated on some occasions by having the corset stays, as they are called, sewn into the bodice of a gown. For the costumes that I have had made for Mary, Queen of Scots, Elizabeth I and a Victorian bustle dress, I have had short "stays" sewn into the bodice of the garment. This makes it much more comfortable, as normal underwear can still be worn, yet the required look of the period is retained.

On the subject of underwear, while it is possible to avoid wearing a corset for some costumes, that which supports the skirt needs to be correct to the period. Wearing a full net underskirt/petticoat beneath a 16th-century skirt will not give the right look. For this period, a farthingale is required. It takes the weight of the skirt and, as you move, has a sort of swing to it which conveys elegance and dignity. A farthingale is also much cooler than a net underskirt to wear on a warm day, and equally, on a cold day, thermal leggings can be worn unseen, providing comfort that I am sure 16th century ladies would have been very grateful for.

Most dresses that you see in paintings were not dresses in the modern sense of one-piece garments but in fact were made up of a bodice and skirt. In the first costumes I had made, I did stick to this, but I found from the start that trying to fasten the two pieces of costume together was not at all easy, and if it was not done properly, they could come undone at the most inconvenient times. It was particularly difficult for the 16th-century costume, as it effectively meant I was wearing one skirt on top of another – literally an "underskirt", often referred to as a petticoat, with a panel of expensive fabric at the front, and another "overskirt", usually of a heavier fabric like velvet. The overskirt had its front panel missing in order to display the expensive panel of the underskirt. These two skirts then had to attach to each other and to the upper bodice. Keeping everything together was hard. Perhaps it was common for these gowns to come apart in their time; history has, sadly, not recorded this. A solution was required! On that basis, I worked with my costume maker, Karen Ashfield, and it was resolved by going against the norm and attaching the bodice to the overskirt.

I did wonder why this was not thought of in the 16th century itself. Further research has revealed that because most women did not have many gowns, they could mix and match their few underskirts and overskirts to create different looks. For the wealthy, this also enabled them to own more clothes. Sleeves often had elaborate inserts which were detachable and therefore changed the look of the gown and made it more versatile. With regards to these sleeve inserts, there was a fashion in the mid-16th century to have these made to match the expensive panel of the underskirt. They often had jewel decoration sewn onto them.

In the 16th-century world, the sleeve insert was often attached with laces over the shoulder, another impossible item to fasten on your own. Therefore,

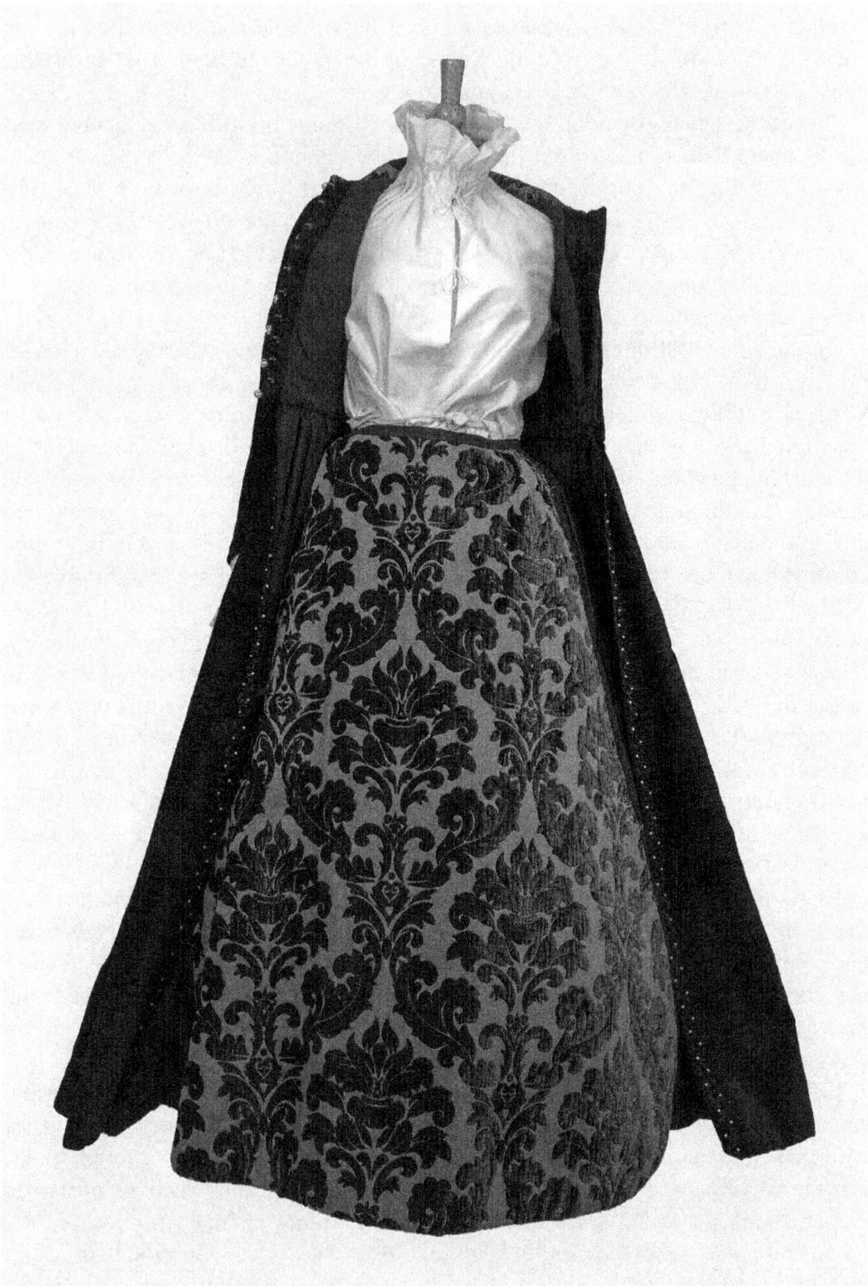

Figure 4.4 Here, you can see how the bodice is attached to the skirt, making it one garment and easier to wear.

Source: © Keith Shaw Buckley/costume from the collection of Artemis Scotland

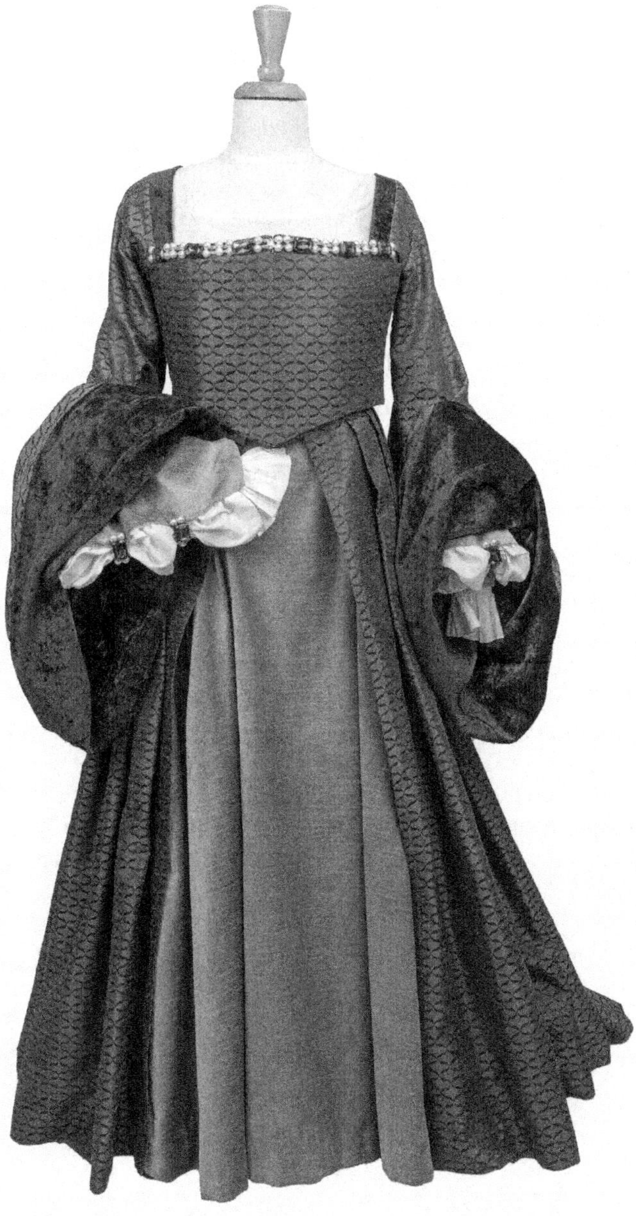

Figure 4.5 The decorative sleeve inserts are made from the same material as the underskirt and also have jewel and pearl decoration sewn on to them.

Source: © Keith Shaw Buckley/costume from the collection of Artemis Scotland

I recommend that if you require detachable sleeve inserts, use press studs or hooks and eyes. However, unless your interpretation requires removal of the inserts for demonstration purposes, I would think seriously about adopting this style, as it is almost impossible to re-attach the sleeves without a mirror. And as this aspect of fashion was reserved for monarchs and nobility, they would not be removing their sleeves in public!

If leather is required in the costume, this, like faux fur, is made to such a high standard to look realistic that there is no need to consider the use of the real thing. I will discuss in the next chapter how to deal with questions about wearing fur or leather, which you may be asked while in costume.

When it comes to hairstyles, you might need to wear a wig. If that is the case, do wear a wig cap underneath it. They are available quite cheaply online and will make the wearing of the wig much more comfortable. As to the wig itself, it can be hired or purchased. Unfortunately, there are a lot of cheap wigs available online which are very unsatisfactory. Often, the images are nothing like the actual wig you end up with, so be very careful. It is best to see the wig before you hire or commit to buying one. It may, however, be the case that you can make it look as if you are wearing a wig by sewing a hairpiece into a hat or headdress or pinning it in under the headdress – that is often the best solution rather than going for a full wig.

You may not be able to afford a wig and feel that your modern hairstyle will ruin the look you are trying to create. This should not really be an issue, as right up to the beginning of the 20th century, women have worn something on their heads. From the wimple of medieval times, the "hood" and beret-style hat of the 16th century, the ever-changing cap that takes you from the 17th century through to the 19th century, with bonnets and hats too, you will be able to find something to wear on your head to solve the problem of your hairstyle. Men have also worn hats through the centuries, but their hairstyles are less problematic – the 18th century being their biggest headache, as most men did wear wigs. Again, a hat can be their salvation. It is not until after the First World War that there is any real issue with headdresses for women, and even then, women wore hats quite a lot.

Jewellery may also be added to achieve the look of a period. Unless the portrayal is of a very wealthy character, it is unlikely that much jewellery will be required because of its expense in the period portrayed. It really has to have the appearance of the time you are portraying. Therefore, if you cannot source such jewellery, it is best to avoid using it.

Taking Care of Costumes

If you have gone to the expense of having a costume made, it is important to look after it. As mentioned earlier, do check with the costume maker as to the cleaning processes you can use on your costume, especially if it has embellishments sewn onto it like beads and braids. It may well be that you can have the costume dry cleaned, but as it will come without a care-instruction label, the dry cleaners will be very reluctant to take it on unless you sign a waiver absolving them of any blame if the cleaning process goes wrong. This is why it is so important to establish what kind of cleaning procedure can be used on the fabric. Some specialist dry cleaners now provide ozone chambers for cleaning costumes that require extra care. This is very useful.

If you are able to wash the costume in a machine, stick to the delicate wash and use a detergent designed for fragile garments. Some costumes will line dry, but avoid direct sun, which might result in fading. Others will need to be dried flat, and for this it is best to lay the costume on towels on the floor with more towels on top; change the towels regularly. If you can do this outside in a garden, the drying process will be much quicker. If the garment is covered with towels, the sun will not be an issue. It may be that the only solution is to hand-wash.

When the situation arises that the costume is being worn regularly, perhaps several days a week over a holiday period, then it is impossible to have it constantly cleaned, but equally it does not make the wearing of the costume very pleasant day after day. Given such a situation, it is to be hoped that wherever you work will provide you with somewhere that the costume can be hung between sessions, as being in the air will help. It is also a good idea to freshen it up before you next need to wear it by spraying it with rubbing alcohol, particularly under the arms. A little tea-tree oil can be added to the rubbing alcohol if you feel the former has a slight medicated smell. It dries quite quickly, and the smell dissipates as it dries. If there is little provision for hanging up the costume at wherever you are working and taking it back and forth is awkward, then spraying it will be useless, as the outfit needs to hang to dry. Hopefully, you will have some form of garment shield already sewn in to help with keeping the underarm area fresh, and it is best to have these attached to your costume with poppers or hooks and eyes so that they can be changed every time the costume is worn. If you have several pairs, it makes the outfit more comfortable to put on over several days until you get the chance to clean it properly. Hired costumes often have these shields already sewn in, and they may not be removable – make sure you check whether you can remove and wash them during a prolonged period of wear. If garment shields cannot be used, which can be the case if the material is lightweight, as with silk, then you may be able to wear something unseen under the costume like a T-shirt, which can be changed daily. Some gowns require a chemise to be worn under the bodice, and it is always a good idea to have several of these made, as they are easy to wash each day, though if you have several, it is not so pressing to wash them daily.

Once the costume is cleaned, it has to be stored. In an ideal world, the best possible solution is to store it flat, wrapped in acid-free tissue paper, in an archive box. However, this is not a practical solution for most people, and I have never been fortunate enough to have the facilities to do so. I have had some of my costumes for more than twenty years and have used the storage process I am sharing with you here.

Always use wooden hangers, as they provide good support and help keep the shape of your costumes. Contoured hangers are best for one-piece gowns, chemises, jackets and similar garments. Stuff the sleeves with acid-free tissue paper to help them keep their shape. Hangers which provide a clamp are ideal for skirts, trousers and breeches. Sometimes, there is a bar at the bottom of a contoured hanger. It is best not to use this, as it can lead to a mark on the fabric if it is left too long on the hanger. Some wooden hangers have an indentation and can also be used for skirts that have hoops on the inside that are there for the purpose of hanging the skirt. However, if hanging for a long time, the skirt can droop, and it puts greater strain on the seams. Wooden hangers may seem expensive, but they are worth the investment and really do last.

Once the costume is on the hanger, the next question is how to protect the fabric from moths. It is now possible to buy moth-repellent garment bags. There is a gap where the hanger comes through the top, so it is important to seal this area with tape so that moths will not be able to get to your clothes at all. If you are unable to buy these, then it is well known that moths hate the smell of cedar, and various forms of preventative measures using cedar can be bought. Lavender bags are also useful and can be hung with each of your costumes in your wardrobe or storage cupboard. Please do not use the old-fashioned moth balls, as it is impossible to get rid of their smell, and it is not at all pleasant to wear anything that has been near them. Whatever you use, make sure you check on your costumes from time to time if they are not in regular use. Fergus John McCann works regularly with me at Artemis Scotland and knows just how important it is to look after what you wear, and he sums it up completely:

> It may sound like a cliché, but look after your costume and your costume will look after you.

Transporting the Costume

When you have to get your costume to the place where you are going to be working, this can seem like quite a challenge. If you are fortunate enough to be travelling by car, you may well be able to take your costume in a garment bag, but that will depend on what kind of changing facility you are provided with and whether you can hang things up. Very often, you may be operating out of a suitcase. My advice is to buy a large, good-quality suitcase on easily manoeuvrable wheels. This then gives you plenty of space in which to pack your costume, footwear, accessories and any small props you are taking. Sometimes, you may find that you need another bag for props – do try and keep it small. If at all possible, keep everything in one case, as it will make transportation and getting on site so much easier.

Always create a checklist of what you are taking. Set it out in the order in which you will be putting on the various items rather than in the packing order. This will be important when in the changing room, as it focusses you on what you need as you move from being you to becoming your character. You will notice that I have included a sheet and towel on the list, which may seem odd. The sheet can be put across a table on which you can lay your costume; that way, you can see where everything is, and if the table should be a bit sticky, it does not get on your

Table 4.1 A costume checklist

World War II costume		
Item of costume	*Packed before event*	*Packed on site*
Sheet		
Hand towel		
Black twin set – short-sleeved top and cardigan		
Skirt		
Pearl necklace and earrings		
Jacket		
Scarf for neck		
Shoes		
Hat		
Gloves		
Small basket containing:		
• Handbell		
• Wooden gas attack rattle		
• Gas mask		
• Whistle		

costume. I have even used the sheet to stand on when the floor has been rather dusty and I wanted to protect the bottom of the gown when changing. So you might want to take two sheets. And at the end of the day, you may well be quite hot and pleased that you have brought a towel with you.

The checklist is very useful at the end of the session so that you can make sure you have everything. You will probably feel quite tired at the end of the day and, when re-packing, miss one vital item that has perhaps fallen behind a chair. The checklist makes sure you have everything and could save a costly journey back to collect the forgotten item. I put my checklist in a plastic pocket with a pencil so no harm comes to the costume; a pen could leak, and that would be a disaster.

Footwear

Not to be forgotten is what is worn on the feet, as it can be a long day in costume, and nothing is worse than ill-fitting footwear. Over the years, I have not succumbed to wearing period shoes mainly for health and safety reasons. Trying to negotiate an historic site or house can be dangerous in shoes that provide little support. Equally, standing on museum floors for long periods without proper supportive shoes or boots can lead to sore leg and back muscles quite quickly, which makes your role as interpreter uncomfortable. For women, I recommend wearing a slip-on, low-heeled court or ballet pump–type shoe. These are unobtrusive and comfortable to wear for a whole day. Given that the costume worn is usually long, it is very unlikely that the shoes will really be seen. When moving into the early 20th century, when hemlines begin to rise, the court shoe is still acceptable provided it is very plain, and as it is still a popular style today, this shoe design can carry you through all the ages. While I recommend sticking to a plain modern shoe, it will likely be different from your everyday shoes. For Helen Cuinn, who has portrayed many characters for me, the shoes are the beginning of everything:

> I always think that to find a character, you have to start with the shoes. Different shoes force a different gait, posture, stride.

From Helen's comment, the lesson is that whatever shoes you choose for your character, make sure you practise wearing them and get the feel of what they are like. You will probably be standing in them for quite a long time. And do remember, if wearing a long dress, it is usually easier to put on your shoes first, as it can be awkward to do so in full costume.

It is a little trickier for men, as their footwear is more obvious when wearing loose knee-length gowns or breeches. Riding boots are always popular for men, but the style of these changes quite dramatically through the ages, and they are expensive. When I have had to provide footwear for men interpreting from medieval times through the 16th century, I have used lace-up jazz shoes, which have a very small heel, and inserted arch-support orthotic insoles. The 17th and 18th centuries are really awkward, as the men's shoes had heels and were quite a decorative part of the overall outfit. On these occasions, I have hired shoes from organisations like the ones mentioned earlier. Once into the 19th century, it becomes easier, as men begin wearing trousers, and plain slip-on or lace-up shoes can be worn.

Props

It is best to keep whatever props you want to use reasonably small, as it is likely that you will have to carry them yourself as you interact with visitors. It may even be that you are to undertake a walk around the heritage site, historic house or museum gallery, and then it is crucial that they are kept small enough to go in a bag that you can easily carry and that looks like it belongs to the period you are interpreting. If you are carrying a bag, then visitors are likely to ask what is in it, so make sure it is not your mobile phone and a paper hanky! It might be that you have some gaming dice, a bottle of smelling salts and a cotton handkerchief – you really do not need much as aids to your conversation with visitors. Props can often be part of the character. For example, an 18th-century lady is most likely to carry a fan, which is a prop but also an accessory expressing the period; likewise, a 16th-century male courtier may have a sword around his waist which is part of his outfit as well as a prop.

If required to provide a short presentation/set performance as a character, then you are very likely to need props. It is advisable to lay these out, if possible, in the way you wish to use them prior to your appearance in costume at the set location. You really do not want to be seen carrying things in and arranging them minutes before you begin, as this does not create a good atmosphere and somewhat breaks the spell of the period you are trying to create. If setting up while in costume just prior to delivery, you may also find that the assembled audience want to talk to you, which you definitely will not want to do prior to your appearance. Equally, it is a time when you want to be thinking about what you are about to present rather than where you have put a prop. There are occasions when you have to rely on a member of staff to set out your props, as there is no other way. My advice is to lay out the props at home in the way you wish to work with them on the day and then take a photograph of them in situ and send it to your contact in the organisation. If there is any reason that the on-site team do not think your layout is possible, you will know about it in advance and can work with them to re-arrange the layout. Try to avoid having no input at all into how the props are placed, because then you really will have no idea where anything is. Unfortunately, I have experienced this and would not wish it on anyone. It is really vital to know where the things are that you are going to use – you will have rehearsed what to say and also practised lifting the things from the set place you have chosen. To turn round and find something completely different in that place is very disconcerting.

If you are asked to incorporate a handling collection of objects into your conversation/presentation with visitors, these artefacts are very different from your own props, as these are being supplied by the heritage site or museum specifically to be touched by visitors. Props belong to you, and how much they are handled, if at all, is in your control. This is not the case with on-site handling collections, the whole point of them being that visitors can touch them. It is best not to have any additional handling material in the form of your props on the days you use a handling collection, as this can lead to a confused experience for the visitors.

It is useful for you to have seen the objects in advance of your work, as you need to know exactly what they are. You will probably have questions you wish to ask, and there may even be technical issues to learn about how they are to be handled. It is, therefore, essential to do this early on in your preparation for delivery, as you will need to incorporate this new information into what you prepare for the day's encounter.

The Costume as a Prop

The costume itself can be considered a prop. An example of this can be seen in the use of the character Henry VIII. On entering Hampton Court Palace, one of his favourite palaces, nothing is better shorthand for the court of this king than his familiar silhouette. A costumed interpreter needs no other prop than the costume he is wearing to interact with visitors, as everyone knows immediately who he is. Equally, the palace itself becomes a prop for the king, too, as it provides the context and perfect environment in which to portray this very familiar historical character. The costume does all the work in providing identity, and other props are far less important. With a character as well known as Henry VIII, it is also possible to use him in a modern gallery exhibition without props that distract from the artefacts on display.

Apart from the costume that makes you instantly recognisable, you also need to be able to explain its component parts. For several years, as part of the public programme, Historic Environment Scotland set up a touring event that took place at several locations around the country that had particular ties to the Renaissance – St Andrews Castle, Linlithgow Palace and Huntly Castle. The event focussed on the costume of the period, and Artemis Scotland provided courtly characters representing various fashion changes throughout this period as well as highlighting the trade connections Scotland had with Europe and further afield through the textiles, dyes, trimmings and fastenings being used. At these events, the costumed interpreters were asked lots of questions about their costumes and therefore really had to know all the component parts. The costume of women is often the more spectacular, but 16th-century male courtiers were known for their lavish clothes and the fascinatingly named codpiece. Fergus was part of this tour, appearing as a 16th-century gentleman at the court of Mary, Queen of Scots and here he reinforces the importance of understanding what you are wearing:

> Your job is to know how to put on and wear your outfit accurately. Plus, you may have to explain your costume. This is especially true of older, high-status costumes, as they're so unfamiliar to contemporary audiences. Many is the time I have had to explain my codpiece!

In order to explain the codpiece, Fergus had first to explain about hose. Men did not talk about wearing breeches. Breeches were called hose (sometimes trunk hose); stockings were called "nether hose". Hose in the earlier part of the 16th century was joined to the nether hose by ties, but by the mid-16th century, it was separate. The nether hose was kept up with garters tied under the hose so they could not be seen. Before hose, men wore long tunics, and any form of covering of the crotch was not required. Once hose became the thing to wear, it was necessary to find some way of protecting oneself from constant exposure. The original cover was a triangular piece of cloth – the point was stitched to the hose and the other two corners fastened to the doublet so that it could be removed easily. This flap gradually became more padded and eventually became the codpiece. Showing off one's masculinity in the 16th century was important and was associated with ideas of chivalry, honour and romance. The codpiece became the way to cover all of this very effectively as well as provide a very practical function. Sometimes, men even gave their codpieces a name! This explanation emphasises how important it is to know all that you can about your costume. Who you are is important, but so is knowing what you wear. Never underestimate the power of costume.

5 *Hello Everyone, My Name Is . . .* Techniques for Preparation and Delivery

All Set to Go!

You have done your research and created your realms with the key messages for your interpretation incorporated into your preparation, so all you have to do is put on your costume and step out on site or into the museum gallery. Nervous? No need for that – everything is here to make sure you are ready and that your delivery is all that it should be.

You

Apart from all the work that you have done in creating your character to use as a means to deliver the key messages chosen for the particular project and planning the costume and props, the thing that is often overlooked is the importance of preparing yourself for walking out before the public. It is all very well being told that the event begins at 11.00 and that you should be out for interaction with visitors for 11.15, but you have to consider how long it is going to take you to get ready both literally and mentally. As part of this process of preparation, you have to factor in travel time as well as getting on site, finding the dressing room, unpacking, getting into costume, making sure your personal items are secure while you are working and making sure you know where and when you can take your break, and most importantly you also need to prepare your mind for your work. All these may seem obvious, but when you are new to costumed interpretation, it is good to know what you should prioritise in your preparation time and even if this has been your profession for some time, it is useful to be reminded in order to combat complacency. No one gives their best by dashing in at the last minute, struggling to put on their costume and then rushing out on site, out of breath. Over the years, I have perfected the groundwork required to get into the right frame of mind as well as into your costume.

How long it takes to get into your costume depends on how complicated the costume is. It is best to try it on several times at home and time yourself so that you really know how long it will take. When you have several sets of timings, go for the one that is between your slowest and fastest and add on few extra minutes, as the chances are that once on site, it may take a little longer. If your character

DOI: 10.4324/9781003260226-6

requires makeup, go through the same process; then you will know exactly how long it takes. Do the same with your hair if it requires a particular style or you are wearing a wig. You need to know how long this takes too. It is also useful to factor in the possibility that you may require protection from the sun, so add that to your to-do list. Use a good-quality sunblock that does not require constant application and remember to apply it before you put on your costume, as some creams stain fabric.

As you will know your timings from your practise sessions at home, allow yourself at least an hour for the changing and preparation. Remember, this is the time you allocate in the changing room and does not include getting there either by public transport or by car, parking your car if you came in one and getting into the building. However, as advised in the chapter on building your character, you will have made a site visit and hopefully already organised parking at the place of delivery if required or know how long it takes to get from the bus stop or train station to the location, as well as where you will change, leave your own possessions securely and have your lunch away from the public eye. Therefore, you will know how long this will take in addition to the hour you need to transform yourself into whoever you are to be for the day.

Once in the changing room, using your costume checklist, first lay the sheet you have packed on the table (which you have requested in advance) and set out the constituent parts of your costume in the order that you will put them on. When packing, it is not always possible to place things in the order of wearing, but it is useful if you can construct your checklist in the order in which you need to wear the items, as shown in the chapter on costume. This means you have everything to hand as you need it. Remember that you may also have a couple of props to take with you.

You want to be as relaxed as possible. If you are on edge and feel tense, you will convey this in your delivery. You may, of course, feel a little nervous but that is very different from feeling stressed. Here are a few techniques that can help you to feel ready for your day.

- Warm up your voice.

  For those of us who use our voices for our work, it is worth getting into the habit of doing a few exercises every morning to warm up the voice regardless of whether it is a day of costumed interpretation or a day of relaxation. Ten to twenty minutes a day helps to strengthen your voice and stops you from straining it. Warming up your voice is not just about repeating various sounds; it also involves various stretches and breathing exercises to eliminate tension. All of these contribute to a healthy voice. Lots of sites online suggest various exercises, and it is through trying them out that you will find what suits you. It is best to do these first thing in the morning, because you will not have time to go through this before getting into costume.

  When in the changing room, within that hour, do a few purely vocal exercises. For this, I suggest tongue twisters, which will just give that extra bit of help to strengthen your voice for the day ahead.

- Hydrate.

  Drink plenty of water in that hour before you go out to meet the public, as this will greatly help your vocal cords to work. You need to keep well hydrated through the day as well, especially if you are working outside and it is warm. However, you do not want to be seen drinking from a plastic bottle, as that does rather ruin being in character. The management will not be averse to you taking a break for a drink of water, as it is certainly not in their interests to have you faint on site or lose your voice.

  You might be offered a cup of tea or coffee on arrival. Lovely as this may seem, it is really better to stick to water unless you can guarantee it is decaffeinated, as caffeine is dehydrating and does not do any good to the voice. Most actors and singers also avoid taking anything with milk in it up to an hour before performance. This is good advice, as milk appears to stress the vocal cords and leads to you wanting to clear your throat a lot as you speak, as I can testify from experience. Just stick to water.
- Prepare your mind.

  The routine you establish for yourself in the changing area helps to get you into character. It is up to you whether you do a few voice exercises before you get into costume or after, but what is important is to have a few quiet moments to yourself. Visualise yourself in the location(s) where you are to be during the day, have a few imaginary conversations in your head and if possible, move around in the costume gradually taking on your persona. Having this quiet, tranquil time to yourself, imagining what is about to happen before you go out is, I find, essential to being relaxed and ready to take on the day ahead.

These may not seem like techniques of delivery, but they really are, because if you have not prepared yourself physically and mentally for the day, you will be exhausted in the first hour. It is hard work, even though it seems to others that all you do all day is float around in a costume, chatting to people. That is, in essence, the trick – make it look as if that is what you are doing. The time spent getting ready – the research, character building and practice – builds your confidence and, whether you are aware of it or not, radiates from you and puts people at their ease, enabling you to be a costumed interpreter.

To Script or Not to Script – That Is the Question!

The very word "script" instantly conjures up the impression of something that has to be memorised and learnt verbatim – and therein lies the problem. Many costumed interpreters hold up their hands in horror – at least metaphorically speaking – if the word "script" is mentioned. To them, it suggests a play which does not allow for them to react to visitors because they have been provided with the words they have to say and no others can be used. Equally if all that has been learnt is the script, then visitor questions that do not relate to it cannot be answered easily, and the costumed interpreters are left with nothing to fall back on but to make something up, which I have seen happen. A script also suggests an order in which things must be said, and if a couple of lines or even a few words are forgotten, panic sets in at trying to work out if not saying them matters. Nevertheless, you cannot go out before the public without having some idea of what to say.

This is where the research that you have done for your character and how you have absorbed the key interpretive messages of the organisation into this development become important. The example provided here is from an event I delivered for Historic Environment Scotland at Linlithgow Palace using the character of Mary of Guise. The event was advertised as "The Other Mary", and the message to convey was that Mary of Guise had strong associations with Linlithgow Palace – in fact, probably more so than her daughter, the future Mary, Queen of Scots who was born there.

Using the following example, let us imagine that you are portraying the character of Mary of Guise, the French wife of James V and mother of Mary, Queen of Scots, at Linlithgow Palace. Your brief for the day is to engage in conversation with visitors. There are no scheduled performances, but if there seem to be a number of visitors who are curious at your presence yet reluctant to engage, it is suggested you give an impromptu performance. Visitors will be informed that Mary of Guise is in the palace, and advertising for the event has promoted it as "The Other Mary – Mary of Guise remembers her time spent at Linlithgow Palace". You have been asked to highlight her links to the palace through her husband, James V, the birth of her daughter and her early widowhood as the mother of the new queen of Scotland. These three messages are the information that you will disseminate in character:

1 Mary of Guise, Linlithgow Palace and James V

- Her first time at Linlithgow Palace was in June 1538 on the royal progress from St Andrews to Holyrood Palace following her arrival from France the week before to meet her husband, James V. She had married by proxy in France earlier that year.
- On first seeing the palace, she is recorded as having said that it "is as fine as any castle in France" and as having been enchanted by its location on the edge of the pretty loch.
- She and James were back at the palace in January 1539, taking with them visitors from the French Court.
- They spent Christmas 1539 at Linlithgow and were there into the new year, as it was here that Sir David Lindsay performed his play *A Satire of the Three Estates* in January 1540. (Note – this play is the earliest known Scottish play and is written in Scots. Lindsay was the highest-ranking herald in Scotland as well as a poet of some renown at the court of James V.)
- Mary was here for some time in November 1542, awaiting the birth of her baby. James visited her here before the Battle of Solway Moss. The battle was a disaster. James returned to the Palace around the 24th of November and left for Falkland Palace on 6th December.
- Mary gave birth to her daughter on 8th December.

- On 14th December 1542, Mary of Guise learnt of her husband's death in Falkland Palace, and on that day, her baby became Mary, Queen of Scots.

2 The Birthplace of Mary, Queen of Scots

- The church beside the palace rather than the chapel inside the palace is where the baby, Princess Mary, was baptised. It is unlikely that Mary of Guise will have attended the baptism, as royal protocol following birth was for the baby's mother to stay in her chamber and recover.
- Roman Catholicism was the religion of Scotland at the time, and this dictated that a newly born child must be baptised as soon as possible in case of illness and death. No baptism would mean no heaven for the baby. Baptism was usually performed the day after birth. The reason for choosing St Michael's was that this baby was also a princess and heir to the Scottish throne, so it was important that she was seen by a wider circle of the court than was already in the palace. They would see that she was healthy and would be hopeful of her staying that way.
- On 14th December, her new baby became queen of Scotland.

3 Widowhood and Mother of the Queen

- Mary of Guise was trapped in Linlithgow Palace – it was traditional that the mother of a child monarch ruled as regent, but the death of James so close to Mary's birth complicated things considerably:
    - o Strict rules of etiquette demanded a royal widow remain in seclusion in the days following bereavement.
    - o A queen who had given birth was not allowed to leave her apartments for one month after the birth of the child.
- Her greatest fear was that James Hamilton, Second Earl of Arran, would become regent. He had a claim on the throne (grandson of James II's eldest daughter), and if the baby, Mary, should die, he would be king.
- On 3rd January 1543 her worst fears were realised – the Earl of Arran became regent.
- In mid-January, Mary of Guise left her baby in the palace and went to her apartments in Holyroodhouse, where Arran was now living. A skirmish between Arran and Cardinal Beaton left Mary fearful for the safety of her baby, and she returned to Linlithgow Palace.
- No sooner had she arrived back than Arran sent a large number of his own men to the palace, saying that the baby queen should have a larger retinue appropriate to her rank. She now feared even more for the safety of them both and endeavoured to move to Stirling, which was her castle.
- Arran forbade them to leave the palace.
- She was stuck there until 26th July 1543. Somehow, she managed to persuade Arran to let them go to Stirling Castle.
- There is no evidence to suggest she ever returned to Linlithgow Palace.

While you will know all these facts, they are not scripted but are incorporated into all that you know about Mary of Guise up to this point. Remember, it is worth knowing a bit more about her so that you are not caught up in answering questions beyond the period you are interpreting. Perhaps a visitor has asked about your return to France – this was in 1550, and what you have here is everything relevant up to 1543, which would also be reflected in your realms for this character. You can get round this by saying something like, "You must be mistaken. I have no plans to return to France". The visitor may say that you went in 1550. Your reply could be, "Well, as it is only 1543, I will look forward to what is to happen that year. Thank you for telling me".

I refer to this kind of delivery preparation as a "loose script", as it outlines why your character is in this particular place. However, you do not have to provide the information in any order or with any particular words. You may give all the key messages to some people; others may only want to know about where you gave birth to Mary. There will be those who want to know how the palace compares with those in France. Some may want to know a little about what your life is like as queen and being married to James V. With any of these scenarios, you will be glad for the work you did in developing your realms, because you will know who you are and can provide the desired information.

While I do not greatly favour scripts, inevitably, there are occasions when I break my own rules – and that is for costumed guided walks. When undertaking a walk, you have a set route, and you do need to be precise and accurate, because you are explaining some fact about the building or who lived there or what happened – and perhaps all three things. If you look back to Chapter 3 and the walk with Mary, Queen of Scots, you will recall the detail that has to be learnt; hence the need for a script in advance of delivery. It does not mean you have to stick slavishly to every word, but it provides what you need to know about each location at which you stop. Sometimes, within a guided walk as a character, you may wish to refer to another historical person by quoting something they have said. On such an occasion, there is no harm in writing this down into a notebook which you read to those on the tour with you. There are now many notebooks available that look as if they are leather or at least more in keeping with older times. If you cannot find one, then omit the reference, as a spiral journalist-type notebook does rather ruin the appearance of what you are trying to create. On the subject of notebooks, I have provided them on several occasions for interpreters portraying authors of the past, particularly when they have been conducting walking tours, as it means they can quote from their "own work" accurately.

Here, you see Laverne Edmonds as Catherine Sinclair on a walking tour around New Town Edinburgh, reading a few sentences. This image also highlights one of the great issues of walks led by costumed interpreters – modern intrusions about which you can do nothing. On the various occasions that I and others working with me have conducted such walks, it appears that the participants are happy to suspend reality and allow their guide to talk of their past, point out things associated with their life and equally help them across a road with traffic lights!

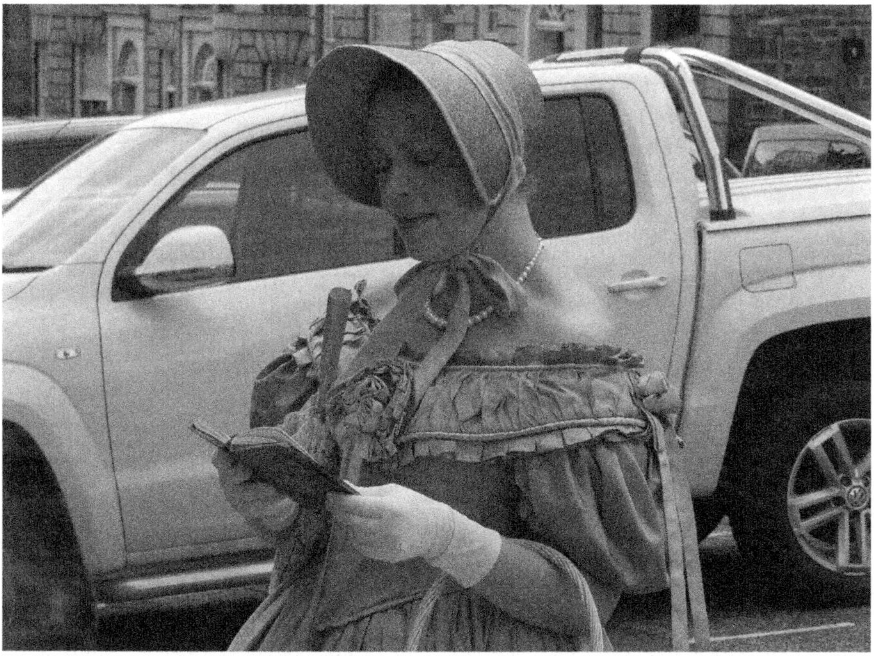

Figure 5.1 Catherine Sinclair reads a few words she has penned on a previous occasion.

Source: © Jackie Lee/Laverne Edmonds, costumed interpreter for Artemis Scotland

Accents and Dialects

Considering the portrayal of a person like Mary of Guise, who was from another country (France in her case), the problem arises as to whether to use an accent. This is quite tricky. You may feel that to do the character justice, an accent will convey more about who they are. Equally, you may feel that within your particular chosen accent, you should introduce a regional dialect. However, remember that costumed interpretation is not a play. You are there to interpret the historical significance of the character to the place or museum object. How and what you say must give further meaning to any information already on site or what is being consumed in audio guides. If you use an accent and possibly a regional dialect as well, this can also make what you are saying less intelligible to visitors, especially to those from other countries who are finding it hard enough to tune in to English, never mind English spoken with a French, German or other accent. This also relates to the use of regional dialects by costumed interpreters and the use of "local" words that are hard to explain. Some regional phrases associated with particular dialects in the UK have become more mainstream thanks to television and film, such as "Why aye, man" meaning "yes", used by those who are from Newcastle-upon-Tyne and the area referred to as Tyneside, or "quine" meaning "girl", used by those speaking

Doric in the North East of Scotland. Overall, however, using dialect adds a layer of complication to interaction, as the costumed interpreter may have to explain the meanings of unfamiliar terms as well as why they are being used.

Another issue with regards to using a different accent or dialect is that unless it is done extremely well, the voice and tone can sound like caricature and can be suggestive of prejudice and racism. It can also imply that you are impersonating the character rather than interpreting their significance. Impersonation is not the same as costumed interpretation, as it suggests comedy, even fraud, in the presentation of the character. Costumed interpretation is about helping people understand life in the past, not making fun of it. Humour can be used to convey a piece of information on an aspect of life which may seem ridiculous to us nowadays, but not to the detriment of the integrity of the presentation. What you are trying to do is get the visitors to connect on a personal level, to empathise with emotions generated by what you are telling them and to feel that these people of the past really had a life, whether at the court of James V or more humble locations like a mill or servants' quarters.

Engagement Skills

As you are now fully aware, costumed interpretation is more than dressing up and looking the part. You have to talk to people, because if you do not communicate with them, your even being there is pointless. It is the interpreter's job to keep the conversation flowing. Equally, you also need to know when to stop talking!

1 Catching the Visitor's Attention

You might be lucky and find that visitors are keen to speak to you and come straight over. There will, however, be occasions when you must coax them into engaging with you and initiate conversation, and when this is the case, it is best to use a greeting to which the visitor can respond. Here are some examples:

- How do you do?
- Hello, how are you today, good sir, madam?
- Have you come far?
- You must be travellers, as your clothes are so strange to me. Do tell me where you have come from.
- Can you help me?
- Can I help you?
- Your face is familiar, but can you tell me your name?
- Ah, I had heard there were some people of quality here today. Do tell me where you are from.
- I see you are carrying an umbrella. Are you expecting rain today?
- My name is John. What is yours?

These opening questions set people at ease. For those who are unsure about talking to someone in costume in case they are asked by that character to do something that they feel will make them look or feel silly, this form of introduction can help to engage them for whatever comes next.

It might well be that you sense that they are reasonably sure who you are interpreting and equally think they know lots about you, in which case, it is best to just ask them outright – "Do you know who I am or anything about me?" If the character is someone famous like Charles Dickens or Florence Nightingale, people always think they know these historic figures well. Usually, this is not the case at all, and you are immediately provided with an opportunity to get straight into your work.

However, sometimes visitors do not feel comfortable enough even to answer a question, and if they are from another country they may not have the language skills to do so. In such situations, a rhetorical question breaks the ice, for example, "I know what you are thinking: Why is Mrs Lydia Bole here in this house? Well, allow me to let you in on a little secret . . ." Another such question might be a kitchen servant saying, "Have you met the lady of the house? Well, let me tell you, her lemonade recipe is not all it seems – I'll tell you more . . ." Visitors do like to be included in a tale that appears to have some kind of secret attached to it as if they are in on some kind of conspiracy.

Of course, you have to hope that the front-of-house visitor services have prepared those who are arriving by highlighting to them that on this occasion there is a costumed interpreter on site who is portraying a particular period and character relevant to the site and that they will be doing this as if they are alive in this particular point of history. If there is a specific location where you are based, then that too should be pointed out. Otherwise, whatever approach you use will be useless. There is nothing more frustrating than having to spend most of the day explaining who you are and why you are there! However, I have worked out from my years in the profession that there is an escape route from this problem of endlessly telling people who you are by slipping in a little more information than just your name and why you are here. For example, you may say something like, "I can see you are wondering who I am. Do you think my clothes make me look important?" Or perhaps, "What kind of work do you think I might do in this sort of clothing? Do you think what I am wearing is suited to this job?"

And that way, you can move the visitors into a more engaging activity in which they try to work things out from the questions you are asking and what you are wearing or doing. Such questions are almost rhetorical – they could be answered with a simple shake or nod of the head. What you have provided for yourself is an opportunity to progress your interpretation of the site, object or exhibition and the key messages you wish to convey. There is usually a solution.

2 Using your voice

It may seem a rather obvious thing to say, but if you are talking to people you do need to be heard. Clear annunciation is as vital as your pronunciation of the words you use, particularly for visitors whose first language is not English. This echoes what I said earlier about the problems that can arise if you also decide to use accents and dialects. As I have said before, you are there to interpret an historical period and relay a set of messages the organisation you are working for want their visitors to know about. You also have to be confident as you speak. Falling over your words because you feel a bit nervous is really not an option.

When you are in conversation or addressing people, they need to hear what you are saying, and you may be working in a location where there is other noise around you, so making yourself audible is essential. However, this does not mean that you should shout. Those who have made the decision to spend their leisure time at a particular place want to enjoy themselves, feel comfortable and not be scared by a person in strange clothes yelling at them. This means projecting your voice, not shouting at people. Voice projection is often seen as a skill only used by actors, but public speakers, tour guides and costumed interpreters use it too. It is not difficult, and there are lots of free online tutorials that show you what to do, but basically voice projection means that you breathe using your diaphragm, which makes your voice stronger and therefore louder. The voice exercises that I suggest you do daily will also make it easier for you to use diaphragmatic breathing. If you shout loudly, it will damage your vocal cords over time, and shouting can sound quite aggressive and sometimes out of control. However, if you learn how to project your voice, you will manifest confidence as well as volume.

It is also important to add nuance to your voice, and by that I mean adding subtle distinctions in how you say things to get your point across. Much is written about voice tone with regards to how businesses address their customers in their correspondence, but when it comes to writing about physically using voice tone, it is much more difficult because the skill is a practical one.

I mentioned earlier in the chapter that inviting people in on a secret can be a great way to awaken interest. Closely related to this technique regarding tone is that of sharing a very personal story with your audience, and this can be used most effectively when the costumed interpreter is faced with a challenging point to get across. During the four-year commemoration of the First World War, I was engaged on numerous occasions to portray a Voluntary Aid Detachment (VAD) nurse, usually known as VADs. These women were unpaid volunteers, most of whom came from well-off middle-class family backgrounds. They had been sheltered from the world and being alone with a man in a room would have ruined their reputation. They received only the most basic of first aid training and were expected to pay for their own uniforms. They were catapulted into a world of horrific injury, given the lowliest work in less-than-appealing conditions and, in the main, surrounded by death. Somehow, these experiences had to be conveyed to visitors by me in a spotlessly clean, freshly pressed and starched VAD uniform. This is a common costume dilemma for interpreters who are giving life to characters who are unlikely to be clean for very long.

For this particular piece of interpretation, visitors were invited to join me at specific timeslots, my clean uniform explained away by the fact that I was about to go on duty but had heard there were some new recruits (sometimes men were employed as VADs, usually on the surgical side) and had been asked to give them some advice. Here, it was less of a sense of letting people in on a secret, more that of sharing something personal with them, giving an insight into my daily work which would soon be theirs too. While it was necessary to make sure everyone could hear, it was still possible to create the sense of purpose by using a soft tone of voice, speaking quite slowly and deliberately and occasionally pausing for a few moments. This enabled me to express my horror about what was happening around me while also suggesting that I and the others soon to join me had an important role: to help relieve the suffering of the wounded soldiers. Equally important was the body language I used. While folded arms are seen as intimidating, clasped hands are not, as they can so easily be unclasped and the hands used in a welcoming gesture. Thus, with the use of my voice and body, I was able to express what it was like to be a VAD.

3 Body Language

I have referred to using both my voice and my body in telling the story of the VAD. Body language, sometimes referred to as non-verbal communication, is as important as the sound of your voice and is made up of four elements, each linked to one another:

- Eye contact: It is important to make eye contact with visitors, as this will help them interact with you and make them feel confident to do so. It will also help them to remember what you are saying.

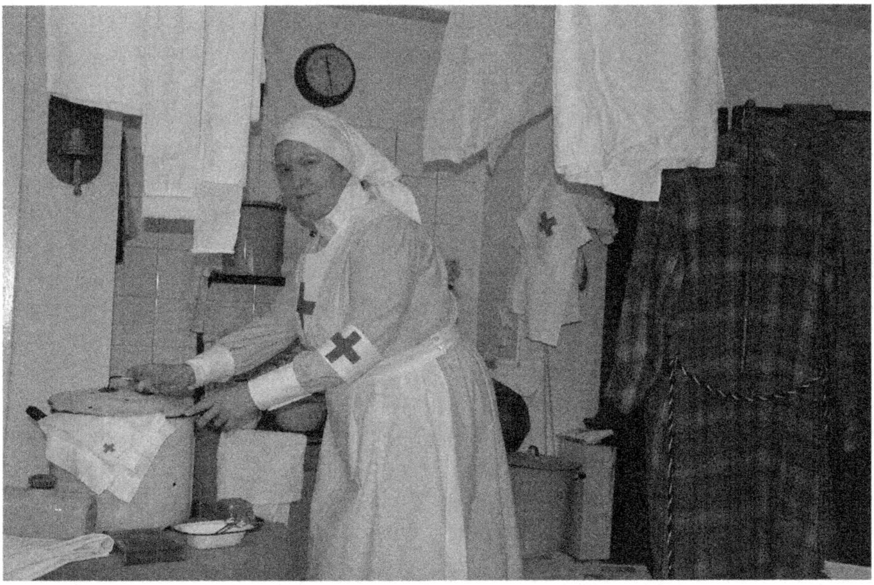

Figure 5.2 With a variety of props to hand, the VAD nurse has plenty of material with which to talk to her audience.

Source: © Keith Shaw Buckley/Jackie Lee of Artemis Scotland, costumed interpreter

- Facial expression: The whole gamut of human emotion can be communicated using your face which can be seen by all the visitors with whom you engage, regardless of whether they speak the same language you do.
- Gestures: These are particularly useful if you need to break eye contact and move everyone's gaze to another area or feature and is done by moving your head to the side and pointing to the object to which you refer. Other gestures include beckoning, pointing, nodding or shaking the head, raising eyebrows and waving. While gestures are non-verbal, they are often part of what you are saying.
- Posture: How you stand or sit is crucial to how you portray who you are and will depend upon the social position of the character. Within the concept of posture is that of personal space, and here you must decide on how close you are prepared to be to the visitors. Whether you are engaged in interpretive conversation or presentation, you must feel as comfortable as the visitors with the space between you.

Using these four elements of body language, which interlink, ensures that no matter what character you are interpreting, you can engage the visitor. It is also important to note that our body language and facial expressions are vital to those who are Deaf or hard of hearing, as is your clear pronunciation of words, as they may be lip-readers.

Here is an example of how you can use the various elements of body language. Let us imagine you have been asked to interpret a character who must portray a degree of gravitas as they converse with visitors. This does not mean you have to look intimidating. Use your body to signal that while you may have serious things to say, you are not in fact scary. Stand tall and use open gestures to attract people to you – beckon to them to join you or hold your arms out with your palms upwards, which again means you can use a beckoning action to bring them over, and of course, make eye contact. This non-verbal communication is not at all threatening and may well make the visitors inquisitive about what you have to say. Once they have approached you, your voice can take on a thoughtful tone before you embark on whatever the serious matter is you wish to discuss with them, and your facial expressions will reinforce the nature of the conversation you have with them.

This is of no use if the visitor is blind or has some form of visual impairment. The likelihood is they are with a sighted person. In such cases, your voice tone takes on greater significance, and any opportunity you can provide to touch surfaces or objects will be appreciated. You may even feel that it is appropriate for the person with sight difficulties to feel some part of your costume – the sleeve of your gown or doublet, your skirt or perhaps gloves – to enable them to understand what you are wearing for your character. This is very much a personal decision on your part.

Props

It is often better to be doing something as people enter the space in which you are located. If you are a monarch, that might be more difficult. Nevertheless, it is worth making the effort to look as if you are busy doing something – you might be seated and looking at some documents or perhaps looking round the room as if to say, "well, look at what I have here"; anything is better than just staring at the door through which the visitors are coming. Some simple activity like looking at what is in your bag can be enough to make people arriving in the space you occupy feel comfortable. You can then greet them with one of the suggestions I have already made, such as, "Hello, how are you today, good sir, madam?" "Greetings, dear friends. I imagine you are wondering what I have here in my bag".

Where at all possible, I like to have a small collection of reproduction objects to use as part of my interpretive conversation. There are many companies that make excellent replicas, and most museums and historic sites have some of these available, which they may provide for costumed interpreters to use. I have, however, built up a small collection of things over the years which are very portable and particularly useful if at a site where I am on the move most of the time. Bags of some description have been around since the time of the Ancient Egyptians, who had bags made from linen and papyrus. From the 11th century, there is evidence of drawstring bags used as part of a woman's accoutrements, and this form of bag remained in use right through to the 18th century, when they were referred to as reticules. By the early 19th century small beaded or tapestry bags with a chain handle and small clip clasp made their appearance in Europe, rather like modern evening bags, with leather handbags first emerging in Britain from the mid-19th century. This means there is always a way of carrying a few things around with you and staying in period. For a lady at court in the 16th century, I carry a couple of bone dice, a small key and a linen handkerchief, all of which can be talked about with visitors, who always want to know what is in my bag. The dice are for playing backgammon – having your own set of dice is a status symbol; the small key is for my jewel box; the linen handkerchief is for those moments when a lady might have to wipe a tear away or even blow her nose. The same items can be used right through to the 18th century, and as you make your way through the centuries, it will take you from high status to upper middle class. By the 18th century, there may be two keys, one for jewels and the other for a tea caddy.

Also, by this point, women may have had a few coins in their bag and most likely a fan and perhaps a pencil and dance card from a previous evening at the Assembly Rooms. The Victorian lady would not have carried dice, as these would be seen as quite immoral; more likely, she would have money in a purse, smelling salts, a notebook and pencil and the ubiquitous handkerchief, now cotton and not linen. From these very simple props, I can involve people of all ages and lead them into other topics of conversation and engagement with their surroundings.

It is also possible to carry a few things if you are a male character, as from quite early on, men wore small leather pouches attached to their belts. These could also contain dice as well as a few coins; whether they are gold or not depends on the status of the character and gives opportunity for further discussion. As a male character, it is quite likely you will have a sword hanging from a belt around your waist, and this too is a useful prop for engagement.

Whether you are male or female, the objects in your bag are small; therefore, allowing visitors to handle them may be difficult, especially if you have quite a crowd round you, as keeping track of the objects can be tricky. Nevertheless, providing what could almost be called a "show-and-tell" conversation enables engaging discussion and participation. Whatever you do decide to have in your bag, remember it must represent some aspect of the period you are interpreting and not include your mobile phone and car keys.

It may well be that you choose not to carry props with you, as it is inappropriate to your character, but remember, your costume is a prop, too, as I have pointed out in the previous chapter and whatever period in which your costume belongs, the various constituent parts will have particular names. For example, in medieval times, both women and men wore garments referred to by the following names and in the order given here – kirtle, cotehardie and surcoat. The difference was in their length – to the knee for men and the ankle for women. The cotehardie (tight fitting to show the contours of the body, often with ornamental sleeves) or surcoat (loose fitting, rather like a tabard and with no sleeves) could be worn on top of the kirtle (plain long-sleeved gown), or all three garments could be worn at the same time. If you were wealthy, it would be unusual to be seen only in the kirtle; if you were poor, this is all you would have to wear. Women wore a variety of headdresses throughout this time, the most common being the wimple (a headdress that covered the whole head, sides of the face and neck), while men were often bare-headed or wore a hood or large beret-like hat with a small brim. The intricacies of such costume detail fascinate visitors, who often sigh with relief that modern clothing is uncomplicated and comfortable to wear.

Touching the Past

While the props in your bag are likely to be replicas, there is nothing like letting visitors touch the past. Young and old alike enjoy the experience of handling something used by a person many years ago, and for blind and visually impaired visitors, this is a particularly rewarding activity. If the organisation are able to provide original objects that can be handled, then do take up this opportunity, as it really does enhance the senses and imagination. It may be that you can demonstrate what some of the objects were used for which is even better. Such demonstrations can be done as part of a timed interactive presentation with a group or people. This means you show them what to do or how to use the object, and they then copy you. I have done this on many occasions when providing "classes" on how to drink tea in the 18th century. As part of my "class" on manners of this time, I ask those attending to imagine they have a cup in their hand. After I show them the proper way to drink from the cup, they then use their imaginary cup and copy the action. When the "class" is over, there is an opportunity to come forward and handle several cups of the period. Another way of doing this is on a more one-to-one or small-group basis, in which you are stationed near the objects, and as you chat to people, you include the objects in the conversation and encourage visitors to hold them.

As an example of the latter, I remember at a Doors Open Day at 5 Charlotte Square, Edinburgh, original objects of the 18th century were laid out on a large table. On this occasion, my fellow interpreter and I were there as Mr and Mrs Grant, the first occupants of this address. We chatted to the visitors and picked up objects as we spoke, handing these things to the visitors. The response that such interaction receives is always interesting, as people are fascinated to think that they are holding some item used by another person from another time, and it makes a real connection with the past.

If the event spans the whole day, you will have to take a break at some point. It is therefore important to arrange that either the objects are removed in your absence or a member of staff is stationed near the objects so that they are not damaged through inappropriate handling. Touching and holding original objects should always be supervised.

While showing people how to use objects is a demonstration of an activity, so is showing them how to do something like curtsy, bow, dance a particular set of steps, sit in a refined manner for a portrait, use a fan as a means of communication or adopt an "attitude" – all rather eccentric forms of mannered behaviour of the past and of which there are many examples. Demonstrating any of these apparently strange manners to your audience first and often showing how ridiculous they appear to be puts everyone at their ease, and if they choose to have a go at doing them, that is wonderful. Equally if they choose not to, that is also perfectly acceptable. No one should ever be forced to take part if they do not want to. Cajole by all means, but if it is obvious that participation is not for them, let it be. Being made to do something which they feel is embarrassing or which they feel makes them look foolish will not enhance their experience. Some visitors are quite happy to watch and possibly ask questions, but not actually take part. You, the costumed interpreter, have still provided them with a meaningful encounter and piqued their curiosity – they did stay and watch, after all, and maybe even asked questions; for them, that has provided a satisfying outcome.

Where Can I Get an Ice Cream?

There is nothing more frustrating than meeting a costumed interpreter who refuses to come out of character to help a visitor. While you hope that the visitors have been prepared to meet you on site and know that you are presenting as if it was, for example, the 16th century, speaking to them in first-person, this does not mean that they believe that by some magical process, they have travelled back in time. Everyone knows it is pretend.

To the visitor, you are just another member of staff, albeit one dressed rather unusually, and if they want to know where the toilets are or how to find the gift shop or where they can buy an ice cream and you are the only person they can find, they will ask you. It is to be hoped that you are not in the middle of a conversation when they ask, but it can happen, and you have to deal with it and not just hope they will get fed up waiting and go away. If you are in mid-conversation, the best thing to do is to say something like, "Excuse me, ladies and gentlemen, boys and girls. I must just take a few moments to help this person" then take them to one side and explain or direct them if you can. There is a problem if you do not know where to find what they are looking for, so I advise that before going on site, you familiarise yourself with the location of the toilet, gift shop and café/restaurant, which can be done during your pre-visit to the site or museum. Sometimes, they may be looking for a particular object or feature at the museum or site, and you cannot be expected to know where everything is. The best thing to do is direct them to one of the front-of-house staff who will have the means to show them where to go. Once you have sent them on their way, you can return to the visitors with whom you are conversing. Some may have left if they are on a tight schedule, but it is my experience that most will stay and will appreciate that you have been courteous and helpful to the confused visitors.

Everyone knows it is a game and that they have not really time travelled, but you can get visitors who so enjoy being part of the make-believe of the moment that they play along with it. On one occasion at Edinburgh Castle, when I was portraying Mary, Queen of Scots at the time just after the birth of her son, a visitor asked if I had any thoughts of going to England. I answered that I would very much like to meet my cousin, Elizabeth, one day, which might mean I would have to travel there unless she came to see me in Scotland. This visitor then informed me that I should never think about going to England because they just knew that something bad would happen to me. I thanked the particular person for their concern, and we smiled at one another. For the rest of that day, the same visitor kept returning to check that I had no plans to visit south! Clearly, the visitor was enjoying this interaction, and it was causing no difficulty to others wishing to engage in conversation with me; this particular visitor did not monopolise me, aware that others wished to chat too.

To mark the 60th anniversary of the coronation of Elizabeth II, a young property manager at an historic house was keen to do something quirky that would attract a different audience. For this, she suggested something with a more vintage 1950s feel, and for this event, two popular Artemis Scotland characters were born: Muriel and Jasper, portrayed by me and my partner. The suggestion of the property manager was that they should provide advice on how to have the perfect 1950s home. We ran the two-day event as if we were interior designers of the period – Muriel specialised in homewares and décor, while Jasper dealt with fabric and wallpaper – there to give advice and tips on how to achieve the quintessential '50s look on a budget. We developed a handling collection for the event and prepared handout sheets on some design aspects and colouring-in sheets for younger visitors. Those that attended enjoyed seeing 1950s period-pieces in a very different context, and we were kept busy with conversation and "advice sessions" over the whole two days. People were encouraged to come in costume to make the event more immersive. One couple were so convinced that we were interior designers specialising in the mid-century vibe that they wanted to book a consultation with us to decorate their flat! We took them to one side and explained that while we did know a lot about mid-century décor, we were not experts in design and were here as costumed interpreters to explain the various developments that took place in this period that radically altered what people's homes looked like. They took it in good part and said they would use the sheets we had provided and the examples we had shown to do some research for their home.

It would seem, therefore, that while everyone knows that time travel is impossible, some people are more than happy to go along with the premise and throw themselves wholeheartedly into the game.

The Tricky Visitor

The majority of visitors are wonderful to be with, and at the end of the day you feel that you have had a very satisfying time at work. Unfortunately, however, a few visitors can be tricky. For some, it is almost as if they see you as a kind of joke because you are in a costume, and they think you are there for them to poke fun at. In other cases, they may monopolise your time with irrelevant questions and become quite aggressive if you do not answer them to their satisfaction. Some try to catch you out and muddle you on your facts, and there are also those who delight in trying to bring you out of character, though there can be times when this is something you must do. There is also the amateur historian who is always sure they know better. Mark Kydd, who is a very experienced performer and has worked with me for many years, provided this example from an event he was doing at Edinburgh Castle for Artemis Scotland, which sums up this particular predicament:

> I was playing Sir Walter Scott at Edinburgh Castle. My audience at one point consisted of a lady and her eleven-year-old son – she had made a point of bringing him along, to use me as a sort of living history lesson. This was absolutely fine until she started taking issue with some of the things I was saying (I had played Scott many times following meticulous research; I would never state anything as "fact" unless I was able to verify it from at least three different sources). I remained polite but stuck to my guns in terms of recounting Scott's history. The moral of the story is beware of amateur historians, who often seem utterly convinced they know better than you do.

Vera Rennie, who was a volunteer at the Tall Ship *Glenlee* when we ran our training course there in 2009, is now a staff member of the learning team. She reinforces this point with her comment:

> You may encounter during your delivery the resident expert. The resident expert's sole purpose is to not enjoy the experience but to show you how much they know.

These examples demonstrate how important it is to do your research, as Mark and Vera have done. Sometimes, all you can do is tell the story you know to be correct and agree to disagree at the end of it.

The visitor who wishes to have you all to themselves all the time is another difficult situation which you may face.

At an event at which I was Queen Victoria as a widow accompanied by Sir Henry Ponsonby, her private secretary, a particular group of visitors became quite fixated on being in "the queen's presence" and followed me around the room, pushing their way to the front, to the annoyance of others there. My fellow interpreter tried to move them away, suggesting that they come and look at the objects that were on a table and that he would explain to them their significance to the queen. They wanted to know if the queen was coming too, and he said she would be coming soon. They did go which enabled me to engage with other visitors, but they were clearly quite annoyed that they had been removed from being with the queen and were quite vociferous about it. Eventually, I went across and was told by them that "the man" had spoiled their visit, as he had taken them away from me. They then left. Interestingly, at the end of this event, during the debrief before we left the site, we were praised by the front-of-house staff for how we had dealt with the situation, as this particular group had been problematic elsewhere at the site. It was definitely an awkward situation, but as there were two of us it had been possible to move them, even though they were not pleased. However, something had to be done, as they were obviously ruining the "meeting the queen" aspect of the event for all the other visitors in the room.

It is not so easy if you are a single interpreter on site. I have also portrayed Queen Victoria on a number of occasions on my own. One particularly memorable episode involved a group of youths who were rather drunk. They wanted a photo with me but also wanted me to wear a pair of sunglasses and to put their arms around me. While you do not want to be rude to anyone, equally no one has the right to touch you or make a fool of you. There is definitely a line that visitors cannot cross. In such situations, it is acceptable to break character if you do not feel able to deal with it. Walk away and seek assistance. With regards to this incident, I remained in character. Being a monarch does give you some leeway to assume a rather imperious manner and put the offending visitors in their place for a few moments. It bought me time so that I could summon some help, because it is often the case that these things take place at some distance from official eyes. Whether this is on purpose or not is hard to tell. I suspect on this occasion, the youths were too drunk to work that out. However, the point is that you are not there to feel threatened. Such behaviour is not acceptable, and you should never feel you have to brazen it out and just get on with it. Others around you will also see what is happening, and you might find they come to help you, but equally, they are unlikely to take on those under the influence of alcohol. Visitors will understand if you have to step out of character to make yourself safe, because the likelihood is that they may well feel threatened too. It is rare, but it is as well to know that this kind of thing can happen, and you must protect yourself. Vera Rennie has clearly experienced this as a costumed guide on the Tall Ship *Glenlee* and reiterates that it does not happen very often:

> There might be a disruptive visitor who got out of bed on the wrong side that day or has been at the cooking sherry. This might be the time to seek assistance (in character if possible) from a hopefully nearby staff member if a subtle glare or moving the group to another location doesn't work. Thankfully, this is rare.

On a similar subject, you may find that suggestions with sexual overtones are made to you that are distinctly uncomfortable, and this can happen to both men and women. My most difficult and serious situation arose when I was portraying the character of Mrs Jean Armour Burns, wife of the Scottish poet Robert Burns. During her lifetime, she had nine children and had put up with the philandering lifestyle of her husband with his extra-marital affairs. For the series of events being run over a week, I found I had a particularly attentive male visitor who returned repeatedly through the week. He never asked any questions but kept coming to the room in which I was based and hanging around the room in a rather menacing way. I notified the on-site staff, and they kept an eye on him. On the last day, there he was again. Only one member of staff was on duty, as the other member had phoned in sick and there had been no opportunity to get a replacement. All was well until right at the end of the day, when a group was buying souvenirs and the staff member was occupied in the shop. The room I was in had no visitors until in he came and said to me, "Are you good in bed?" This is definitely the type of moment in which one must come out of character and summon help. The staff member came immediately, but the man had already left, probably shaken by my scream. I was, needless to say, somewhat upset. The staff member emptied the building and closed early. When I was changing, I noticed the same man still hanging around outside. The staff member left the building with me and walked me to my car. Fortunately, the man did not follow me, and I did not see him again. I should have followed it up with the museum management or reported it to the police, but I did not. I was busy with another commission and early in my career. Fortunately, it has not happened again, and if it did I would not neglect to report it.

Costumed interpreters are popular at late-night events in museums and sites. Such events are often centred around a special exhibition and aim to attract a younger crowd. Activities are run as part of the evening that link to the exhibition. Costumed interpreters are there to run activities relevant to the story of the exhibition as well as to promenade around the event, engaging in conversation and posing for photographs with those attending. There is usually a bar. As a result, encounters with people who have had too much to drink, like the youths mentioned earlier, do happen.

One of the male interpreters who works for Artemis Scotland had a particularly difficult time with a group of women at a late-night museum event. They followed him around and made suggestive comments, accompanied by attempts to touch him inappropriately. It was a busy evening, and the only solution was to come out of character, give a firm "no" and move away from the group, making it clear their behaviour was unacceptable. He also reported it to the front-of-house staff at the event and to the management later on.

The lesson from these examples is that you should never be put in a position of feeling uneasy or threatened. From these incidents, I have learnt that if I or anyone who works for me is on a site or in a gallery on their own as an interpreter, part of the risk assessment must include provision of a site member of staff being close by for their safety. This is harder if the costumed interpreter is roving around the site or gallery; however, it is possible to stay in areas within sight of front-of-house members of staff. Management must recognise the importance of your safety. Never allow yourself to be put in a vulnerable situation. Fortunately, these threatening situations do not occur very often. Those recounted here are the only ones encountered in my professional career of over twenty years. However, they did happen, and it is better to be prepared and know what to do should anything arise.

The "Crystal Ball" Technique

You will, on occasions, find yourself in a situation in which you have to deal with questions that reference modern values and ideas which are alien to the period that you are inhabiting. As you are delivering in first-person, this could potentially be quite difficult to deal with unless you are prepared.

While some aspects of human behaviour of the past are amusing, some are utterly barbaric. From a British historical perspective, this is demonstrated by values that considered "white foreigners" as suspicious and those who were ethnically diverse as dangerous and often, as in the case of slavery, humans who were somehow lesser beings than white people. This can be seen in art, literature, diary entries, correspondence, newspapers and official documentation of the past – sources that you will use in your research. The connections to slavery and the slave trade are everywhere. For example:

- Many Georgian-built country houses have direct links to plantation ownership and other colonial connections. For example, Alexander Callander made his money in India and bought Preston Hall outside Edinburgh, which he had re-built in the classical style.
- The by-products of the trade – the raw materials brought back from the Caribbean, sugar, tobacco and cotton – provided work in the new factories springing up around Britain, thus connecting not only the factory owners but also the workers.
- The growing banking sector provided the funding for both the slave trade and the new factories and paid dividends to investors. It is very likely that the investors knew their dividends were gained from slavery connections.

Colonial influence was not limited to the Caribbean, as the empire expanded across the world, covering 10 million square miles of land by the beginning of the 20th century. As with slavery, home-based industries provided the goods to send out to colonists, and the raw materials and resources of the various countries of the Empire secured Britain's prosperity. This was of course to the detriment of the colonised countries. Involvement in the Empire was rife.

The National Trust in England has nearly one hundred properties which have links to slavery and colonialism; in Scotland's National Trust, nearly a fifth of its buildings and monuments have the connection. Houses owned by other organisations across the UK have links to slavery as well as the wider empire. It is now recognised that the stories of these places need to be told on a much wider basis, and much is being put in place to do this in an empathetic and respectful way that works with an overall policy to decolonise history.

The problem you face as a costumed interpreter is putting this darker side of history into perspective as you operate within these heritage spaces that originate from colonial connections. It is all very well to be on site to portray an amusing aspect of 18th-century etiquette, but you may find yourself in the position of answering a question that references the house's connections with slavery or some other aspect of colonialism. On one memorable occasion, I was in this position.

In the middle of the session on the language of the fans, with the ladies in my group waving their fans at the gentlemen, a visitor made it very clear that he and his family were uncomfortable about this sort of activity taking place because it ignored the house's connections with historic slavery, and I was just reinforcing the trivia of country-house life. Surely, I knew that this particular house and all its fancy furniture and décor were here because of the proceeds of slave labour. This was the story I should be telling, not some silly thing about waving fans about. The dilemma here was that the organisation had set up bookable fan sessions in a cordoned-off area of a public room, and therefore, visitors passing through the room could see what was going on. The layout of the house meant that the visitors had yet to see a new exhibition at the end of the tour that featured the neglected history of where the money had come from to build the house and the owner's connections to the Caribbean. Information about this exhibition was in the new guidebook, which these visitors did not have, and while there was mention of it on a poster, it could be easily missed on arrival. In this case, I used my imaginary "crystal ball", a technique I have developed to enable me to look into the modern world and see the future or to enable me to come out of character to explain a difficult issue. This is possible because as I have already made clear, everyone knows this is a game and that I am not a time-traveller. Equally, I do have to deal with the fact that I have spent all my time while in their company speaking as if I am from the 18th century and dressed accordingly. The crystal ball, therefore, is very useful. In this case, I said something along these lines:

> Ladies and gentlemen, boys and girls, looking into my imaginary crystal ball [I pretend to pick up a ball and look into it], I can see that in your time, many people want to know more about where the money came from to build this house and have discovered it was earned in a very cruel way. The owner ran several plantations in the Caribbean and was known to be a horrible master to the many slaves he owned. In later years, his family benefitted from the compensation paid to slave owners when slavery was abolished in 1833. If you proceed to the rooms at the very end of the tour, you will find an exhibition that explains more about the owner's connection to what is called the Triangular Trade. I understand why you find my particular session on manners and etiquette of the period frivolous given the way in which the owner made so much money. It is, however, very unlikely that the owner's wife, who he married on his return from the Caribbean, or his daughters would have had

> much idea where he had made his money, that not being their concern. Also, the education of middle-class women in the late 18th and early 19th centuries was not a priority and would have concentrated on making them marriageable rather than knowing much about the world. The behaviour that I am showing to you all gathered here today would have been very recognisable to them. You will be pleased to hear that there is an exhibition that you will come to shortly that will provide more detail on the owner's connection to the slave trade. Once I have finished my session with the audience, I will be happy to answer your questions, though I am sure that the house stewards will also be able to help you. If those of you seated here have time to stay to the end of the session, then I will put my crystal ball to one side and finish the lesson.

The visitor who had asked the question left with his family, and I finished the session. At the end of the day, the house manager told me that the family who had wanted to know about the slavery connections had said that they wished to pass on their thanks to me for treating their question with respect. For this event, I was fortunate that there was an exhibition in place explaining the family connection to the slave trade. This will not always be the case. If this had been the situation in which I had found myself, I would have provided the same information about the family and then added:

> There is nothing here that explains that connection. I suggest that you speak with one of the members of staff on site today, who should be able to help. I will also be happy to chat with you when I have finished this session with the assembled group in a few minutes.

There is no doubt it is unsettling to have such an interjection in the middle of a session, but it must be dealt with respectfully, as a valid point is being made.

I have used the "crystal ball" technique on many occasions as my means of explaining things that the character would not have known at the time. In the case of Queen Margaret of Scotland, many people ask, "Why are you called St Margaret?" She died in 1093 and was made a saint in 1250, so the "crystal ball" technique is a simple way of providing an answer to this predicament.

It is not only historical facts that require the use of this technique. Many costumes, particularly those of early periods, use fur as a trimming or integral feature of the garment. In Chapter 4, I pointed out that there is no need nowadays to use real fur or leather, as the faux versions look very realistic. However, because they look so realistic, you may get some visitors saying how cruel it is to kill an animal to use on clothes and question why you are doing so. As I suggested in Chapter 4, it is a good idea to have a sample of the faux fur or leather from your costume available for visitors to see and handle. My explanation for wearing fur on my costume for the 11th-century Queen Margaret is as follows:

> Ladies and gentlemen, boys and girls, to answer your question about why I am wearing fur, I must have a look in my imaginary crystal ball. I can see

> that in the time period that you inhabit, it is regarded as cruel to kill animals and use their skin or fur for clothing. In the time to which I belong, this is not the case. Being the Queen, it is a sign of my great importance and wealth. In my time, there are regulations which dictate who can wear certain fabrics and which fur is associated with a person's position in society. These are called sumptuary laws. Only members of the royal family are entitled to wear ermine, which is what I am wearing around my neck and on my sleeves. Now, while it seems very cruel, the fur has a very practical use as well as being decorative and showing one and all that I am a member of the royal family. The fur keeps out the cold and means I am warm. It is also used to line the inside of my clothes and hats for the very cold days of winter. Remember, the only heating I have is a fire. I can see from my crystal ball that in your time, you have lots of fabrics and materials you can wear that keep you cosy in the cold, and this means that you don't have to wear fur, and you have lots of ways to heat your homes. You also seem to have many options for keeping dry in the rain. I have no alternative but to wear cloaks made from animal skins, as this is the only waterproof covering available to me. I hope this explanation helps you to understand the reason I am wearing fur today. I can also reassure you that thanks to the technology of your world, no animals have been harmed, as you can see from the samples of fur on the table.

This technique I have developed has proved very useful throughout my career in costumed interpretation. I recommend that you use it when you have to step out of character for a few moments to provide an explanation that will otherwise tie you in knots if you attempt to justify your historic stance while those around you question your morals.

Storytelling

By virtue of being in costume and being a character, you are already telling a story visually. Your invitation to the visitors to join you in your world – "Ah, I had heard there were some people of quality here today. Do tell me where you are from" or "My name is John. What is yours?" – is also the beginning of your story because you are asking them to be part of your world and discover something about it. A story is a great way to get across key messages and is at the core of all heritage interpretation, as it helps people make connections between lives of the past and the present day. In most cases you will be telling stories that are true, but sometimes there may be reference to a myth or legend that has developed about a place, object, the person that you are for the day or other people associated with your character.

An example of this from my work is the story of Flora MacDonald. As part of a series of events in 2016 marking 270 years since the Jacobite Rebellion, I was engaged to tell the real story of Flora MacDonald's involvement with the famous escape "over the sea to Skye". The opportunity to set the record straight on her relationship with Bonnie Prince Charlie enabled me to dispel the myth that the two of them were romantically involved and, equally, the long-held belief that she was a wee Highland lass overcome with the prince's handsomeness. Research most certainly revealed that this was not the case at all and that she was a well-educated, intelligent woman who understood the risks, was involved in the planning of the escape to Skye and was incredibly wily with her captors, thus enabling the prince to further evade his own capture and also protect herself from severe punishment. Telling this story as Flora brought greater meaning to the unravelling of the myth and also enabled visitors to question the character. A list of facts would not have done the job. The power of the story enthralled the visitors, and the opportunity to question Flora clearly helped them see how important her role was and far removed from that of an impressionable young woman bowled over by the apparent charms of the prince. The story also tied in with other interpretation on site about the romanticisation of Scottish history by writers like Sir Walter Scott and later by the Victorians. Throughout the day, I had people returning to me and telling me they had just discovered how stories had been altered to make them more romantic and thanked me for telling my story. Job done, as is often said! The example of the Flora MacDonald story demonstrates that it is possible to change long-held views through storytelling.

Stories do not have to be about people; they can also be about objects. However, as these objects have been designed and made by people, the human element is always there which is why stories hold so much fascination. The story of why a spiral staircase in a castle twists one way rather than another, why lavender is grown in a garden, how the table is laid for a dinner party – all of these are interesting and reveal aspects of past lives and how people have lived. Much is made of connection within heritage interpretation, whether that be to an old building, the landscape, an object or a person associated with these things, and the tool to make this connection is the story. The connection you are trying to make is one of emotion, to get the feeling of how lives were once lived.

As a costumed interpreter, it is important to remember that the story cannot be too long – three minutes is about enough, but you might manage five minutes if you have your audience in the palm of your hand, so to speak. The important thing is to read their reactions, and if they start to get fidgety or are looking at their watches, it is clear it is time to reach your conclusion. This means you must have several versions of the story in your head. Sometimes it is just best to ask, "Do you have five minutes to spare while I tell you about what it's like to work in this mill here in Cromford that Mr Arkwright keeps calling a factory?" Or "I am sorry you have to be on your way soon, but have you about three minutes to spare? Good. I can tell you a bit about what it is like here".

For those new to the interpretative story through costumed interpretation, its key components are:

- Personalise the story – not many people would remember the story of the Gunpowder Plot if it was just presented as a list of facts and dates. Adding in a person, in this case Guy Fawkes, makes it easier to relate to the narrative. Because you are in costume as a character, you have this element covered already.

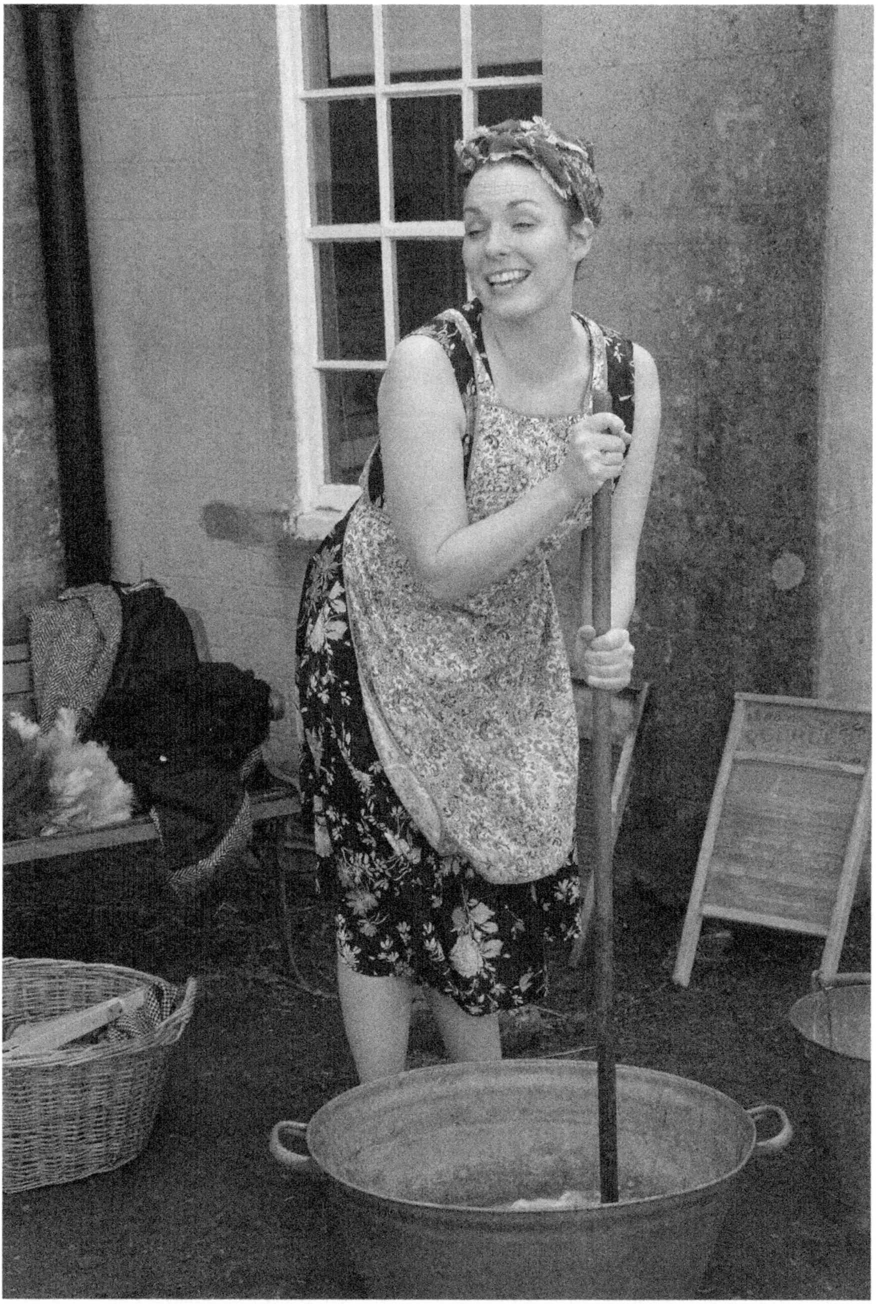

Figure 5.3 Sadie tells the assembled visitors what it was like to do her washing while demonstrating the actions.

Source: © Keith Shaw Buckley/Eilidh McCormick, costumed interpreter for Artemis Scotland

- Use descriptive words that paint a picture and enhance the setting in which you are telling the story, be it a grand house, a thatched cottage or the middle of a battlefield. Similes and metaphors are useful as well. The following examples demonstrate the difference these can make:
    - The grand house has such gleaming windows.
    - The roof of the thatched cottage is as thick as a loaf of bread.
    - The wind blew across the battlefield like a bellowing bull.

For those listening to the story, you have immediately created an image for them.

- Incorporate an action for them to do in the story, thus enabling them to participate even in a small way. You could ask them to feel the stone used to construct the building, the grass beneath their feet once trodden on by an advancing army or the walls of the cottage that surround them or to handle props or period objects related to the story you are telling.
- Make sure it has a beginning, a middle and an end.
- Practise the story to make sure you have the timing just right for your three- and five-minute versions.
- Do not be afraid to improvise a little once you have done it a few times. As long as you know exactly what you have to get across, you do not have to use exactly the same words every time unless you are tied to a script. You will soon get the feeling of whether the visitors are enjoying it or not.

Using these elements, you can be confident of telling stories that will inform as well as engage and enlighten and even entertain. The interpretive story is a useful tool for the costumed interpreter to convey the key messages in a memorable way, as it is a proven fact that humans like to listen to stories, no matter what age they are. This technique is also particularly useful when you have a large gathering of people around you and it is inevitably less easy by virtue of numbers to engage in conversation.

Make Them Laugh – or at Least Smile!

There is no harm in using a bit of humour. I find it works best when you draw analogies with something well known from the modern world which chimes well with what is happening in the time period you are interpreting. This also reinforces the idea that there are some things which never change and it is possible to compare and contrast past and present. As an illustration, when leading a group on a walk in the New Town of Edinburgh as Mrs Grant, the 18th-century occupant of No 5 Charlotte Square, in character, I refer to the state of the roads and the general complaint that walking round the New Town is like living on a building site – really, the town council must do something about the state of the roads – dresses are being ruined, and this is just not acceptable. This raises a smile from the visitors, as there seems always to be a part of the Edinburgh road system that is being dug up, making travel difficult.

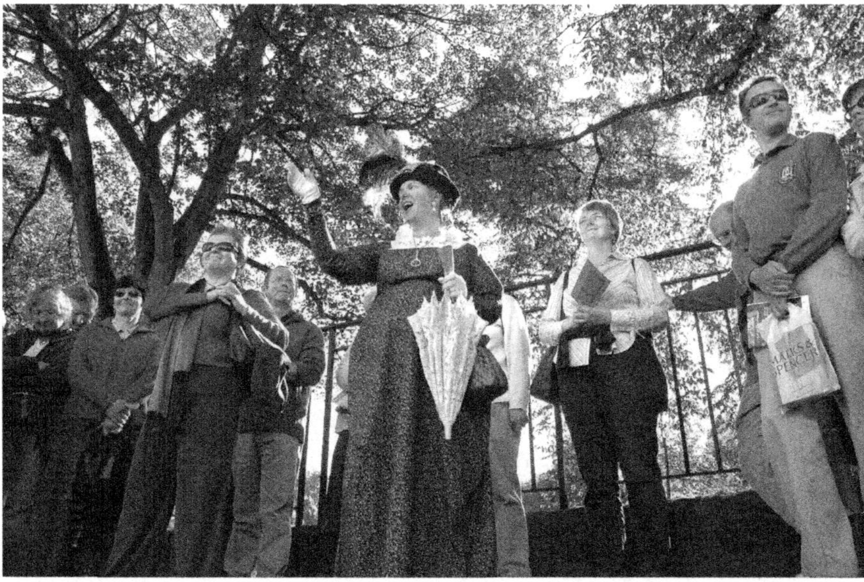

Figure 5.4 Mrs Grant on her walk around the New Town of Edinburgh.
Source: © Witch Creations/Jackie Lee of Artemis Scotland, costumed interpreter

My advice is to keep an eye on what is happening in the locality where you will be working several days before you get there. There may well be something going on that you can pull into your interpretation that enables visitors to see the parallel between then and now, as with the roadworks in Edinburgh. You may also spot something on site that you can link to – perhaps on a windy day, you notice someone's hat blowing away. You could then point out that is why you have ties on your hat and a few hat pins, as this prevents such calamities happening.

There are of course things within the courtesy and etiquette books of the past which are really funny that your character can use to effect. Looking back to the medieval period, women's earlobes were regarded as attractive. In character as Queen Margaret of Scotland, who had eight children, I explain why women wear wimples: "It's to cover our earlobes, because as you know earlobes are *so* attractive to men, and having had eight children, I have proved beyond doubt that my earlobes are *extremely* attractive! And I certainly don't want to enflame any passions here today. King Malcolm would not be pleased!" This raises a smile and often a little laughter too, as it seem so ridiculous by modern standards.

For any high-status characters of the 16th century, you can make something of why it so important to be right-handed. It was the belief then that your guardian angel sat on your right shoulder, while the devil sat on your left. Therefore, to be left-handed suggested you were untrustworthy and under the power of evil spirits. As your 16th-century character, you can say something like, "As we all know . . ."

and explain this belief and finish it up with "Now, hands up – who is left-handed?" In my experience, this usually results in a few chuckles and certainly some smiles amongst the gathered visitors.

You will find many other examples within your research you can use to provide humour in your engagement. A smile or some laughter is also invaluable in putting visitors at their ease and enabling them to enjoy their interaction with you.

Working at a Distance with Another Costumed Interpreter

There have been several occasions in my working life when I have been commissioned to provide two characters for an event at which we have had to work at different locations within the same building yet know of the other's existence and encourage visits to each other. For such events, you need to work out a scenario that realistically links you and in which the visitors can believe. A good example of this is an occasion where I portrayed a housekeeper while my fellow interpreter was the butler. It was not uncommon for a butler nearing retirement to marry a similarly aged housekeeper and set up a guesthouse together. This became the basis for our on-site link.

The scenario for the day was that the owners of the house were arriving "anytime soon" and that I, the housekeeper, and the butler were preparing for their arrival; some staff had not arrived, and I was hoping to recruit a lady's maid and a valet, while the butler was looking for some help in serving afternoon tea and tidying up in the kitchen. Children and adults alike were to be involved in afternoon tea preparations with the butler, while upstairs how to unpack a suitcase and fold clothes for drawers was run by the housekeeper. The layout of the house meant that on arrival, visitors could choose to go straight upstairs or into the main downstairs area. Therefore, I was upstairs all day, trying to recruit new staff by showing them what to do and getting them to have a go at it. The butler busied himself downstairs in the butler's pantry, polishing cutlery and setting trays for afternoon tea. To enable interaction between us, though in different areas of the house, the butler asked those he met if they had met the housekeeper. If they said no, he would reply, "Well, I'll let you into a secret: I'm pretty certain that she's interested in me. I was thinking that we could get married and leave working in the big house now that we are getting a bit older. With our skills, we could run our own guesthouse by the sea". If the answer was yes, they had met her, the chances were they had been told the secret was "a lot of nonsense in that man's head", which enabled the butler to react either crestfallen or reply, "She's just joking; I know I'm in with a chance". This banter between us led to some people, often children, returning back upstairs to relay a message along the lines of "We thought we'd let you know that he really thinks you like him and you're just pretending not to like him. Are you pretending?" If they had not met the butler at all because they had come straight upstairs, I would say, "I'll let you into a secret: if that butler thinks I am running a guesthouse with him, he is very much mistaken. Don't go believing what he has to say about me". This approach kept both children and adults interested in the characters as well as the activities.

Make your connection with the other interpreter realistic enough and it will add to the enjoyment and the experience that the visitors, young and old alike, have while there.

One Last Tip

From Vera Rennie again, of the Tall Ship *Glenlee*, a sound piece of advice:

> Don't flop dramatically on the nearest chaise longue when the session has finished; always be out of sight of the visitors before you return to the present day. Leave picking up a bag of chips on the way home till you are well away from the site; you may be recognised by your guests from earlier in the day.

And a last reminder from me: if you are taking your break in an area different from where you have left your belongings, make sure you have moved any food you have brought with you before you get into costume. You do not want to be seen carrying a supermarket bag across a courtyard while dressed as Henry VIII or anyone else for that matter!

6 Working with Different Audiences

It is very likely in your career as a costumed interpreter that you will be engaged by organisations to work with specific groups. Sometimes, these sessions take place in areas away from the public gaze, as is often the case with school classes and vulnerable groups. While the techniques of engagement outlined in the previous chapter are applicable in how you work, you will find that there may be other expectations of you, and it is worth taking this opportunity to examine these here.

School Groups

Educational programmes which use costumed interpreters provide an interesting way of engaging pupils with their heritage and helps them to understand some difficult historical concepts through participation. The opportunity to be in a different environment outside the school and with someone other than their teacher leading them through a learning experience is very different from being in a classroom. It helps children to develop important social skills such as interaction with people who are not familiar to them, in this case the interpreter(s), museum/site staff and those encountered on their journey, as well as direct learning skills such as curiosity, collaboration with classmates and problem-solving. Sometimes the organisation can provide the children with costumes to wear, which enables them to become fully immersed within the historical world.

An understanding of the school curriculum is useful but not essential, as museum and heritage education staff have the necessary experience to guide you on what they require you to deliver. There will be key messages to convey as there are with any session – that is, the things that the museum or site have which contribute to the period of history being studied. While this is important and is what is bringing the class out of the school, the focus will be on the learning outcomes the session/workshop provides, as these will be what sells the experience to the teachers, who will know what they want their class to achieve from the visit. It is rare for there to be no financial cost involved for the visiting school, whether as payment for the session and/or transport costs, plus the administration involved to take a class out of school, so every teacher is keen to see that the booked session is worth the money. As a result, it is common practice to ask you to contribute to the organisation's lesson plan or, in some cases, to construct your own. The plan

DOI: 10.4324/9781003260226-7

is then available to schools so that they can see that the learning provided will be all that they require of it. Much of the information for the plan will be provided by the organisation's education officer; your contribution will be to outline how you will work with the pupils during the session and what is involved that will tick all the right boxes for the teacher. In discussion with the education officer, you will already know:

- the historical period
- the kind of character you will be, though not necessarily the name
- the topic to be covered
- whether there are objects that you are to incorporate into the session
- where the session is taking place – it might be several places
- the length of the session
- the time the school will arrive
- the age of the pupils with whom you will be working
- any special educational needs that are to be addressed
- the key messages
- the skills that the pupils will learn from the activity
- the scenario
- the learning outcomes

Guided by the above information and liaising with the education officer, you can create the lesson plan that you will deliver to the pupils.

With regards to character creation for school sessions, it is quite often the case that you will be presented with all the information that you need on the character by the education officer. If you will be playing a generic character, the teacher will be less interested in information that you have on who you are, as you will be seen merely as the conduit to achieving the learning outcomes. If you are portraying a real person from history, the lesson plan will outline why your character is important as the means to the end, once again the focus being what the children have learnt on site that they could not learn in the classroom. There are occasions when you may be approached to provide the same character you have developed for an event or public programme if the education officer has seen you as this historic character and recognises the potential for school workshops.

One of the first school workshops I developed was for the National Museum of Rural Life that features a teacher in 1939 and her new class of recently evacuated children. This session has been used regularly for many years because of the excellent feedback it has received from schools, and I feel it is a good example of how it is possible to use a costumed interpreter to deliver a session tailored to the needs of the curriculum as well as enhancing the overall experience offered to the class by inviting them to time travel. Children enjoy using their imaginations, and this supposed time travel aids their creative development and collaboration skills. The whole class are in this together, so the experience is shared, and it is recognised that shared experiences help children's personal, social and emotional development.

The original premise for the workshop was to give children the experience of coming to an historic farm setting of the kind many evacuees would have arrived at in 1939. To make the session workable, a reason had to be found to move the children from the museum building at which they arrived up to the farm without "breaking the spell" of being back in time. By chance, I knew of a project that had recorded women's experiences of the Second World War, and in amongst them was a teacher who had been moved from Glasgow to the Isle of Bute to cope with the influx of children from the urban areas. The schools on the island were overflowing, and to do their bit to help the children continue their lessons, local people offered all sorts of buildings that could be used as classrooms, including farm buildings. I was able to secure permission to use this story as the basis for the workshop. The woman who was the teacher asked to meet me and told me a bit more detail about her time on Bute, adding I could use it in my workshop if I could find a way. "It'll make it more real, how it really was. And you can use my name for your character, but remember, you'll have to be strict. That's how it was then, strict but fair". She said that the children from Glasgow were overwhelmed by being away from home. Most had never been away from their parents other than to stay with their grandparents. Some had difficulty distinguishing between hens and ducks or horses and cows. Her point was that there were few books in working-class houses and little chance of going to the cinema, where they might see such things. "There was no internet then, remember", she added. To give them exercise, she used to take the children on walks around the island. "They hated walking, because we were out in all weathers". To get over this obstacle, she made them sing in unison as they walked, which took their mind off the walk and also made them move faster. They sang songs like "One Man Went to Mow" and "Ten Green Bottles".

In consultation with the education officer, the following *outcomes* for the session emerged. The workshop would enable the pupils to:

1 learn how life changed for children who were evacuated to the country and compare and contrast the life of the evacuees in 1939 to their lives now
2 understand how different life was for these children with the outbreak of war as well as recognising the constant factor in their lives at that point was school
3 appreciate how different school was in 1939, with the need for children to learn how to put on a gas mask and what to do if ever caught in an air raid, as well as do their lessons
4 discover what it would be like, as a child, to live on a farm away from your family during the Second World War
5 investigate the bothy where the prisoners of war slept while working on the farm and understand how the Second World War affected the lives of both sides fighting in the war
6 think about the significance of why they were given labels to wear.

From these outcomes, the teacher would know that her class would be taking part in a stimulating learning session which also had a sensory element embedded within it. The walk to the farm along the path would be an unusual occurrence for children used to being transported everywhere by car, as would the smells and sounds of the countryside. Combining these elements with the historical components meant the workshop would provide a rounded experience. It was also decided that to ensure the final outcome could be achieved, every pupil would be provided with a label on which to write their name. It was suggested that they make up an address rather than use their own in case they lost the label. The class would also be asked to make gas mask boxes, and a template for this would be provided with the booking confirmation.

Knowing these outcomes and using the additional information I had learned from Miss Moffat, I was able to construct a scenario and outline how I would make this an authentic learning experience for the classes. Here is my lesson plan.

Table 6.1 Sample lesson plan

Evacuees

Costumed character: Miss Moffat, the new teacher for the pupils evacuated from Glasgow to the country.

Time: 10.30–11.45; 12.30–13.45
Level: Upper Primary
There will be flexibility on start times given that some schools may have transport issues and arrive later than expected.

Location: Learning Centre and at the Farm of the National Museum of Rural Life

Historical Date: It is Monday 4th September 1939, the day after war has been declared. The pupils are at their new home in the country and about to go to school.

Scenario: The majority of pupils were evacuated on the 1st and 2nd of September, so the children are still nervous about their new life. The only familiar aspect to them is the school day, and even that will be different. When they arrive at their new school (the museum), there is not enough room for all the children at what is a small rural school (imagination). However, the local people want to help the children and offer various buildings as classrooms – the most common being farm buildings. Mr Reid of Wester Kittochside (the farm the children will walk to) has offered this class a building for their lessons.

Objects/props: handheld school bell; gas mask, ARP rattle, whistle

Key Messages:

- While it might seem like an exciting adventure at first, most evacuees had no idea when they would next see their parents.
- Teaching methods were very different and gave little scope for children to ask questions or contribute to lessons.
- Gas mask and air raid drill had to be learnt quickly.
- Walking to places was more common both in town and country then, and the walk to the farm from the museum reinforces some of the differences in life compared to nowadays.
- Many of the children evacuated had never been to the country before and certainly had not been on a farm. This may be the case for the 21st-century pupils also.
- Why they wore labels when they were travelling.

(*Continued*)

Table 6.1 (Continued)

The Workshop

Pupils will be met by the interpreter out of character at the museum entrance – a short introduction on what is about to happen will be given along with a few basic questions to help set the scene. Sample questions include:

- Why were children moved from towns and cities to the country?
- What is the name given to children who were taken from their homes?
- How do you think you would feel if this happened to you?
- When was war declared?
- What do you think school might be like back then?

The interpreter tells the children that they are about to step back in time and become evacuees. If they have brought gas mask boxes, she will explain that she wants them to imagine there are gas masks inside which she will later ask them to pretend to put on. If there are no boxes, she will ask them to imagine the boxes as well as the gas masks. She also informs the children that her name is Miss Moffat, and she is their teacher for this immersive workshop.

She informs them that she will ring the school bell she is carrying, and that will be the signal that it is Monday 4th September 1939. This is their first day in their new school and the first whole day of the war, and they are to imagine themselves as evacuee children as they take part in the activities.

The bell rings, signalling "stepping back in time".

Miss Moffat greets the class. She then splits the class into two groups – girls and boys – as would have been the way of doing things at that time and lines them up before taking them to the museum's learning centre, which will be set up as a classroom, with benches and a blackboard on an easel.

Miss Moffat organises where they will sit on the benches and asks them to remain standing until she gives them permission to sit down. From the beginning, pupils will notice the strict behaviour of the teacher, which allows little freedom of expression and questioning as would happen in a current school setting. This provides the pupils with an instant contrast to their learning lives today.

The session will proceed:

- Still standing, Miss Moffat will make a short prayer, asking for their safe return to their families once the war is over.
- Seat them and set out the class rules:
  - o no shouting out
  - o no chatting – just concentrating on what they have to learn, because it will save their lives (gas mask drill and air raid practise)
  - o hands up if they want to ask a question.
- Mood of class changes
- Demonstration to the class of how to put on a gas mask; prepare them for gas mask and air raid drills – go over this several times with them to reinforce the stages. They then copy your actions.
- Schoolwork – whole class chant tables and spell words set out on the old-fashioned blackboard on an easel. While this way of working is unfamiliar to children today, the short session of it within the workshop highlights how different school learning was then with little or no opportunity to question.

- Intersperse lesson with "surprise" gas attack alerts, during which the children have to pretend to put on their gas masks and are praised for doing it well.
- The class will be prepared for the short walk to the farm – there will be two roads to cross on the way up and they must wait until Miss Moffat has said it is safe to cross.
- Coats on and line up at the door, ready to leave the building.

Outside on the way to the farm

- On her way up, Miss Moffat will stop and point out various aspects about the farm.
- She will also emphasise the importance of shutting gates in the country – something town children evacuated to the country often did not understand. Class will be asked to identify animals in the fields.
- Whole class sing "Ten Green Bottles" as they walk along – walking pace quickens as they do so.
- Once they have arrived at the farm, the pupils will be taken into the building to the side of the milking parlour. They will be told that this is their new classroom. There will then be another gas mask drill and a check on what to do in an air raid.
- Miss Moffat will then come out of character, using the school bell as a "marking device", and explain that the real Miss Moffat had done a lot of the things they have done today with the evacuees she taught on the Island of Bute – what they have taken part in so far was the real experience of children in 1939.
- The interpreter then takes questions from the class.

Exploring the farm

- Now out of character, the interpreter explains that the class are to explore the farm and its buildings and that they are to divide into three groups. (In the information sent to the school after booking, it will have been stated that the class should be divided into three groups for part of the activity and that having this done in advance saves time during the visit.)
- The class will now split into their three groups, led by the adults in attendance as well as the teaching staff. Question sheets will be provided to help the accompanying adults to highlight features in the three areas and pose questions.
- Each group will have an opportunity to explore:
  - o The farmhouse kitchen
  - o The bothy, home to the prisoner of war
  - o The farmyard buildings

The interpreter will be present throughout to help the groups and will draw together the various elements of the whole workshop before taking her leave of them. The final question will be about why they are wearing labels.

Session ends.

The class will return to the museum accompanied by their teacher.

A school workshop needs a tight frame on which to hang the whole session. The lesson plan ensures that everything that the classroom teacher requires to be covered is in place and it is worth the effort of getting the class out of the school. For the children, this is likely to be an experience that cements learning that the teacher has been working on with them in the classroom as well as providing new stimuli to their curiosity. In addition, it is recognised that learning outside the classroom helps children grow in confidence as they learn to navigate the world in a safe environment. The lesson plan provided here demonstrates the importance of the children participating in the session as much as possible. The learning experience must be different from what they would normally encounter in the classroom; hence the variety of locations, each with its own set of tasks assigned to them:

- The classroom created in the learning centre provides an insight into formal education during the war.
- The walk to the farm gives the children the sense of being in the countryside and discovering a new world, as the evacuees did in 1939. The walk also echoes that of the real Miss Moffat.
- The farm, with its yard and outbuildings, provides the children with a sense of what life could have been like for evacuees.

Built into the lesson plan are ways of helping children absorb historical concepts like change and continuity, as well as life in the past. It is rare to find a topic in history which completely focusses on what happened to children, and this makes the evacuee session particularly valuable in establishing empathetic understanding of these difficult concepts without a heavy-handed emphasis on how it is being done. As well as gaining an understanding of the underlying ideas about the point of studying history, the pupils are learning to think critically and ask questions and then draw conclusions from what they have done during the workshop.

The session is designed to be immersive, support classroom teaching and provide further stimuli for the teacher to build on back in the classroom, all of which it has succeeded in doing. The proof of its success is that when offered to schools by the museum, it books up quickly. Having delivered this now for many years, I do feel that the pupils get an insight into what life was like for the evacuees in 1939. With the right preparation before the session, children are excellent at using their imaginations and being absorbed in the moment. As the workshop is not being led by their teacher, they cannot judge exactly what will happen and the strictness of Miss Moffat, though not as strict as I am sure she was in reality, is something very different to what they are used to. The session always begins at the museum entrance in full view of visitors, the reason being to engage them as soon as possible in the strangeness of school life in 1939. Here, the children are lined up with boys in one line and girls in another and marched down to their new classroom. On one occasion, when I returned to the museum at the end of the workshop, the front-of-house staff told me that I had certainly played the part well, as several visitors were rather surprised to find such an old-fashioned and strict teacher still at work. The staff were able to tell them not to worry; it was really a history lesson that took the children back in time to experience what life was like in 1939 for those evacuated. Suitably enlightened, the visitors all agreed they wished they had been able to take part in something like that when they had been at school and what a good idea it was. I feel sure the real Miss Moffat would be pleased her influence remains the inspiration for the leader of this workshop.

Not all school sessions with costumed interpreters are run at museums or heritage sites. Some schools prefer to have an interactive experience in the school or classroom, particularly if they are in remote locations and travel is difficult. Most freelance costumed interpreters deliver workshops directly to schools by focussing on a particular topic or period. It is impossible to provide for every period that is covered in the school curriculum, as you are dependent on having the costume; the school will have nothing they can provide. Over the years, the most popular sessions I have run regularly in schools are Meet Mary, Queen of Scots, The Victorian Schoolroom, The Victorian Servant and The Homefront and Rationing in the Second World War. For all of these, I have costume and over the years built up a collection of props and original objects that can be used with the class. The lesson plan for such a session requires consultation with the teacher on what they want the class to learn from the experience. You can then show in your plan how you will achieve this through the various participative activities you include.

Few studies have been done on whether engaging children in this way makes any difference to their learning of history, but in contrast, there are many sweeping statements that interactive learning in this way trivialises history. In Chapter 1 "'Seeing It for Real . . .?' – Authenticity, Theatre and Learning in Museums", the research project by Anthony Jackson and Helen Rees Leahy in 2005 investigated the use of costumed interpretation at the Imperial War Museum and the People's History Museum in Manchester. The case studies of several museums in the USA featured in *Living History* by David B. Allison (2016, Rowman & Littlefield) also examined the effect that first-person costumed interpretation had on pupils, and smaller studies have been carried out in Norfolk and Dumfries. These research projects all have in common the conclusion that children are more receptive to ideas when they experience them through some form of physical activity; the doing of something stimulates them, and while the subject might be serious, there is a sense of having enjoyed what they have done and remembered it sometime later. While the evidence is small, it does highlight that this form of learning has its place. From my perspective, I have found it a very rewarding method for teaching history, and I have the advantage of having taught history in a classroom as well as in character at heritage sites and museums. I am in the fortunate position of sometimes meeting young people again further on in their school life and even after they have left school. On these occasions, they have come up and said things like, "I remember when you came to see us as the Victorian teacher and we did writing on slates that made a strange noise". One particular time at a visit to the local vet, I met a trainee who said she was sure I was the lady who was "on the *Titanic*", and I had shown them what life was like to be stewards and stewardesses to the wealthy on board. "It's about the only thing I can remember from primary school", she added!

Special Educational Needs (SEN)

Some children within the school system require additional support to help them learn effectively. It is impossible for the non-educational practitioner to be skilled in accommodating all of these; however, you can make slight adjustments to workshops that make it an excellent learning experience for everyone. For example, if you are delivering a session similar to the evacuee workshop, some children might find the strictness of the teacher quite a difficult concept with which to cope. A quick exercise at the beginning of the workshop along the lines of "Miss Moffat smiling" then "Miss Moffat not smiling", repeated several times, makes all the children smile and relax and helps those who are struggling with the strictness. Sitting in total silence in a "Victorian schoolroom" is also very challenging and unnatural. It is still possible to achieve the ambiance of 19th-century education with a little chat going on in the background. The class will be comfortable and get more out of the session than sitting looking terrified to move in their seats or speak out of turn, and you will not spend the whole time saying "Class, be quiet!" Do not forget all those techniques from the previous chapter, as many of them are equally applicable to working with schools.

When a school confirms their attendance at a workshop in a museum or heritage site, it is the usual practice to inform the organisation whether there are any pupils in the class with SEN who are accompanied by their learning assistant. This is useful to know in advance, because if the children are taking part in a practical activity, for example, learning a court dance with Mary, Queen of Scots, you will have to accommodate the learning assistant(s) within the class group. Notification may also highlight a child with hearing impairment in the class and the request that you wear a microphone provided by the teacher. Again, knowledge of this in advance means you can plan how to fix it on to your costume. It also means that you are aware of the necessity to speak more slowly with clear enunciation to enable lip-reading.

If for any reason there is no information provided that indicates there are pupils within the class who require extra help, this does not mean that there are none. Sometimes, confirmation of the school booking is last minute. Learning assistants will still accompany their pupils; it is just that you will not know they are coming in addition to the teachers and parent helpers who are also there. Nor will you know of any small amendments you might have to make. One of the tools of the trade, so to speak, is certainly to be prepared for anything and think on your feet, literally! In such situations, this is when you are glad you have done all your background work, prepared a lesson plan and have the necessary techniques to deliver the session. Nevertheless, there are times when you will be dumbfounded, as on the occasion I was asked by a child, "Mary, Queen of Scots, what is your favourite sea creature?" After a pause, I said "The dolphin – after my first husband, the Dauphin of France. What is your favourite?" The child's reply was "the seahorse", but she liked dolphins too.

The Deaf and Those with Hearing Impairment

In 2015, I was approached by a student from Heriot Watt University who was on the MA (Hons) course of British Sign Language (BSL). Part of her studies was related to Deaf people in society and working with Deaf communities. She chose to study and investigate the provision made within Scottish tourism for this group and how their experience could be improved. The student had been on a costumed guided walk I had delivered as Mrs Grant from the beginning of the 19th century for Edinburgh World Heritage and the National Library of Scotland related to food shopping along the Royal Mile and felt it would work well with Deaf people and their families. Would I be willing to work with a BSL interpreter to provide this walk for her group? This interested me greatly, as I could not quite work out how my input would be of any value, as I personally could not provide BSL. She said that I already spoke clearly, which enabled Deaf people to lip-read, and I was good at using my body expressively to communicate certain feelings. She also added that the Deaf people in her group had hearing family and friends, and this walk would be more inclusive than a dedicated BSL walk. Needless to say, I was very interested. As an interpreter in costume, I found it fascinating to work alongside another form of interpretation.

From this project, I learnt that the essential components for an engaging encounter with a costumed guide and BSL interpreter on a walking tour for a mixed group where some are Deaf, some have hearing impairment and some are hearing are as follows:

- Provide a script of the tour to the BSL interpreter and flag any technical words within it that might be tricky to translate into sign language in order for this to be worked out in advance. It is helpful if you can describe what this technical word means, as this may be the way the word is explained. For example, on this walk, I would talk of luckenbooths, the name given to small, locked shops in the area around St Giles Cathedral. The advance notice meant that the BSL interpreter could work out a way of describing these.
- This is an occasion when you really do need a script, and you need to stick to it on the day of delivery as this is what the BSL interpreter will have learnt. A sudden recollection that you decide to add will not be appreciated.
- Walk the route with the BSL interpreter before the event. This means you can:
    - practice the content together
    - refine the route – decide on the best stopping places that will ensure you and the BSL interpreter can be seen clearly and are not in shadow, which is very important for those who are lip-reading
    - note where it is best to cross the road safely.
- Maintain eye contact, as your facial expression and eyes help to convey the voice tone you are using, which enables the Deaf participant to understand the mood you are creating. This is good practice in any form of walking tour and particularly important to the Deaf.
- Speak more slowly but at your normal volume – raising your voice will alter your lip movement, and this then makes lip-reading difficult.
- While clear enunciation is important, over-enunciation is unhelpful, as it is more difficult to work out what the word is.

- As the Deaf participants on the walk need to watch the costumed guide and/or the BSL interpreter to get the necessary information at each stop, it is crucial that pauses at each stop are longer to ensure that they can look at what has just been described.
- Simple gestures can be useful to suggest mood, such as holding the back of your hand to your forehead as an act of despair if you are perhaps explaining a sad story. Pointing things out is useful too.
- Factor in time for questions from the whole group.

It is still difficult to find opportunities for those who are Deaf or with hearing impairment to have meaningful outings together with their hearing family and friends – most Deaf people are given guidebooks or similar reading material to compensate for there being no BSL interpretation. Some organisations provide a BSL interpreter as a small inset on their hand-held audio-visual tours rather than a dedicated BSL-visual tour. There are now locations that have specific BSL tours on certain days, but again this is awkward for people with hearing friends and family. The costumed interpreter-and-BSL interpreter partnership is rare, but from the walk I undertook for the student, it proves to be a very worthwhile consideration for museums and heritage organisations seeking to provide excellent on-site experiences for hearing and Deaf visitors. I am pleased to say that those who took part on the Royal Mile Walk enjoyed it, and the student gained an excellent mark for her project and went on to gain a first-class degree.

Family Events

When school holidays arrive visits to heritage sites, historic houses and museums become more family focused, often with special programmes put in place to target this audience in particular. In some cases, it may just be that the overall interaction you have with families is to include them in your presentations or conversations, but it is more likely that special events are run to attract families to visit. The important thing to remember about this visitor group is the motivation for their visit. They might want to learn something new or see something different and exciting, but the thing they want most is to enjoy themselves. Their visit may be part of a holiday which brings together different generations or just one of many planned activities over a school break to occupy the children. Whichever it is, they do not want to feel that they are being overloaded with information but rather that they have enjoyed some social interaction and been entertained at the same time, as well as finding out something new and interesting.

Museums, historic houses and heritage sites most definitely want their visitors to enjoy themselves. They also see their role as imparting an understanding of the history and/or heritage of the location in which they are set through the objects they hold or buildings they own, as well as explaining and illuminating difficult concepts that are part of human history that help us understand where we are now and what our future might look like. Such goals do not always fit easily with the idea of having a "good day out". The trick is to enable people to enjoy their visit and learn something meaningful without realising that this was always the organisation's intention – a concept now known as "edutainment", a term first used by Walt Disney in 1954. Disneyfication is a great fear held by heritage and museum organisations – no one wants that to happen. They wish to remain centres of scholarly excellence, yet they want and also need people to visit and engage with their collections. As a result, the term "edutainment" is no longer shunned in quite the same way by these organisations once they realise that it is possible to offer a pleasurable cultural visit that also provides a learning experience within it.

Organisations like to have an activity which involves both children, parents and extended family, not just the children, and for such events a costumed character adds to the appeal of taking part – so much better to learn an old-fashioned skill from someone from the period, even if it is all pretend! As with any role you undertake, you need to research your character to know who you are, but it is quite likely that the character you take on for these kinds of summer activities (very often Victorian characters) are very similar, and what is required on these occasions is knowledge of the location, as you already know your realms. It may well be that the organisation has an activity in mind, but this is not always the case, and you have to think about how you can enliven the visit with something everyone can do without embarrassment to themselves but which is interesting and, hopefully, fun. It is best to keep it simple, and even the easiest of activities takes on new meaning when a whole family are doing it together. Perhaps you are a servant in a large country house and need some help folding napkins or setting out a tea tray. The activity is already part of what you are doing as the visitors come into the area where you are working, possibly a kitchen or pantry. The title for the family event could be "Always busy! Join our Victorian servant in the kitchen and lend a hand as she prepares afternoon tea for the lady of the house", and there you are rushing about, seeming to have too much to do and so glad to see the arrival of some helping hands. For such an activity, you will need a good supply of linen napkins, preferably starched, and a variety of pieces of cutlery, a few trays, several tea settings (cups, saucers, plates) and a few teapots. These things may well be provided for you by the organisation from their handling collection, though they are relatively easy to source yourself. If the house is certain of large numbers, it is best that the activity is in timed slots with set numbers. This means that if you know you are running 6 sessions for 10 people each time, you are prepared with enough napkins and trays to set up for afternoon tea for everyone to have a try at doing it. It also means it provides you with a few minutes between sessions to tidy up before the next group arrives. This way many people get a chance to have a turn at the activity, and it is more controllable for the front-of-house staff at the location.

The sensory experience of making exact folds in the starched napkin and the precision required in laying out a tray provides interesting things to do, and younger children often need a little help from older family members. If the family group is multi-generational, it can also result in grandparents, while clearly not of the Victorian period, reminiscing about times when they were young. For example, it could be about how they had their tea or coffee from cups and saucers rather than mugs. With this simple activity, you have provided an insight to life in a different era, involved families in doing something and satisfied the desire for social interaction within the group and with others around them, namely yourself and other visitors. Being in character, you guide them in the activity and intersperse it with little pieces of information relevant to what they are doing, and you can answer questions too.

It is my experience that any activity that involves some form of table or tray setting is greatly enjoyed by all ages. Popular period dramas on television have certainly created interest in life below stairs as well as the paraphernalia that was required for dining and any form of eating. It all seems rather ridiculous by comparison to the informality of modern living. By the simple act of teaching someone any aspect of table laying, you are creating a link with past behaviour and possibly even ancestors who have worked as domestic servants. For this example, the location was a country house seeking to attract families over the summer, and it was successful in doing so.

There can be occasions when an exhibition in a museum has as its subject matter a topic which is less appealing to family audiences yet is on over the summer months and is likely to have such visitor groups come along. The learning and engagement team are keen to make the exhibition more relevant to their summer audience, and a programme is planned accordingly. This was the case for an exhibition of Victorian photography one summer at the National Museum of Scotland in Edinburgh. It was felt that using a costumed interpreter would be the right approach, and I Artemis Scotland was asked to develop an activity to be delivered throughout the summer that would appeal to family groups. This was to take place in a cordoned-off area in the main hall of the museum and was to be on a drop-in basis rather than booked. This meant that the interpreter would always be on view. From the exhibition, it was clear that there were a number of photographic studios in Edinburgh at that time. We discovered that in 1853, John Moffat opened his first studio in Nicolson Square and moved to Princes Street in 1864, establishing a family business that lasted until 1962 and that specialised in taking portrait photographs of children. Interestingly, information from the 1881 census revealed John's daughter, Ellen, was a photographer and that John employed women in his business, his daughter being one of them. In our research, we also discovered that many studios provided clothes that people could hire at an additional charge if they felt their own attire was not quite up to the mark. This gave us the idea to run a Victorian photographic studio. The museum team provided a selection of period dressing-up clothes and a few props such as a clothes' stand and a chair as well as a background of Victorian Edinburgh. We also sourced some reproduction toys of the type that would have been used to amuse children as they waited for the photo to be taken. There was also a small handling collection of original photos.

The premise of the activity was to come along to the session and discover what having your photograph taken would have been like and the best poses you could adopt for a photo. The costumed interpreter of the day, either John or Ellen, talked the family visitors through why they were dressing up and the importance of sitting still, using the handling collection as examples of how to stand or sit. Once everyone was dressed up and in the chosen pose, one of the group could then take a photo with their own camera or ask the interpreter to take it for them. This activity proved so popular – it attracted well over 2,000 visitors, mainly families – that it was extended to the October school holiday. The family engagement officer at the National Museum of Scotland, Alison Rae, said of our provision through the summer and autumn:

> Even if some families just wanted to try on some of the costumes for a photo opportunity, the photographer assistant interpretation character treated them as importantly as those who had more time, questions or apparent prior interest in the subject – offering easily digestible snippets of information as to how they would have posed in those times, what they would have worn, the length of time it took etc. Families were then more likely to stay and continue the interaction, having got what they initially wanted from it and even more besides. Artemis understand different audience needs and can adapt accordingly. They understand the importance of quality and integrity in the public programmes that an organisation presents, while still remaining relevant, innovative and just that little bit playful.

These two examples, the tray setting and photography studio, demonstrate how much enjoyment can be had from simple activities. Whatever they are doing with the costumed interpreter is just one small part of the whole day out, and therefore, keeping it short and straightforward enables it to be enjoyable and meaningful as well. And if the historical aspect seems of no consequence to the group and they are taking part just because they want to do something different, that is absolutely fine – you never know what they might pick up while there and what it might lead to in the future. The organisations have achieved their goal in getting some new people to their sites and perhaps even persuaded some to join their members' group, which would not have happened if the activity had not run. With regards to the museum session, many of the families who come to holiday activities are regular attenders throughout the year at weekends and have got to know some of the staff and their particular specialities. A new face is always welcome, and as with the experience of the schoolchildren playing the part of the evacuees, an unknown person lacks familiarity which enhances the family's encounter of new things to do. In the case of the country house and in common with many such places, there is a reliance on volunteers whose expertise lies in their knowledge of the collections. If a younger audience is to be encouraged to visit, there will be an expectation of there being something to do, and a costumed interpreter portraying even a generic character relevant to the house's history helps to bring the house into context and facilitate an interesting activity too.

Adults

While family audiences are important to museums and heritage sites, so are adults who want to take part in an activity or find out a bit more about a particular subject. Weekend events and activities focused on adult audiences are also part of the calendar in the museum and heritage world as you will see in the next example.

For several years, I portrayed my 1950s character, Muriel Wylie, accompanied by my partner who took on the character of Jasper, husband to Muriel, at a regular May Bank Holiday event, "The Fabulous Fifties", at the National Museum of Rural Life centred around the glamour of the period. The target audience for these 1950s events was adults fascinated by the vintage lifestyle of the period as well as classic '50s cars and the event attracted a wide age range of people. Enthusiasts brought their period vehicles, which were parked around the museum and became a central part of the event. Everything was focussed on taking everyone "back to the '50s". Muriel and Jasper Wylie – our generic 1950s wife and husband who ran an interior design shop that you met in Chapter 5 – were booked for this event too, proving that constructed generic characters could have life elsewhere. Muriel and Jasper ran four workshops a day on topics that had a wide appeal such as fashion, décor, manners of the time and food. In between sessions, we walked around the site, engaging in conversation with the visitors, some of whom were dressed appropriate to the 1950s.

This vintage weekend was held for four years. Muriel and Jasper were at all of these providing tips on how to do most things in the perfect 1950s way. The most popular of the sessions that were run at these events by us were the food demonstrations based on magazine recipes and books of the period, with an opportunity

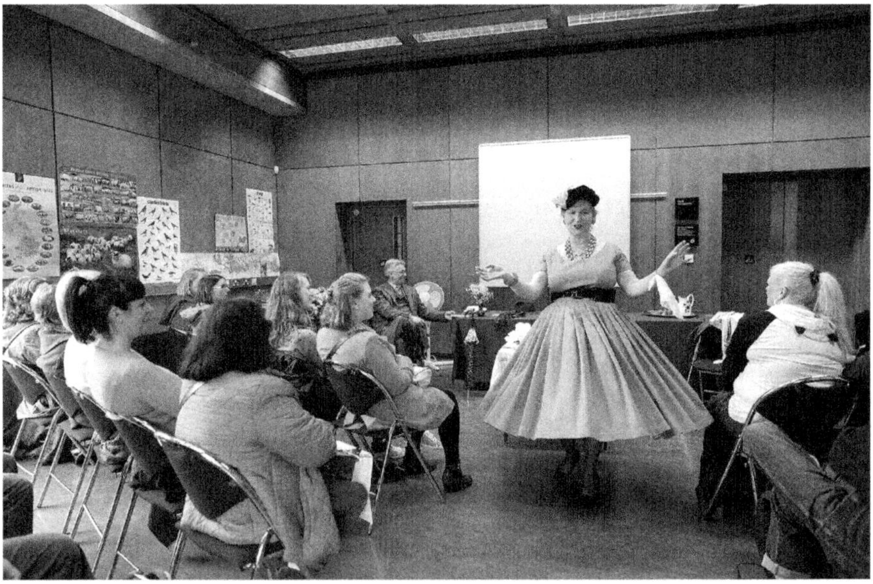

Figure 6.1 Muriel demonstrates how to make the most of a fashionable full skirt at the National Museum of Rural Life's Fabulous Fifties event.

Source: © Ruth Armstrong Photography/Jackie Lee of Artemis Scotland, costumed interpreter

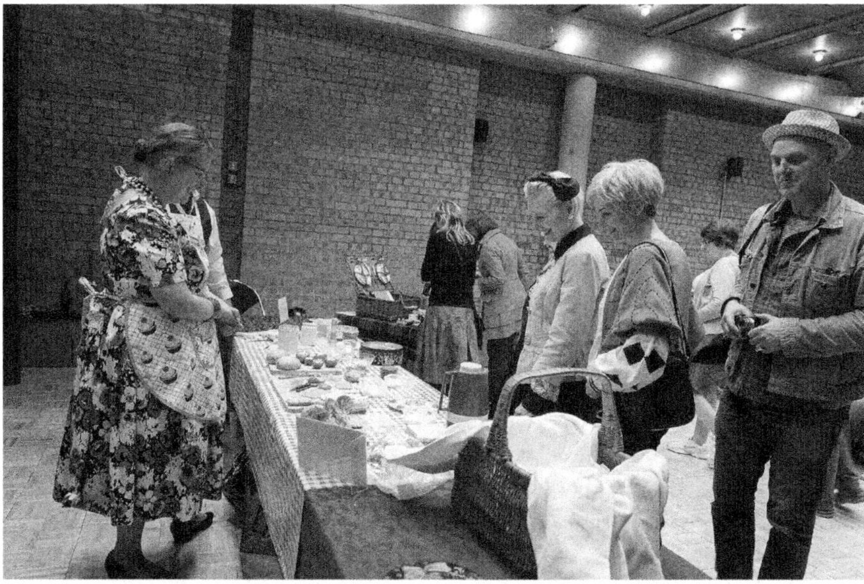

Figure 6.2 The perfect food for a 1950s picnic at National Museum of Rural Life's Fabulous Fifties event provides an interactive experience for those attending.

Source: © Ruth Armstrong Photography/Jackie Lee of Artemis Scotland, costumed interpreter

for people to inspect the samples, though not taste them, ask questions and handle the props.

The success of the photographic studio that we ran for the family events at the National Museum in Edinburgh resulted in this activity being included in the Museum's Late Night opening as one of the evening's participatory events for adults. These Late Night openings are specifically targeted at adults and centre around the current temporary exhibition, in this case the summer one, "Photography: A Victorian Sensation". The anticipated popularity of this activity resulted in two interpreters, John and Ellen (myself and my partner on this occasion), and two museum facilitators to manage the numbers! While primarily a fun activity at the Late Night, there were visitors who took time to look at the handling collection and ask questions about John Moffat's Studio. There were some who said there were studio photos in their family collection from the 1920s or thereabouts with the name Moffat on the back of the photo, and some remembered the name Yerbury, the family who took over the Moffat business in 1962 – we were required to look into our crystal ball on several occasions! Several people came back to see us that evening, having been round the exhibition, saying how much they had enjoyed it and that they really felt for the Victorians who had had to sit so long in their heavy clothes while the photo was taken, having had a try at it themselves with us.

What is clear from these examples is that adults really do like many of the things that children enjoy – they appreciate the chance to try on costume, do something different and handle objects of the past and are interested to learn new things as long as it is not done in a didactic way. It is worth noting that the dynamics of the event do change depending on whether it is during the day or at night, as alcoholic refreshments served in the evening tend to shift the emphasis from education to entertainment, and the costumed interpreter may well find that their interaction with the visitors is more for fun than anything else. However, as we found with the Late Night at the studio, while some came just to dress up and have their photos taken, others wanted to talk about Victorian photography.

Working with the Elderly

It is less common to work specifically with elderly people as a group in their own right. As mentioned earlier, it is more usual to meet older people who are out with their extended family for the day. However, it is worth considering how to adapt your approach if you should be invited to help with a reminiscence group or perhaps with those in the early stages of dementia.

For the Diamond Jubilee in 2013, marking sixty years since Queen Elizabeth II's coronation, we were invited to take part in a community project with a group of retired women who met weekly for companionship in a rural and remote part of Scotland. It was unusual for them to have any outside interaction, but the organiser thought it would be fun to get involved with the celebrations to mark sixty years since the queen's coronation, and there was funding available to support commemorative events. There was also a feeling that some of the members were beginning to show memory/cognitive difficulties, and perhaps a chat about when they were young would be good. Our Muriel and Jasper blog, based on our two 1950s characters and usually portrayed by myself and my partner, was familiar to the organiser, and it was thought it would be good to have these two characters come along to one of the weekly get-togethers to provide a facilitated conversation and stimulate some memories. We put forward a suggested format for the day, which included dressing the room with bunting and providing coronation souvenirs to handle as well as several reproduction crowns to provide sensory prompts for conversation. We felt it worked better if we came along on the pretext of collecting information for our characters, Muriel and Jasper, as to pretend to be from the 1950s could be very confusing to some and, equally, might look as if we were imposing on their memories and perhaps even making fun of them. We felt it would be better to return for a second visit and recount what we had learned from them. As part of our visit, we arranged that along with their usual cup of tea, Victoria sponges and empire biscuits would be served as a further inducement to conversation. We sat with the women and encouraged them to handle the objects we had brought along, and some of them remembered boxes of shortbread in the local shops with pictures of the queen on them that were far too expensive for them to buy. They loved the crowns and had great fun trying them on, especially one woman who was partially sighted and was quite overcome by the fact she could see the crown and coloured stones quite clearly. Gradually, over tea, the conversation flowed, and they were transported back to their youthful days as young mums looking after their children, which was the overwhelming memory rather than a day filled with street parties and coronation chicken, which they all unanimously agreed was a modern invention of the 1980s! Their idea of party food was potted meat and salmon paste as a special treat, and then the conversation moved on to rationing, and the coronation was largely forgotten, except that the local policeman had invited schoolchildren into the police station to watch it on a television he set up for the purpose.

On our second visit, we went dressed as Muriel and Jasper and constructed the session as us seeking their advice and approval on how we looked – had we got the early 1950s look right for a couple going out to a party; were we too formal/informal? – and whether we were portraying this period accurately. We recounted the things we had learnt from them on our last visit and asked their permission to use what we had learnt in our future presentations in other parts of Scotland. We wanted to demonstrate to them that their stories were of great value and should be shared, not forgotten. I am delighted to say that they were happy for us to retell their tales, and it was clear that they felt we appreciated what they had said. We continue to share their stories as our characters, Muriel and Jasper.

I found working with this group to be very moving. The sessions themselves were fun and full of joy, but there was, at the beginning, a sense of "no one wants to hear what we have to say; we are old now". The realisation that what they had to say was interesting to others and that we wanted to hear these things produced a flow of conversation from them all. Their contributions were appreciated and live on in our characters. This was certainly not a typical example of "a day in the life of a costumed interpreter", but it does highlight that the skills associated with our work can be used in reminiscence work provided there is flexibility in approach.

The National Galleries, National Library and National Museum of Scotland have combined forces to provide a programme of culturally related events in Edinburgh for those living with dementia and their carers. Each of these organisations provide a monthly get together themed around some aspect of their collections, which they promote as "socials". In July of 2019, I was invited to portray Queen Victoria to this group to tie in with the Museum's exhibition, "Wild and Majestic: Romantic Visions of Scotland", which highlighted the origins of how Scotland has represented itself to the wider world from the late 18th century onwards. Within the exhibition, there was a particular feature on the influence of Queen Victoria and Prince Albert, whose love of Scotland's scenery and its history resulted in the purchase of Balmoral and contributed to making it more popular as a country to visit. The "Museum Social" has a format which is stuck to rigidly, as this is of benefit to those who have dementia as they learn the routine and are not confused by something new happening.

- Arrival, find a seat and make yourself comfortable
- Welcome from the community engagement team who run the programme
- Tea, coffee and cake and chat

- An informal speaker on some aspect of their collections or current exhibitions
- An opportunity to ask questions
- An activity that relates to what the speaker has said
- Farewells

The brief for my presence at the social as Queen Victoria was to keep it light and amusing and relate it to things they were likely to know. I therefore concentrated my "talk" around the queen at Balmoral and recounted the kind of things that I as Queen Victoria liked about being here – being woken every morning to the sound of bagpipes; the dramatic scenery for walks with Albert; riding in the hills; sketching; dancing Scottish reels in the evening. I referenced Sir Walter Scott's novel *The Bride of Lammermoor*, as it was this book which Victoria claimed had made her fall in love with Scotland. I also added that while at Balmoral, I adopted many Scottish customs such as taking a nip of whisky in my tea and being surrounded by as much tartan as possible. There was much laughter and quite a lot of questions, one relating to the fact that I seemed far more "amused" than I was usually shown to be! I was invited to stay on for their activity, which was making a tartan rosette, and wandered around the tables, admiring their handiwork. At the end of the session, several of the participants came up to speak to me directly. One man in particular was keen to tell me that he had been a solicitor whose company had done work for the Balmoral estate and that he had been involved in some of this work; he had even visited the castle. When he moved off to get his coat, his wife, who was his carer, thanked me and said that this was the most he had said in ages and that the mention of Balmoral had really caught his attention, and he had been chatting to her about it through the whole session. As I learnt later, he continued for some time after, as demonstrated by the feedback on the event. Laura Bennison, the community engagement officer at National Museums Scotland, was present at the Social and commented on the reaction of the participants:

> I just wanted to say another big thank-you for making Friday's Social event so memorable. We've had some really lovely feedback via email including one woman who said how much fun it was and it had provided the stimuli for a really good conversation with her husband which they are having less of these days. Thanks for bringing all your props and enthusiasm and good humour. . . . It was lovely to see so many people chuckling away and embracing their chance to speak to Queen Victoria!

These two examples demonstrate that the experienced costumed interpreter can add an interesting dimension to events with elderly people who have some form of impaired cognitive functioning, the most common of these being Alzheimer's disease. Referencing things that are familiar to them in some way may result in you ending up in some time period that has nothing to do with your character, but in this instance, it really does not matter. No one is trying to put you off deliberately; it is just that you have said something which has triggered a memory about which they can speak with confidence, and that is a very worthwhile achievement.

Visitors from Further Afield

When on holiday, we all enjoy visiting places of interest, and these are often heritage sites, historic houses and museums. We do it when at home and abroad, and so do others when they come to our country. People can be independent travellers or arrive in larger tour groups with a translator. For any costumed interpreter who has a group of visitors from another country before them, it is extremely unlikely they will be able to speak other languages sufficiently well to do their whole interaction in that other language. The techniques associated with welcoming gestures and expressive body language go some way to explain what you are doing and why you are there. However, for many, seeing you and having their photo taken with you is sufficient; and if that is what makes the visit special for them, then that is perfectly acceptable to everyone.

There is always a way of making everyone feel that they have had some form of interaction with you. As demonstrating some simple skill is part of your tool kit on many occasions, this is a simple way of providing engagement and a sense of experiencing some aspect of life in the past without a word spoken; and everyone appreciates a smile, no matter where they are from.

7 Running a Costumed Interpretation Programme

Over the years, I have come across situations in which the person who has been assigned the management of a costumed interpretation programme has not done this before and there is little guidance on what is required. The intention here is to remove any worry about embarking on such a programme by providing a collection of tips on what to do to produce a fantastic visitor experience for your organisation.

Who Should Do the Job?

If you are given this opportunity of setting up a costumed interpretation programme, the first decision you have to make is whether you are going to recruit from your volunteers or permanent staff or engage freelancers as and when you need them. In most cases, it is a combination of volunteers and professional freelance costumed interpreters brought in to meet a particular requirement of an exhibition, for events at heritage sites and historic houses in the summer or provide characters relevant to a site as part of a public programme and for educational and outreach work.

If you embark on recruiting volunteers or full-time staff to provide the costumed interpretation, it is important to avoid those who see this as an extension to their "am dram" involvement – this is not going to be a performance on a stage; it will be direct interaction with the public. Nor is it a "bit of dressing up" done for fun. I speak from experience, having been involved with several sites where it has been made known to me, sometime after my being employed to deliver a character – in each case a Victorian from around the 1880s – that there would be volunteers on the day who just "love to dress up and are all involved with amateur dramatics so know what they are doing". On the day, it turned out they had very little idea how to interact with those who came. Their costumes were also an issue – the Victorian period is from 1837 to 1901 and encompasses many fashion changes within it. I can assure you all the fashions of the period were represented on these particular days! You want your visitors to enjoy themselves, but you also have clear goals and messages you wish to convey through costumed interpretation that you feel cannot be conveyed in any other way. You need a clear interview process that enables you to select those who show that they have a motivation and

DOI: 10.4324/9781003260226-8

desire to interact with the public as well as an interest in the subject matter they will be interpreting. I suggest that when you interview, whether it be for volunteers or staff, you consider an interview process which involves these elements:

- The candidate prepares a short presentation, no longer than ten minutes, on an historical character or event they find interesting which will demonstrate their versatility, originality and communication skills. Costume is not required.
- You provide an object and ask them to describe it and its uses to an imaginary audience group such as school pupils. Keep the object to something simple such as a wooden spoon, a pudding basin or a teapot. There is no use providing something complicated.
- It is important that the candidate can work alone but also be part of a team, because while they might be the only person in costume, their contribution is part of the overall visitor experience. Everyone, from the person who takes the ticket money to the front-of-house on-site personnel to the costumed interpreter, is part of making it a good day out for those who come. Therefore, whoever becomes the costumed interpreter(s) must be able to fit in with everyone, so make sure your questions enable the interviewee to demonstrate their social skills as well as their ability to interact with visitors.

When scoring their interview on these elements and any further questions that you ask related to the programme for which you are recruiting, your top candidate will have demonstrated:

- their research abilities required for the preparation of their presentation
- their awareness of their audience
- their ability to enthuse their audience by their lively and dynamic presentation
- their great communication skills
- their ability to keep to time and not overrun
- their ability to think on the spot when presented with the object in the interview, which highlights their adaptability and creativity
- their social skills.

Candidates who cannot keep to time, present their information as facts in a tedious or didactic manner or who are unnerved by the presentation of an unknown object will not have the skills for the costumed interpreters that you seek. The surprise object may seem an odd activity to include, but what it reveals is their ability to draw out a story from an ordinary object – the wooden spoon may have been bought in a supermarket, but the tales it has to tell of birthday cakes, Christmas puddings and parties are something to wonder at; a Victorian shoe of a child, worn at the heel, may suggest a child dressed in best clothes for an outing or even a nursery rhyme or fairy tale. It shows the skill of making connections and also demonstrates that they will not be put off if a visitor suddenly produces something they decide they want to show them, which is quite possible.

You may decide to opt for freelance interpreters for your project, and the likelihood is that one of your colleagues will have a recommendation of several people they have worked with before. If this is not a piece of work that requires a tender, then the best method is to invite them in for an informal interview, give them an idea of the project and see what they come up with there and then. This has certainly been my experience, and it is from meetings like this that great things have been born, as in the case of the literary walks in the New Town I developed for a project with the English department of Edinburgh University and the International Book Festival. From this first meeting, the next part of the process is to provide the freelance interpreter with some written information around which they can create their more detailed proposal of what they can provide for you. Once you have their creative response, you are in a position to decide on who you want for your programme.

Training

Regardless of whether you choose to use a volunteer team or permanent staff, they will need training. In most programmes I have come across in which organisations decide to use costumed interpreters, training has been one intense day. Over the years, as part of my business Artemis Scotland, I have provided such courses, which can never provide enough information and are part of the reason I wanted to write this book, which clearly explains how to develop characters and gives advice on delivery techniques. That said, volunteers and staff need guidance on what you expect of them and how they can do it.

For anyone new to costumed interpretation, the most important factor is confidence. While they have had to be fairly confident to get to the point of being chosen as a result of the interview, they still need to be reassured that they are doing a good job and providing what is required. If using volunteers, it is also in the interest of your organisation to keep them as part of the team, having already invested all this time in recruiting them. As they are giving up their time for no remuneration, they could easily walk away at any moment if you do not provide them with appropriate support, which manifests itself in some form of training. Equally, you may have to factor in the real possibility that there will be a high turnover amongst your voluntary staff.

The first thing you must do is tell them who they are to portray and provide some basic information on why you have chosen these characters and how they relate to what you want them to present to visitors – the key messages. To help your new team become self-assured in their delivery, I recommend that you focus on building confidence through boosting their communication skills in the training. However, before you embark on the detail of how to communicate on site, I suggest you encourage them to communicate with each other, and this can be achieved with the following exercise:

- Observe how your group sit with each other on arrival.
- After welcoming them, put them into pairs but not with the person they have chosen to sit beside. Mix them up.

- Now ask them to introduce themselves to each other and provide a few interesting facts about themselves.
- Time it, giving them each two minutes.
- Once the four minutes are up, bring the whole group back together.
- Now ask each person to introduce their partner to the group and tell everyone about who they are.

This will not be what they are expecting and is an excellent way of breaking the ice and fostering a good working relationship. It demonstrates listening skills and hearing good things about yourself from someone else does help you feel more confident, even from someone you have just met. There is generally a bit of a buzz in the air after a session like this and also a more relaxed feeling that enables you to move on to concentrate on the key points of communication with visitors. With possibly only a day in which to do this, I recommend that you focus on:

- Guidance on character development – the three realms
- The principles of communication with the public:
    - o use of space
    - o body language
    - o gestures
    - o facial expressions
    - o paralanguage – things like volume, tone, speed of speech, pauses
    - o open questions and inviting a response
- Barriers to communication:
    - o visitors' perceptions, knowledge, values and beliefs
- The importance of interaction
    - o creating a presence through your character by what you are wearing
    - o thinking about ways to interact with visitors through the costume; for example, key features of what you are wearing that can be explained
    - o conversation
    - o presentations
    - o use of props

Those who have been selected by you for your costumed interpretation programme have already demonstrated their research abilities, as proven through your interview, which means that they will relish the prospect of developing their realms for their characters. Most importantly, they must master the more varied elements of communication with the public, as outlined here. This is what will give them the confidence which, when in their costume interacting with the visitors, will ensure an engaging interaction.

Talking of costume, do not forget to factor in practice sessions for costume wearing. Those new to costumed interpretation, whether volunteers or staff, will need to learn how to put the costume on, what it feels like to wear for a prolonged period and, in some cases, how to sit down in it. At Edinburgh Castle, I am known as the Mary, Queen of Scots who can sit! Apparently, a previous costumed interpreter was always nervous of sitting in her costume in case she damaged the farthingale that supports the main part of the gown. Since then, I have always made sure anyone who works for me knows how to sit in their costume. (And in case you are interested in how to sit in a farthingale, you make sure you do not sit on the supports but on the fabric between them.) Apart from getting used to wearing their costumes, make sure your costumed interpretation team know how to care for the costumes to minimise repair costs. Show them how to hang their costume and where it goes in your costume store when not in use.

If at all possible, factor in a dress rehearsal. Perhaps as part of their training, an afternoon could be organised for volunteers with other organisational duties to come along and be "visitors" on site. Or it might be that several local groups could be invited for a free visit on a set day when the site is closed to the public to critique their experience in return for their free entry, thus giving the new costumed interpreters an opportunity to practise their skills and feel confident for when they meet the public.

It is also vital that they become familiar with the heritage site or museum gallery where they will be working, and you must encourage them to spend time at the locations where they will be. As part of this process, this means they will come into contact with those already working there, which leads to a crucial element to the achievement of your costumed interpretation programme – that of integrating the costumed interpreters with the visitor experience and interpretation teams already in place. Building a good a relationship with those working there really is fundamental to the overall success of your costumed interpretation programme and mitigates against an "incomers" or "them and us" view, which can be a barrier if not dealt with from the beginning. This enables delivery of your programme as a seamless and harmonious operation. Never exclude the staff who are already established providers of front-of-house services to visitors from opportunities to meet the costumed interpreters and interact with them. Everyone should be included in briefing meetings and, if at all possible, invite the visitor experience team to the training session to see what the costumed interpreters do. Encourage them to communicate with each other as much as possible and see each other as part of the whole team who engage visitors in the on-site experience on offer.

Should you have decided on using freelance costumed interpreters, who effectively arrive ready to go on-site on the day they deliver, make it easy for them on arrival. If they are coming by car, provide a parking space that is convenient for the unloading of their costume and any other equipment they might have. Inform the security staff of their arrival too. No one needs the hassle of having to prove who they are before they cross the threshold to do a day's work; it is stressful and adds to the feeling of being somewhat marginalised. Unfortunately, it has happened to me on many occasions, and it really does not help in preparing for the day ahead. An invitation to a briefing meeting on arrival is also a useful means of welcoming the freelance costumed interpreter(s) and introduces them to everyone. This means that they feel included in what is happening and not that they are just the "dressed-up extras", and the other bonus is the permanent staff will not feel threatened by their arrival.

Dotting the "I" and Crossing the "T"

Several administrative duties are essential to put in place which will guarantee that your costumed interpretation programme runs efficiently, and this section provides a checklist of the things you must not forget to do.

1 Risk Assessments: The health and safety of visitors and interpreters is equally important.

- As with all work involving visitors, their safety is paramount. Therefore, as with any other activity you run, a risk assessment for the costumed interpretation programme is essential.
- Irrespective of whether you choose to use volunteers, permanent staff or freelancers, everyone must be made aware of the organisation's policies on child and vulnerable adult protection.
- It is also imperative that a risk assessment is carried out to ensure the safety of the interpreters, considering such things as the location of changing facilities and the route to where they are working on site – it may involve a lot of steps, and their costume might make this difficult.
- Organisations have a duty of care for their staff, whether they are permanent, voluntary or freelance. Managers need to ensure that the costumed interpreters feel safe on site and can get help from front-of-house staff if they feel threatened or vulnerable. The volunteers and freelancers also need to be informed of what to do if a major incident takes place on site or what to do in the event of fire. They also need to know who to access for first aid for visitors and themselves.

2 The Costume

- If this is the first time you are running a costumed interpretation programme, make sure you leave yourself plenty of time for sourcing costume, as it will have to be made for your particular project, and that takes time. Allow at least six weeks for costume construction and be very clear in what you want from the costume maker.
- Take a photograph of each costume you are using in the programme, as these can be used for comparative purposes when repairs are required. It is also essential to check the condition of all your costumes regularly. Provide your costumed interpreters with a logbook in which they can record any costume malfunctions as they happen. This enables you to keep track of repairs.
- Fastenings, hems, seams and trimmings are the things that are most likely to need attention on a fairly constant basis. Therefore, it is good to have someone who can come in once a month and check over everything and make sure these repairs are done as soon as possible.

- It is also good practice to clean the costumes properly at the end of the project, which will ensure they last much longer.

Freelance interpreters provide their own costume and will therefore have their own methods for its care.

3 Provision of Changing Facilities

- While this may seem an obvious need for costumed interpreters, it is surprising how often it is neglected in the planning process. It is not at all acceptable to offer a toilet or a cleaner's cupboard where the interpreter has to navigate round cleaning products, mops and brooms as a place to get changed. This is even more important in the post-COVID world. Basic requirements are a hygienic area with a table, chair and long mirror with good lighting in the room. While getting into costume is, in essence, the same as putting on a uniform to be part of the team, it is a more complicated process, often involving corsetry and lots of fastenings, so the last thing anyone wants is to be in a small space and unable to move properly. That also does not enable your costumed interpreters to go through their routines which help get them into character.
- If possible, provide access to lockers for personal items. If this is not possible, arrange to have the room being used for changing locked when the costumed interpreters are working, but make sure they can get into the room when on their break.

4 Rest Spaces

- When the costumed interpreters are having their break, it is important that they have access to facilities away from the public eye that enable them to have a warm drink and heat food if they wish. Having spent their morning speaking to visitors, they need a chance for some quiet time.
- If the usual staff facilities are too small to take extra people, given that some costumes take up a lot of room, time everyone's break periods in such a way that the interpreters can use the staff facilities.

5 Preparing the Visitors

- As I have highlighted on several occasions in this book, visitors need to know what is happening when they arrive at a heritage site, museum or historic house. If there are to be costumed interpreters there, they should be informed where they may meet them and whether there are any particular activities taking place that involve participation with the interpreters, because they may, or may not, wish to take part.
- Although visitors are more used to finding people in costume on site, most prefer to know what is happening in advance – it is their day out, so they will make the choice of what they want to do.
- Advertising the programme in advance will attract those who most delight in such interaction and deliberately visit for that reason. For those

out for the day who come upon your site or museum without any knowledge of what is on whoever is their first point of contact, whether it be a car park attendant or the ticket seller, should enthuse about what there is to do at the site and how this is your chance today, for example, to meet Lady Redbourne and Thomas, the butler.

- Not everyone takes everything on board as the car is being parked or ticket money paid. Therefore, a simple programme issued with their tickets can be provided saying what is on that day. It need be nothing more than an A4 sheet outlining the activities – something like "Today in the Drawing Room you will meet the lady of the house, Lady Redbourne, at her sewing. She would really enjoy a chat with you while she waits for the butler to bring her afternoon tea. And look out for Thomas, the butler in the pantry. He may need your help to get the tea ready".
- If it is a timed participatory activity, a list of timings and the location on this information sheet will enable visitors to decide whether they want to join in or watch from afar. An extra A-frame sign at the entrance is another means of alerting visitors to something happening. Some places may have the facility to make loudspeaker announcements or have screens which provide information about what is on that day.

6 Communicating with Freelancers

- If there has been a change of management during the set-up of the costumed interpretation programme, do make sure that the new person in position is fully briefed on what they are taking on and that any freelancers employed for the programme are notified of the change. It does happen; it has happened to me twice! On both occasions, I was booked to provide a costumed character at particular locations for several weekends in the summer. By the time I arrived, a new manager was in place who was dumbfounded by my arrival, as no notification had been passed on of these planned events. It all worked out in the end, but I would have preferred if it had not happened at all.

Evaluation

No matter where delivery of the costumed interpretation takes place, you need to find out if it has provided engaging visitor experiences and met your objectives. If the programme is for several months, evaluation will be required at set periods throughout its delivery to ensure that the interpreter(s) stay on message and as a form of quality control. It also helps the interpreters to develop their skills and gives an opportunity to commend them for their input throughout the programme – everyone likes a bit of praise and appreciation. Full evaluation will also be required at the conclusion of the programme. It is also important to invite the costumed interpreters themselves to provide evaluation of their experience on site to ensure that any issues that arose can be corrected for future work. You will also have to evaluate the project from the perspective of the visitor.

Evaluation of the Costume Interpreters

At the beginning of the programme, it is important to observe the interpreters at work on a regular basis (I would suggest weekly for the first month) and adopt an approach that is not overly critical, particularly if you are using volunteers. For this, my recommendation is to take on the role of coach. This enables you to develop a relationship that supports the interpreters as they strive to achieve the best possible visitor experience as well as providing regular recognition of their work and feedback on any elements that they may need to modify or develop further. As part of this coaching approach, self-evaluation by the interpreter is an excellent tool to use. Maintaining a diary, or any kind of notebook, in which they record aspects of their day's work enables the costumed interpreters to keep track of their own delivery and be aware of where they feel they may need help with a particular technique while also recording what they have thought has worked well. This means that you can recognise their success while helping with their areas of concern. The interpreter then feels that they are being valued as well as being provided with advice on how to improve their skills. Here is an example of what I mean by recording aspects of the day.

From entries like these, you can see that the interpreter has used their initiative with regards to the table location and is already building up a good relationship with front-of-house staff.

There is some difficulty with enthusiastic visitors staying too long and concern that children are a little restless, but these are all solvable issues with a bit of gentle support from the organisation. Please do encourage your costumed interpreters to use some form of recording their progress. It is enormously helpful to them and you.

Table 7.1 An example of how a costumed interpreter records their work experiences over three days as part of a self-evaluation programme

June
Friday Interaction with audience using objects went well as it was a small group. Think I might be better with the table nearer me to keep an eye on the return of the handled props; currently table too far away from the window where I normally stand. Not sure that the children in today found the dance very easy.
Saturday Table in new position thanks to front-of-house staff who helped move it nearer me. It was much better here especially as more people visiting today. I felt more comfortable.
Sunday Spent a long time speaking to one family; feel I may have neglected other visitors as a result. Any advice on how I can move them on without feeling I have insulted them? Object handling went very well today – a lot of interest in the cups with no handles and the manners that are associated with tea drinking. Definitely better having the table nearer me. Room stewards very helpful at directing people over to me.

Table 7.2 Sample evaluation form to be used for costumed interpreters

Character:	Location:					
Time and date of evaluation:						
Name of evaluator:						
Score from 1 to 6 where 1 is poor and 6 is excellent						
Observational comments on arrival						
Appearance	1	2	3	4	5	6
Greeting visitors	1	2	3	4	5	6
Open and inviting towards visitors	1	2	3	4	5	6
Interaction with visitors	1	2	3	4	5	6
Conveyed key messages	1	2	3	4	5	6
Tone of voice	1	2	3	4	5	6
Conversational style/presentation	1	2	3	4	5	6
Use of facial expression and gesture	1	2	3	4	5	6
Eye contact	1	2	3	4	5	6
Use of props	1	2	3	4	5	6
Object handling	1	2	3	4	5	6
Interaction with other staff on site	1	2	3	4	5	6

Once coaching them into their role has been achieved, evaluation can be done every three or four weeks, depending on the length of the project and the level of proficiency you feel they have reached. The fairest way to approach this is with a scoring sheet that enables you to measure their performance and gauge improvement. Do remember that evaluation should be a positive experience. No one can do everything perfectly, but if you have chosen them and nurtured them into their character role, they cannot possibly be scoring nothing but ones and twos. Use evaluation as a positive experience rather than as a negative tool to find fault. Here, you will find an example of an evaluation sheet that can be used for costumed interpreters.

There may be other things that you wish to add. However, it is best to keep the form short and stick to important elements that are key to providing an engaging and memorable visitor experience.

Visitor Evaluation

While evaluating the delivery of the costumed interpretation programme, you must run a parallel evaluation that examines what your visitors have thought of their experience. The likelihood is that the costumed interpretation programme is only one part of what you are offering to the visitors, and your evaluation of their experience will cover the whole day with the costumed interpreters featuring as part of what they have encountered and interacted with during their visit.

Observing visitors' interaction with your costumed interpreters is one of the best ways to see how well it is working. You can judge from their reactions how well they are responding to the various activities, conversations and/or presentations that are being initiated by the characters. Through your observation, you can measure dwell time and compare it to how much time they spend on other installations or features you have at your site, and this will help you determine the success of your costumed interpretation programme. It is a good idea, when welcoming your visitors, to mention that someone is around that day observing activities taking place as part of the planning process for future events; that way, they will not be put off by meeting you several times on their way round or wondering why someone is paying particular attention to their conversation with a character. You will not be incognito, as you will have your organisation's ID badge, but it is more reassuring for a visitor to be told what is going on that day. It is not advisable to do this every day, as while your observation is aimed at the visitor, you will also be watching the interpreters which can be quite unnerving and create a feeling that you do not trust them. Set aside one day a week for your visitor observation, and make sure all on-site staff know which day it is.

The question then arises of what to do on days when you are not observing your visitors – you still want to know if they have enjoyed their outing. For this, I suggest the use of a visitor book in which people can make comments, and provision can be made for them to indicate how far they have travelled and how they heard about your site. This, of course, only gives you a general overview of the day. If you want some targeted feedback on the costumed interpretation programme, you could consider a set of blank postcards with a couple of printed questions, as provided in the example here.

This is more of a hit-or-miss method of acquiring information, but it might just be better than nothing. I have seen it used successfully, but it does have to be obvious and not tucked away in a corner.

It is harder to capture visitors' views by formal written evaluation because it means you have to stop them and ask questions, thus interrupting their visit. For that reason, if you choose this approach, keep the form simple, and do not ask too many questions – no more than a page. Explain that their responses will help your organisation to improve the visitor experience of the future and that it will only take a few minutes of their time. Remember to thank them at the end and reiterate how much you appreciate their contribution. Following is my example of such a form for evaluating a fictitious site called Brown's Cotton Mill.

It is tempting to add additional questions. You might want to invite the visitors to join your mailing list or become members or friends of your organisation. Appealing as this might be, it is not evaluation. What you are asking your visitors to do with this sample form is give a little thought to choices that will help you work out what you might want to change for the future or what they feel has been a complete success. If you are a large organisation, it is possible that you will have

Table 7.3 Sample questions printed on a blank postcard for visitors to complete on the day of an event

We hope you have enjoyed meeting our characters from the past.

Who was your favourite? Please circle or put a tick beside your favourite.

Mr Simpson, the mill manager

Bella, the mill worker

Maggie, the mill worker

What did you enjoy most about your visit to the mill?

Table 7.4 Sample evaluation form for visitors

Event: 1820s Mill Experience **Date and time:**

Circle the number which most accurately reflects the visitors' assessment of the day.

(1 = poor → 6 = excellent/very valuable)

Costumes and presentation	1	2	3	4	5	6
Interpreters: Mr Simpson (the mill manager)	1	2	3	4	5	6
Maggie (mill worker)	1	2	3	4	5	6
Bella (mill worker)	1	2	3	4	5	6
Friendly and informative	1	2	3	4	5	6

In what ways do you feel that this costumed interpretation presentation has contributed to your visit?

We would like to know if you enjoyed the other elements of your visit to our mill. Please rate these as above.

The guided tour of the mill	1	2	3	4	5	6
The working machinery	1	2	3	4	5	6
The audio-visual show	1	2	3	4	5	6
The objects available for handling	1	2	3	4	5	6

Did you visit the café and enjoy your visit? Yes [ ] No [ ]

Do you like the range of gifts in our shop? Yes [ ] No [ ]

How could we improve your experience of our mill?

a dedicated team assigned to the evaluation of all you have to offer; for a smaller set-up, this is an unlikely luxury. Whether large or small, it is, however, important to see if the reasons you had for choosing to implement a costumed interpretation programme have been fulfilled from the perspective of both the visitors and the costumed interpreters.

When It Is All Over

When the project has ended, it is also important to carry out a further round of evaluation with your costumed interpreters to consider the success of the programme as a whole. This way, you will see if the objectives you originally set have been achieved. Your evaluation of what visitors have thought of their interaction with the interpreters, which will have been carried on in parallel with that of the interpreters, will feed into your final overview of how the project has worked. By now you will have coached your costumed interpreters, observed their work and scored it accordingly, so you will know their work very well. This final meeting will help you both to recognise the achievements of the programme and learn how things could be done differently next time.

Before you close the door on the costume store at the end of the project, remember to celebrate the successes you have had, many of which may well be totally unexpected.

Conclusion

Now we have come to the end of the book. I hope that everything I have set before you is useful. I am sure that those of you who take up the challenge to become costumed interpreters will discover many new and interesting ways to develop these skills that I have shared with you even further, and I look forward to seeing that happen. Some of you may be in the position of managing a costumed interpretation programme, and I hope that what is here will also help you in your work.

You will have gathered from everything within this book that I believe that it is a very interesting way to explain and engage people of all ages in their history and to appreciate the heritage around them, both that which they can see and that which they cannot in the songs, stories and various other factors which make up our cultural heritage. Used skilfully, it connects people, places and events in a sensory experience. For example, the swish of a gown in a medieval hall, the sound of a lute in a 16th-century dance at a castle, the texture of a starched linen napkin in a Victorian dining room and standing on a former battlefield with a soldier of the First World War are more likely to linger longer in the memory if visitors have been involved in the experience.

Involving the audience in a session on how to bow or curtsy or taking a promenade in an 18th-century drawing room or perhaps joining a Victorian butler in polishing the cutlery or a Second World War housewife on a shopping trip with her ration book – such activities give the visitor of any age a peek into the past and how our ancestors may have lived. Dr Richard Irvine is a volunteer costumed guide at Verdant Works, a jute mill museum in Dundee. I met Dr Irvine at a training day that I provided for all of the volunteers at Verdant Works who were interested in costumed interpretation. The aim of the day was to encourage their volunteers to try costumed interpretation and help them with character development. Dr Irvine had already begun to create the persona of Mr Forrester, the fictional mill manager, and the training day provided some useful tips, which has resulted in him being the mainstay of their costumed interpretation programme at the museum. I asked him if he would like to contribute a few words on why he chose this form of heritage interpretation. He said:

> For me, costumed interpretation breaks down many barriers by putting a human face to history, by making it accessible, real and digestible.

DOI: 10.4324/9781003260226-9

Mark Kydd, who we heard from earlier in the book with regards to his portrayal of Sir Walter Scott, echoes what Dr Irvine says:

> I find that recounting history through character and anecdote is the most direct and engaging way of bringing historical characters alive. I feel that I'm a custodian of the life of the person I'm portraying and have a duty to represent them in a vibrant and even-handed way; direct engagement with the public is what makes these figures memorable and ensures their stories stick.

He has portrayed many famous historical characters, ranging from Bonnie Prince Charlie and Sir Walter Scott to the less well known Davie Kirkwood, the Red Clydesider imprisoned in Edinburgh Castle during the First World War, and their stories were in a good pair of hands with Mark. The costumed interpreter recognises their responsibility to portray their characters in a respectful manner while engaging the visitor in a way that is not didactic.

Accessibility and direct engagement were seen in action at the country house where I and my fellow interpreter were the housekeeper and butler mentioned in Chapter 5. The event was popular and ran for several years and, to our delight, attracted a repeat visit from an elderly lady who had herself been in service. At each visit, she shared her experiences in conversation with the butler, thus enhancing his knowledge and fascinating the other visitors. She recalled details like washing coins from bed-side tables with hot soapy water each evening and replacing them while the household were at dinner. She also told of the gardeners sweeping the dew off the grass with branches of broom tied together before they used the mower. One summer, her son returned alone and stood at the back of the small group in the butler's pantry while the butler demonstrated how to clean a copper pan as instructed by the elderly lady in previous years. There was no conversation on this visit, just a smile from the son at the back, a nod and a whispered "thank you".

This is not an easy form of interpretation, as it requires a multi-tasking approach with considerable knowledge and understanding of historical context and, of course, your character as well as engagement and delivery skills and techniques from the world of acting. There will be unexpected weather, challenging visitors and fire alarms. The costumed interpreter has to be able to think on their feet in both the past and the present. Not all audiences are the same. Dr Irvine, whose main role is as a costumed guide, puts this very well:

> In my role I consider flexibility and adaptability the key points of importance. The purpose of the costumed guide is engagement, to communicate with visitors, to ensure they appreciate or discover a little more about Dundee's textile industry when they visit the museum. Therefore, I need to utilise methods that reach out effectively to as many visitors as possible . . . what I actually say and do is not fixed; a primary school group is different from an adult couple or a family.

This essential flexibility of approach is echoed by Laverne Edmonds, who has worked with me for many years and has portrayed everything from Queen Margaret of Scotland to a land girl in the Second World War:

> When performing in this type of work it is so important to have as much knowledge and information about the historical character and era as you can. You never know what you could be asked. Having had a good theatre training and experience in improvisation is beneficial too with this work. Knowledge, thinking on your feet and good people skills make for the best experience for both actor and visitors . . . and I have never finished a job without a sense of achievement and having enjoyed the experience.

Of course, costumed interpretation is nothing without the costume. As Fergus John McCann, who has performed as Lord Darnley as well as Sir Walter Scott, a 19th-century golfer and a steward on board a 20th-century ship, his advice is:

> Dress to impress. A big part of costumed interpretation is, obviously, the costume.

There is no doubt that the costume can have quite an effect on both the visitors and the interpreter, as Stephanie Falls, who has been Mary of Guise for Artemis Scotland for several years, recounts:

> I found wearing the costumes in the same place that Mary had once been, e.g. Edinburgh Castle and Linlithgow Palace, particularly powerful in terms of getting into character. I remember first walking around Linlithgow Palace, where she had given birth to her daughter, Mary, Queen of Scots, and being hit with the realisation that this woman had lived and breathed, loved, and lost within these very walls. I think that knowledge adds an immediacy and passion to the telling of stories to audiences and is the perfect way of getting history off the page and into people's hearts and heads.

Chris Lee, my partner in work and life, also knows how much wearing a costume can change how people react to you as well as how it makes you feel:

> It's amazing how the costume (in this case, that of a First World War colonel in a military setting) allows you not only to manage a lively class but also to see at firsthand the power such a uniform commands. I got a huge amount of pleasure from being saluted and deferred to by the real soldiers at Fort George, simply because they recognized my rank. I was even saluted by the real colonel!

And from me, I reiterate what I hope this book conveys to you: the great joy and privilege it is to tell the stories of the past through the medium of costumed interpretation. I look forward to seeing you in action one day at a site or museum.

Fergus has had the uncanny knack throughout this book of summing up my thoughts most succinctly:

> Costumed interpretation involves a lot of effort: research, practice, performance, judging how to walk the line between immersion and education. So it's always deeply satisfying when you can walk home at the end of the day, knowing you've found that difficult balance; not only informing and entertaining your audience, but making them hungry for more knowledge.

However, the last words in this book are from an elderly visitor I had the pleasure of meeting at an event near the beginning of my career in 2000, which sums up why I continue to work in the field of costumed interpretation: "Why wasn't history this interesting at school?"

Bibliography

Addison, J. (1816). No. 102. Wednesday, June 27, 1711. In *The spectator, with sketches of the lives of the authors, and explanatory notes: Vol. 2* (pp. 86–89). Alex. Lawrie & Co.

Allison, D. (2016). *Living history: Effective costumed interpretation and enactment at museums and historic sites*. Rowman & Littlefield.

Anderson, J. (1984). *Time machines: The world of living history*. The American Association for State and Local History.

Anonymous. (2010). *The handbook of etiquette: Being a complete guide to the usages of polite society*. Kessinger Legacy Reprints. (Original work published 1860)

Benson, A. C., The Viscount Esher (Ed.) (1908). *The Letters of Queen Victoria: A selection from Her Majesty's correspondence between the years 1837 and 1861*. John Murray.

Braun, M., Costigliolo, L., North, S., Thornton, C., & Tiramani, J. (2016). *17th century men's dress patterns 1600–1630*. Thames & Hudson.

Carr, R. (2014). *Gender and enlightenment culture in eighteenth century Scotland*. Edinburgh University Press. https://doi.org/10.1515/9780748646432

Castiglione, B. (1967). *The book of the courtier* (G. Bull, Trans.). Penguin Books. (Original work published 1528).

Coltman, M. (2009). *My memories of growing up in Welwyn Garden City, 1929 to 1947* [unpublished manuscript]

Cosh, M. (2003). *Edinburgh in the golden age*. John Donald Publishers.

Crowfoot, E., Pritchard, F., & Staniland, K. (2006). *Textiles and clothing 1150–1450*. Boydell Press.

Devereux, G. R. M. (1983). *A book of Edwardian etiquette: Being a facsimile reprint of Etiquette for women, a book of modern modes and manners by "one of the aristocracy"*. Allen & Unwin. (Original work published 1902)

Douglas, H. (1993). *Flora MacDonald: The most loyal rebel*. Alan Sutton.

Edwards, L. (2017). *How to read a dress: A guide to changing fashion from the 16th to the 20th century*. Bloomsbury Academic. https://doi.org/10.5040/9781474285919

Edwards, L. (2020). *How to read a suit: A guide to men's fashion from the 17th to the 20th century*. Bloomsbury Visual Arts. https://doi.org/10.5040/9781350071193

Eserin, A. (1995). *Welwyn Garden City*. The History Press.

Filler, R. (1985). *A history of Welwyn Garden City*. Phillimore & Co Ltd.

Fraser, A. (1970). *Mary Queen of Scots*. Weidenfeld & Nicolson.

Friendship, E. (2013). *Creating historical clothes: Pattern cutting from Tudor to Victorian Times*. Pavilion Books.

Galt, J. (2009). *The annals of the Parish*. Serenity Publishers, LLC. (Original work published 1821)

Glassberg, D. (1986). Living in the past [review of the book *Time machines: The world of living history*, by J. Anderson]. *American Quarterly*, *38*(2), 305–310. https://doi.org/10.2307/2712857

Graham, H. (1961). *The social life of Scotland in the eighteenth century*. Adam and Charles Black. (Original work published 1899)

Graham, R. (2014). *Bonnie Prince Charlie: Truth or lies*. Saint Andrew Press.

Guy, J. (2004). *'My heart is my own', the life of Mary Queen of Scots*. Fourth Estate.

Hartley, C. (2014). *The gentlemen's book of etiquette and manual of politeness*. Hesperus Press Ltd. (Original work published 1860). https://doi.org/10.2307/25528144

Hartley, F. (2017). *The ladies' book of etiquette and manual of politeness*. Dover Publications Inc. (Original publication 1860). https://doi.org/10.2307/25528144

Hayward, M. (2020). *Stuart style and the Scottish male elite*. Yale University.

Hibbert, C. (2001). *Queen Victoria: A personal history*. Harper Collins.

Horn, P. (1986). *The rise and fall of the Victorian servant*. Alan Sutton.

Hugget, J., & Mikhaila, N. (2013). *The Tudor child: Clothing and culture 1485 to 1625*. Fat Goose Press Ltd.

Jackson, A., & Leahy, H. R. (2005). 'Seeing it for real . . . ?'- Authenticity, theatre and learning in museums. *Research in Drama Education: The Journal of Applied Theatre and Performance*, *10*(3), 303–325. https://doi.org/10.1080/13569780500275956

Jenyns, S. (1729). *The art of dancing, a poem in three Canto's*. W.P.

Johnson, C. (2009). *The king's servants: A Tudor tailor case study*. Fat Goose Press Ltd.

Johnson, C. (2011). *The queen's servants: Gentlewomen's dress at the accession of Henry VIII*. Fat Goose Press Ltd.

Lam, H. (2020). Embodying Japanese heritage: Consumer experience and social contact at a historical themed park. *Journal of Intercultural Studies*, *41*(3), 1–18. https://doi.org/10.1080/07256868.2020.1751598

Lee, C. (2012). '*The lights have fused, Mr Coltman': The story of Alec Coltman and his life in the new town of Welwyn Garden City* [unpublished manuscript]

Longford, E. (1964). *Victoria R.I.* Weidenfeld and Nicolson.

Magelssen, S. (2007). *Living history museums: Undoing history through performance*. Scarecrow Press.

Malcolm-Davies, J. (2004). Borrowed robes: The educational value of costumed interpretation at historic sites. *International Journal of Heritage Studies*, *10*(3), 277–293. https://doi.org/10.1080/1352725042000234451

Malcolm-Davies, J., & Mikhaila, N. (2006). *The Tudor tailor: Reconstructing sixteenth-century dress*. Batsford.

Marshall, R. (2008). *Mary of Guise Queen of Scots*. NMSE – Publishing Ltd.

Petrie, A. (2010). *Rules of good deportment, or of good breeding, for the use of youth*. The British Library. (Original work published 1720)

Racinet, A. (2006). *The costume history from ancient times to the 19th century*. Taschen. (Original work published between 1876 and 1888 in six volumes)

Riley, N. (2017). *The accomplished lady, a history of genteel pursuits c1660–1860*. Oblong.

Roth, S. (1998). *Past into present: Effective techniques for first-person historical interpretation*. The University of North Carolina Press.

Schuessler Bond, M. (2019). *Dressing the Scottish court 1543–1553: Clothing in the accounts of the lord high treasurer of Scotland*. Boydell Press. https://doi.org/10.1017/9781787444256

Sheridan, T. (2010). *A course of lectures on elocution* (Print ed.). Gale ECCO. (Original work published 1762)

Sheridan, T. (2018). *A general pronouncing and explanatory dictionary of the English language* (Print ed.). Gale ECCO. (Original work published 1780)

Swift, J. (2007). *A complete collection of polite and ingenious conversation*. Hesperus Press Ltd. (Original work published 1738)

The Duke of Hamilton. (1991). *Maria R, Mary Queen of Scots the crucial years*. Mainstream Publishing.

Thomas, A. (2013). *Glory and honour: The renaissance in Scotland*. Birlinn.

Thomas, K. (2018). *In pursuit of civility: Manners and civilization in early modern England*. Yale University Press. https://doi.org/10.2307/j.ctvzpv6kq

Tilden, F. (1957). *Interpreting our heritage*. The University of North Carolina Press.

Tyrell, A. (2013). *Vintage dress patterns of the 20th century*. Batsford.

Vickery, A. (2009). *Behind closed doors: At home in Georgian England*. Yale University Press.

Walker, J. (2016). *Elements of elocution*. Wentworth Press. (Original work published 1781)

Walker, J. (2018). *A critical pronouncing dictionary and expositor of the English language*. (Original work published 1791)

Watkins, S. (2001). *Mary Queen of Scots*. Thames & Hudson.

Whelan, F. (2017). *The making of manners and morals in twelfth-century England: The book of the civilised man*. Routledge. https://doi.org/10.4324/9781315524894

Index

Note: Page numbers in *italics* indicates figures and page numbers in **bold** indicates tables on the corresponding page.

Printed in Dunstable, United Kingdom

63589698R00100